FOOD, GENDER, AND

POVERTY IN THE

ECUADORIAN ANDES

Mary J. Weismantel

WAVELAND

PRESS, INC.

Prospect Heights, Illinois

For information about this book, write or call:
Waveland Press, Inc.
P.O. Box 400
Prospect Heights, Illinois 60070
847/634-0081

FOOD, GENDER, AND

POVERTY IN THE

ECUADORIAN ANDES

This work is dedicated to two people: to DR. JOSEPH B. CASAGRANDE, my first adviser, who did not live to see its completion; and to NANCY CHALUIZA QUISPE of Zumbagua, my achi wawa, who was born during the year I lived with her family.

CONTENTS

ILLUSTRATIONS

Figures

Plates (between pp. 86 and 87)

ACKNOWLEDGMENTS

This book could never have been written without the support of a great many people and institutions. Most of the research was funded by a Fulbright-Hayes grant, but I am also grateful for financial support received from the Graduate College, Department of Anthropology, and Center for Latin American Studies of the University of Illinois at Urbana-Champaign. Fieldwork in Ecuador was done under the auspices of the Instituto Nacional del Patrimonio Cultural del Ecuador. A brief period spent working for the Sacha Runa Foundation as a consultant on the ethnographic content of Tigua paintings also contributed to my own research.

Among the people I would like to thank, my gratitude goes first and foremost to the people of Zumbagua, and especially to my compadres, the *familia* Chaluiza of Yanatoro, who opened their homes and their hearts to me, as well as to the many other residents of the parish who befriended me and showed great tolerance, patience, and humor in letting me share a little of their lives.

Second, I would like to thank the faculty, students, staff, and spouses of the Department of Anthropology and the Center for Latin American Studies at the University of Illinois. The deepest gratitude is due to Norman Whitten, who has given me an enormous amount of support, guidance, and friendship, both in Ecuador and in Urbana, since I began my graduate studies. I am greatly indebted to him and to his wife, Sibby. Enrique Mayer has shown unfailing patience and compassion during the sometimes tortuous progress of this work, and especially in the difficult days of proposal writing. During the actual process of writing this work, Ann Anagnost offered friendship and counsel in my darkest hours, as well as inspiring many of my brightest moments. I have fond memories of hours spent arguing and discussing with Mahir Saul, whose intimidating intellect is matched with great curiosity and a very kind heart. All four of these scholars have provided tremendous intellectual stimulation and emotional support; this work reflects their direct and indirect influences in many ways.

Ideas, information, good advice, and kind words have also come from other past and present faculty members of the University of Illinois, in-

Acknowledgments

cluding: Frank Salomon, Carmen Chuquín, R. T. Zuidema, Donald Lathrap, John Stewart, Charles Keller, and Paul Drake, all of whose knowledge and insights have contributed to my education and to this work. I also owe an intellectual debt to the Unit for Interpretation and Critical Theory of the University of Illinois.

In Quito, I am most especially grateful to María del Carmen Molestina Zaldumbide for her continued assistance and for the warm personal kindness and courtesy she has always shown me. She is especially to be thanked for making available some of the ethnohistorical materials on the Augustinian hacienda of Zumbagua. María Mogollon of the Fulbright Office has also been a good friend. I am also grateful to the staff of the Catholic church and the Subcentro de Salud in Zumbagua for sharing information and offering friendship and comfort during my fieldwork.

Last but not least, I would like to thank the family and friends who have given me their love, friendship, and many different kinds of assistance during this long process: writing and visiting while I was in the field; encouraging me when needed; taking care of correspondence, academic and financial affairs while I was away; housing my possessions, my cat, and occasionally myself during the many upheavals associated with doing fieldwork; and generally providing me with an emotional haven during several homeless years. Space does not permit me to mention everyone who has helped me, but I would like to acknowledge my parents, Bill and Jeanne Weismantel, as well as Ronnie Kann, Annette Nekola, Lucy Whalley, Kay Candler, Paco and Katy Unglaub, Misha Kokotovic, Tom Aleto and Karen Elwell, Bruce Rapkin, Cathy Echols, Victor Ottati, Diane Vanek, David Minor, Diego Quiroga, and Byung-Ho Chung. I would also like to thank Mark Stone for his beautiful maps, and Stephen F. Eisenman for some thought-provoking discussions about the concepts of ideology and hegemony.

NOTE ON THE USE OF SYMBOLS

For the purposes of this text, with the exception of common English expressions such as "and/or," the slash (/) is used to separate two contrasting terms (for example, savory/sweet), while the backslash (\) is used to separate terms that are equivalent. The backslash is most commonly used when both the Spanish and the Quichua names for a food are given, the first term being the Spanish and the second the Quichua. In these cases, I am giving the terms used in Zumbagua; frequently, usages in the parish vary from standard usage. Zumbagua Quichua is filled with Spanish loanwords, many of them now obsolete in Spanish itself, such as the "Dyusulupagui" said in giving thanks (from Spanish "Dios se le pague," may God repay you), or the "Alabadu" or "Alabay" said upon entering a doorway. Spanish spoken in the area likewise utilizes a great many words of Quichua origin, so that the designation of a term as Spanish or Quichua in this work is understood to refer to the way it is currently classified by Zumbagua residents, not to its etymology or to standard Latin American or Iberian usages.

I have departed from one Quichua grammatical rule in several places in this text. When using a single Quichua term in an English sentence, I have not used the Quichua plural *-kuna*, but rather have appended an *-s* where necessary, as the *-kuna* is confusing to those who have no familiarity with the Quichua language.

When citing works for which an English translation is available, I have given the date of the original publication, accompanied by the relevant page numbers from the translation. Both original and translation are listed in the bibliography. Similarly, when I have cited an edition other than the first of a work in English, both editions are listed in the bibliography.

FOOD, GENDER, AND

POVERTY IN THE

ECUADORIAN ANDES

INTRODUCTION

This book is about the lives of the people of Zumbagua in the first half of the 1980s. Zumbagua, an impoverished rural parish of the Ecuadorian Andes, while ethnically unique, is undergoing processes of change—economic, social, and cultural—that are strikingly similar to those affecting rural areas throughout the Third World. Thus, while the data presented here will be of interest to Andean scholars, the general perspective of this book will also be valuable for those who have observed the same processes elsewhere.

Despite its obvious debt to the traditions of symbolic and structuralist anthropology, this book's subject is not the esoterica of Zumbagua culture. It is not about the secret knowledge of Zumbagua shamans: the sacred stones that represent the holy places, the rites of sucking and blowing, the all-night healing sessions thick with *trago* fumes and cigarette smoke, the covert early-morning burials of evil bundles. Neither does it detail the fiesta cycle: the dozens of costumed players, *vaca loca, yumbo,* and *danzante,* each belonging to specific fiestas, from Niñu Fishtu at Christmas to Wagra Fishtu, the seven-day harvest festival in late June. The symbols analyzed here are not sacred, but secular and mundane: toasted barley flour and white rice, chickens and guinea pigs, bread and candies. My subject matter is the ordinary rituals of everyday life: the early morning grinding of barley, known by women physically as the rhythmic motion of back and arms and thighs that begins each day from childhood into old age, and familiar to men as a comfortable, intimate scene of family life; or the evening meal, the senior woman of the family sitting dominant by the cooking pot, controlling her family through the etiquette of serving. The locus of analysis is not the church or the plaza but the kitchen, that warmest and most central place in the Zumbaguan household, the heart of daily life.

Although my focus on food and cooking differs from that of many anthropological studies, like most ethnographies this one attempts to depict a way of life holistically: it says something about love and money, art and politics, land and families, work and play. The limited range of foods eaten in Zumbagua is a reflection of the parish's environmental setting in the western Cordillera of the northern Andes, high enough to be above the limits of cultivation for many crops. At the same time, the increasing role of manufactured and imported foods in the diet illuminates the influence of the economic and political milieu.

In the semiotic structure of its cuisine, with its "wet" meals and "dry" meals, thin soups and thick soups, Zumbagua shares a Pan-Andean indigenous culture. But some aspects of local cuisine, such as the relative values placed on grains and tubers, speak of the region's history as a society bound for three and a half centuries into the oppressive hacienda system. And the impoverished calendar round of *fanescas* without fish and Finados without maize, which is becoming familiar in the 1980s, is one of the ways in which the people of Zumbagua are now discovering, like the postbellum blacks of our own nation, the bitter ironies of political emancipation without economic opportunity. Lastly, the use of food symbolism in parish discourse speaks of the bitterness of the people of Zumbagua about their role in the nation: newly enfranchised, they feel the powerlessness of a rural indigenous population in an impoverished Third World nation in which the politicians value their urban, Hispanic constituency above all others.

The everyday practices of cooking, dress, and speech provide the medium for expression of controversies and contradictions inherent in Zumbagua life today, many of which center around issues of being Indian and being subsistence farmers, of assimilating and joining the urban underclass. Questions of whether these options are desirable or even possible, and what relationship exists between cultural choices and economic opportunity, permeate everyday parish life. A sense of urgency fueled by the region's poverty brings into sharp focus the mundane discourses and everyday practices out of which Zumbagua produces an image of itself and of reality.

These controversies are produced in part by social schisms within the parish, schisms that are also expressed by everyday means. Woman and man, old and young, adult and child, rich and poor, Indian and white distinguish themselves from each other by what they eat, how they dress, and what they say. Through these means people establish ideological positions: the needs and desires, conflicts and power differences inherent in their roles. Analyzing the everyday practices of the kitchen as constituted ideology reveals the differentiating effects of socioeconomic change on individuals and their ideological stances. Men who work as temporary migrants in the city are exposed to proletarian values and Latin culture: cumbia music, soccer games, national politics, images of racing cars and pinup girls. They are increasingly alienated in experience and understanding from their wives and sisters, subsistence farmers for whom beauty is a matter of fields in flower and pregnant animals, whose humor

4

is expressed in Quichua riddle-games, their pleasures in myths about magical condors and anthropomorphic bears. These conflicts are exacerbated by the nature of a semiproletarianized economy, which drives women's orientation increasingly inward even as their men turn outward. Both sexes in turn differ from their parents, for whom language, knowledge, and wealth have never been polarized to the same degree according to gender.

Arguments over food and cooking reveal the discordant visions individuals have of their households and of the roles different members should play. Children demanding store-bought bread at breakfast in place of homemade porridge, or old and young quarreling over the hours at which meals should be served, exemplify the conflictive positions of the generations within the household and reveal the divisive nature of processes of acculturation and change. Transformations in diet and cuisine, which in overview seem gradual and inevitable in nature, at closer range are seen to be produced through the interaction of individual actors whose desires clash. Not only the foods eaten within the household, but the relations of power and prestige among its members are altered in these processes, and the reproduction of the household itself is transformed.

This work uses food and cooking, realms of ordinary life, to explore the underlying structures of Zumbagua: a semiproletarianized economy, a racist society, an indigenous Andean culture. Consideration of all of these factors in the creation of Zumbagua foodways makes clear that the structures of economy, society, and culture, artificially separated through the heuristic operations of social scientists, are indissolubly linked in the lived experience of everyday practice. Each chapter, though addressed to specific theoretical and substantive issues, constantly reaffirms their interdependence within practice.

The first chapter is an overview of theoretical approaches to the study of cooking, as diet, as cuisine, and as economic activity. The second chapter contains the type of material with which many conventional ethnographies begin: the geography, natural and political, of the region; demographic data; a brief summary of parish history; and a discussion of some of the major issues of political strategy and ethnic identity confronting the parish today. The third chapter describes the diet of the parish in concrete, specific terms: the foods people eat. The discussion of diet introduces issues of poverty and wealth.

The final three chapters present the main argument. The role of foods in Zumbagua life is considered using three different, yet overlapping forms of analysis. Chapter 4 takes a structuralist approach in differentiating diet from cuisine, the socially made, individually internalized structures by which food is known, and which order its preparation and consumption. The basic structures of Zumbagua cuisine are presented schematically and discussed in terms of contrasts in form and content, as they are used to generate socially meaningful oppositions such as wet season/dry season, special occasion/everyday, male/female, and Indian/white.

Chapter 5 is concerned with foods in their roles as ideologically charged symbols in political discourse, thus providing a detailed case-study of ideological discourse as constituted in the lived experience of a contemporary, "unpoliticized" people of the rural Third World. The symbolism of white rice, as it expresses the interrelated concepts of racial superiority and commodity fetishism, provides a key example of the pressures to assimilate felt in the parish today, while the role of barley is analyzed as a symbol of indigenous resistance.

Finally, Chapter 6 considers how the production and consumption of foods are organized, with particular emphasis on gender roles: the interactions of women in the organization of kitchen work; relations between husband and wife as enacted in the production, acquisition, and consumption of foods; and the power relations within the household as demonstrated in the formal organization of the meal. This analysis reveals the nature of household reproduction and of the social reproduction of the family over time, and thus the transformations the Zumbagua family and household are currently undergoing as they adapt to the structure of semiproletarianized life.

The last three chapters, then, present Zumbagua cooking as an implicit system of signs underlying everyday actions, as a fertile source for the symbols used in ideological discourse, and as a realm of productive practice, the organization of which provides a basis for the social formation of family and household and for the power relations of generation and gender.

This book attempts to achieve two goals. It is an ethnography—a detailed, qualitative description of the culture of a contemporary northern Andean people, modern-day "peasants." And it is a theoretical exploration of a single domain of everyday life—food and cooking—as a tool for understanding social life and historical process.

O N E

Food and Theory

Food and cooking are inextricably linked with culture. It is not only a physiological truism that we are what we eat; what we eat and how we eat it also defines us as social beings. Cooking ensures the material production and reproduction of the social group, but this material process is culturally structured. To cook is to speak and to mean, as well as to make and to do.

A bowl of boiled potatoes or a plate of white rice is at least three different kinds of thing: it is a sign, a symbol, and a product. In the chapters that follow, I consider Zumbagua foods as each of these things. This work begins and ends in material practice. The intervening chapters, however, are concerned with the immaterial life of food in Zumbagua. Chapter 4 is about not diet but cuisine, the categories of thought that underlie practices of cooking and eating. Chapter 5 considers the use of foods as symbols in political discourse, which is a social use of foods at the farthest remove from material life, foods as abstract entities used to symbolize entire social formations.

And yet even in the realm of discourse there is no great distance between symbolic and material usages in actual practice. Ordinary objects such as foods are used as symbols of ideological conflict not so much in clearly defined political arenas as in everyday debates over mundane questions, such as what to eat or what to wear. These discourses are ideology embedded in practice: a neighbor who is seen as pretentious for cooking rice, old men calling young men *lluchu* ("naked" or "skinned") if they dare to walk publicly in the parish without poncho and hat.

There is another way in which the role of material objects such as foods in discourse is inseparable from their role in material practice. When foods become symbols, their meanings are not arbitrarily defined but derive from the roles they play in economic life. An expensive food stands for wealth, a cheap one for poverty; homegrown and handmade are contrasted to store-bought, the well worn to the shiny new. It is because they are ordinarily immersed in everyday practice in a material way that foods, abstracted as symbols from this material process, can condense in themselves a wealth of ideological meanings. A symbol works because it is a thing, a tangible representation of the intangible social and cultural forces that organize material life.

This relationship of material and symbolic in discourse is reversed in the structures of cuisine. When a food serves as a symbol in discourse, it is an object that carries, in the context of that discourse, a symbolic load. The material object becomes a tool for symbolic work, the work of reproducing (or creating or destroying) cultural and ideological forms. In the case of cuisine, symbolic forms exist whose primary purpose is the organization of material production. The rules of exclusion and inclusion that order menus and meals are arbitrary structures whose existence is purely immaterial. They resemble a language, an art style, an elaborate game, and yet they are a practical tool: a woman calls on the laws of cuisine every time she cooks for herself and her family.

Structure: Cooking as Cuisine

Symbols and Signs

Foods as Symbols

A food is a substance; but it can also be both symbol and sign.[1] The anthropological literature is saturated with references to the pervasiveness of food symbolism in social life.[2] Among the earliest anthropological treatises one finds works such as Crawley's *The Mystic Rose* (1927[1902]), which explores the relationship between metaphors of food and of sexuality, and W. Robertson Smith's (1889) treatise on sacrifice, where great emphasis is placed on the commensuality of the shared meal as symbolic of the social bond. This emphasis on the meal as an important aspect of ritual enactments is found in many modern ethnographies as well.[3]

In addition to the symbolism of the meal, the establishment of social bonds through gifts of food has not escaped the notice of ethnographers. Mauss's *The Gift* (1967) discusses gifts of food; every student who ever read Malinowski (1950) remembers pigs and yams; Evans-Pritchard is eloquent on the subject of the sharing of foods as defining social groups (1940:84–85).[4]

In the Andes, where formalized enactments of reciprocity and redistribution play such a critical role in the creation and maintenance of social ties (Mayer 1974; Alberti and Mayer 1974; Fonseca Martel 1972), the gift of food is of profound importance. Rituals of drinking are also important, both in current practice (see Allen's excellent treatment 1978) and historically (see for example Zuidema 1980). Andean systems of verticality (Murra 1975) are symbolized through the exchange of foods from different zones (see for example Bastien 1978, Fonseca Martel 1966).[5]

If foods play such an important part in the symbols and rituals that establish social relations within a group, it is not surprising that they are equally potent expressions of relations *between* groups: "people who eat strikingly different foods or similar foods in strikingly different ways are thought to be strikingly different, perhaps even less than human" (Mintz 1985:3). Food is one of the strongest of ethnic and class markers; consequently, it provides an endless source of metaphorical referents of ethnicity, many of them derogatory, ranging from the Englishman speaking of the French as "frogs" (referring to the presence of frogs' legs in Gallic cuisine), to the lowland Ecuadorian Runa who calls highlanders "barley-gruel-eaters" (Whitten, personal communication). Not only hostility between rival groups but relations of domination make use of food symbolism in this fashion.[6]

The Spanish conquest of the New World brought a variety of cultigens and cuisines into contact, to the tremendous enrichment of both European and American diets. An enormous diversity of foods, from chocolate to potatoes, was introduced to European palates, while Old World domesticates, such as broad beans and barley, and animals, including sheep, pigs, and chickens, transformed the Andean diet. But the Spaniards came as conquerors, and the relations of domination established in the colonial period were represented by the stigmatizing of certain indigenous foods as "Indian," and hence unfit for consumption by non-Indians. This practice of denigration, evident in early sources such as González Holguín (1608), is still very much a part of Andean life.[7] As Andean communities like Zumbagua struggle for self-definition today, foods and ways of eating them are still among the symbols by which social conflicts can be named and confronted.

Foods can easily become highly charged symbols of ethnicity because they speak deeply to us about who we are. Sidney Mintz says that "food preferences are close to the center of . . . self-definition" (1985:3). Some of the first and most deeply imprinted metaphors we unknowingly predicate (Fernandez 1977) onto our unformed infant selves are phrased in terms of what we eat and what we are fed by those on whom we depend.

This deeply personal relationship with foods, which seems to be an inescapable part of the human condition, provides an orectic pole that gives food symbolism its affective power. Because we can use foods to express metaphorically who we are, and because through these symbols we may be motivated to feel and to act, foods and ways of cooking them may even become symbols that polarize factions and create arenas of conflict. Foods become highly charged symbols: expressive, multivocalic, condensing, ambiguous (Turner 1967).

In Victor Turner's masterful presentation of the nature of symbols, he places primary emphasis on the affective roots of symbolic power. While acknowledging that the meanings of symbols are partially derived from what he terms their "positional" context (1967:50–51)—that is, their definition relative to other symbols—he in no way privileges this systemic aspect of meaning. But the power of foods to act as symbols, to express, connote, affect, is based on their also belonging to a semiotic system, a system of signs. Metaphorical imagery depends on the existence of an underlying linguistic structure with which it can play (Sapir 1977); food symbolism can work only because foods are both symbols and signs.

Foods as Signs

In the literature on semiotics and structuralism, foods crop up repeatedly as examples of the kind of objects in social life that form systems of signs. For example, in *Elements of Semiology* (1965), one of the fundamental texts of semiotic theory, Roland Barthes turns repeatedly to the garment system and the food system in his exploration of signifying systems composed of "collections of objects." He finds the food system especially amenable to semiotic analysis, as it has some of the most important properties of language: a unity in the material out of which the signifiers are constructed (47), the double axes of syntagm and paradigm (63),[8] and a distinctly separable *langue* and *parole* (27–28).

Claude Lévi-Strauss, the major proponent of a linguistic model for the study of culture within anthropology proper, also finds the example of cooking a useful one in presenting his project: "The object of comparative structural analysis is . . . a certain number of structures which I seek where they may be found, and not elsewhere: in other words, in the kinship system, political ideology, mythology, ritual, art, code of etiquette, and—why not—cooking" (1958:85). These structures are all "partial expressions" of "this entity . . . called society," chosen as objects of research because they are "especially well suited to scientific study" (1958:85).

In addition to these statements of principle, both Lévi-Strauss and Barthes return repeatedly to foods throughout their work. Meat and honey, cooking and rotting prove to be major themes in Lévi-Strauss's disentanglement of Amazonian mythology (1964, 1966a, 1966b); the aesthetics of Japanese food preparation delight Barthes in *Empire of Signs* (1970), while American food habits are disparagingly explored by him elsewhere (1961), and the nightmarish wonderland of postcapitalist semiotic depicted in Barthes's *Mythologies* (1957) several times is captured through foods.

Nevertheless, neither author has systematically explored the constitution of an entire semiotic of foods within a single cultural system. Barthes discusses the possibilities of analyzing a food system in its entirety without actually doing so (1961, 1965), while Lévi-Strauss in *Structural Anthropology* (1958:87) refers to his brief discussion of cuisine as "a somewhat flimsy example" chosen only because it is as apropos of contemporary societies as of primitive ones.

A full exploration of the possibilities of structural analysis for a study of food and cooking is to be found in the work of Christine Hugh-Jones (1978, 1979). Like Lévi-Strauss, Hugh-Jones writes of Amazonia, in her case of the cultural system of the Pirá-Paraná area of northwestern Amazonia. She uses cooking as a key cultural domain, analysis of which provides access to the structures of geography, cosmology, life processes, and social structures. Interestingly, while other scholars have looked for structure in the combination of foods that make up a meal (Lévi-Strauss 1958:86–87; Barthes 1965:27–28, 83; Douglas 1971), Hugh-Jones instead analyzes the cooking process itself as a sequence of operations, the structure of which is homologous to that of other cultural and natural processes. This isomorphism reinforces the imposition of cultural order on the natural world, and provides in the humble female activities of cooking metaphors by which the larger masculine world of intervillage relations can be expressed and understood.

In her work, Hugh-Jones follows the approach outlined by Lévi-Strauss for the structural study of societies. Within the domain of cooking, an underlying structure is abstracted from the productive activities and social interactions of lived experience. This structure is then compared to similar structures underlying other domains (the construction of houses, the raising of children, the establishment of political formations, the relationship between the sexes, the burial of the dead). In this, she follows exactly the plan laid out by Lévi-Strauss (1958:87), for whom, once the "differential structures" of a cuisine have been discovered, the next step is to inquire "whether they . . . may be encountered (often in a transformed fashion) in other spheres of the same society or in different societies. And, if we find these structures to be common to several spheres, we have the right to conclude that we have reached a significant knowledge of the unconscious attitudes of the society or societies under consideration."

Sign, Symbol, Thing

Hugh-Jones's work stands as a ground-breaking contribution to the study of food systems and to South American ethnography. My own project, however, differs from hers in its conception. It would be possible to demonstrate the isomorphism of structures from the various domains of Zumbagua culture, as Hugh-Jones does; this structure could then be studied in isolation from the economic and social life that produced it, and compared only to other such structures. But while I do not deny the validity of such heuristic isolation of semiotic systems for purposes of analysis, my own project is instead to demonstrate the interaction of structure, discourse, and practice in one domain, that of food and cooking. Chapter 4 presents the underlying structure of Zumbagua foods, the rules that make intelligible social action possible. Analysis of structure is a necessary first step; but the following chapters, instead of comparing the structures of cooking to other semiotic structures, will show the immersion of this system in daily life and its complete interpenetration with other systems: language, society, politics, and the economics of production and exchange. It is the relation between the abstract system of signs and the lived experience through which the system is reproduced that interests me.

In taking this approach, I am following Barthes rather than Lévi-Strauss, semiotics rather than structuralism. Unlike Lévi-Strauss, Barthes sees no need to search for isomorphism between the semiotic systems of various domains. My approach also mirrors general trends since the initial establishment of structuralism as a body of theory. Poststructuralist thought has moved away from structure to the analysis of discourse (Ricoeur 1977, Foucault 1969:27). As Foucault points out, although the study of language and the study of discourse begin with the same body of data, "a corpus of statements, or a collection of discursive facts," their ends are fundamentally different: a linguistic system is established when one has isolated from that body of statements "rules that may make it possible to construct other statements than these" (1969:27). The study of discourse, however, with its emphasis on the event of speech itself, "poses a quite different question: how is it that one particular statement appeared rather than another?" (ibid.). The structure of a language is only a tool, in itself empty of content, but making possible the expression of meaning. It is discourse that reveals the movement of history.

> However banal it may be, however unimportant its consequences may appear to be, however quickly it may be forgotten after its appearance . . . a statement is always an event that neither the language (*langue*) nor the meaning can quite exhaust . . . like every event, it is unique, yet subject to repetition, transformation, and reactivation . . . it is linked not only to the situations that provoke it, and the consequences it gives rise to, but . . . to the statements that precede and follow it. (Ibid.)

It is in the study of discourse—where the "banal," the "unimportant" are analyzed in order to reinsert action, process, intent, and historicity into the study of communication and culture—that analyzing the domains of everyday practice such as cooking can provide not simply the trivial examples of semiosis in society that Lévi-Strauss pictures, but key sources for understanding the movement of society and history.

Current thought has moved beyond discourse to the dialogic, that is, the existence of competing discourses within society (Stewart 1983, Hill 1985), a theoretical approach derived from the work of Mikhail Bakhtin (1968, 1981), and also found in the recent work of Pierre Bourdieu (1977). According to this approach, historical process is not unilinear but the result of multiple voices, formations, and trajectories. In discussing the use of food symbolism in the discourses of race and class in Zumbagua, I will also have recourse to this type of analysis. Only a theory of multiple discursive universes allows exploration of the multiple, coexisting yet unassimilable statements about Indian and white, rich and poor, superior and inferior through which the contradictory position of indigenous people in the modern Andes is expressed.

In the analysis presented here, then, structure remains as an underlying base, one that exists at any particular moment as a functioning and perfected whole, a fact that Saussure made clear in 1916. The challenge now is to discover the relations between underlying structure and the discourses, competing dialogues, and (ultimately) practices of the moment; but this analysis must begin with the system of signs.

The System of Signs

A Potato is a Sign

The foods eaten by the people of Zumbagua are organized into a system of signs. This statement has several implications. First, that it is a *system* of signs implies certain things: its constituent elements must exist in fixed relations to one another, such that they derive part of their meaning from their positions relative to one another. Moreover, this statement that a food system is a system of *signs* implies that each food is itself a sign. The exact meaning of this second statement, that a food can be a sign, must be carefully examined.

A sign, in the metaphor Saussure (1916) has given us, is a piece of paper of which one side is the signifier and the other the signified. Signification, then, is the process of "cutting out" signs, in which both sides are simultaneously separated from the rest of the sheet.

Because the social creation of the world is so invisible to us, the difficulty when first presented with this view of language, as Barthes has pointed out (1965:38–39), is to conceive of the signified as being part of the sign. The signifier "potato" and the sign "potato" seem to be the same, a symbol for a real object, a potato. It is difficult to grasp the fact that the word "potato" stands not for a physical object, but for a concept, a socially produced category "potato" that is referred to by its signifier, the combination of sounds or the written word that represents it in acts of communication. The signifier "potato," the word itself, stands at a double remove from the "real" potato. The word stands for a concept, the concept for a thing: signifier "potato"\signified potato\potato.

Neither the signifier nor the signified is in fact that concrete object, a potato; the signifier—in spoken form as sound or in written form as marks on paper—is if anything more concrete than the ethereal signified existing in the noncorporeal realm of mind or of collective representation. But it is intrinsic to the operation of signs in society that their material/immaterial nature appears as other than it is.

When confronted with the notion that a nonlinguistic area of culture such as food is a semiotic system, similar to a language, the locus of the difficulty changes, though the nature of the problem does not. It is not difficult to accept the fact that cultures do create rule-bound structures that govern the way foods are prepared and eaten. Mary Douglas's "Deciphering a Meal" (1971), for example, gives a clear and convincing presentation of some of the rules governing the food system of the English middle class and underlines the arbitrary and culture-specific nature of such rules by contrasting this system with some conventions of French cooking. Neither is it difficult to accept that some foods have connotative values. Mom and apple pie, birthday cake and wedding cake, all carry evident symbolic weight in middle America.

The problem lies in the notion of semiosis itself. Whereas words, so obviously abstract, seem like signifiers divorced from their signifieds, for concrete objects the problem is reversed. It is difficult to grasp the idea that the macaroni in macaroni and cheese, which so obviously exists as a material object, also constitutes a sign. Macaroni appears to be a signified, a concrete thing, without a signifier: it does not represent, it just is. What we need to bear in mind, again, is the social construction of the world, the collective representations that filter our knowledge of "concrete objects." "As soon as there is a society, every usage is converted into a sign of itself" (Barthes 1965:41). We never know a potato except as "a potato," a culturally designated sign that is simultaneously both object and symbol, both itself and a representation of itself. These "two sides of a piece of paper" are as inseparable in the food system as in language, if not more so. Like the sound of a tree falling when no one hears it, the existence of the signified potato is something we can only imagine. We can only experience it through its signifier. At the same time, the process of signification is itself invisible to us: food is among the many aspects of our lives that people "continue to experience as a simple function at the very moment they constitute it into a sign" (Barthes 1961:168).

People from Ames, Iowa, like those from Zumbagua, eat potatoes; but the Iowan "potato," functioning as it does within its own semiotic system, can never mean or be what a *papa* is in Zumbagua, any more than the French *fromage* is exactly like the American "cheese" (Lévi-Strauss 1958:93). The meaning of the potato in Ames encompasses french fries, potato chips, mashed potatoes on the dinner table at Thanksgiving, and baked potatoes at the local steak house. In Zumbagua its range of meaning is entirely different, all the more so because, to cultivators, a subsistence crop like the *papa* speaks of hoes and harvests as well as of dishes such as *yawarlocro* and *cariuchu*.

Syntagm and Paradigm

The difference between the potato in Iowa and the potato in Zumbagua lies not only in its connotations but also in its role in the semiotic system. The cultural constitution of the "potato" as a symbol rests on its role as a sign, and just as in other semiotic systems, the sign "potato" in a specific food system is largely defined by its position relative to the signs around it. Its shape is formed by the other spaces cut out of the piece of paper around it. Potatoes are contrasted to other foods within a cuisine along two axes, syntagm and paradigm (Barthes 1965:63). (In Figures 6–9, pp. 128–38, syntagm appears as the horizontal axis, paradigm as the vertical one.) Signification may be defined by syntagmatic positioning, by the contrast between the roles foods play in a meal. For example, Mary Douglas (1971) analyzes the British meal as being built upon a basic structure of A + 2B, one main element (meat) and two subsidiary elements (starch and vegetable). In this system, the potato would clearly be a *B*, a subsidiary item. (In Ames as well: rules of cuisine in the United States are clearly derived from British constructs [Root and Rochemont 1976].)

Unlike the British potato, however, the potato in Zumbagua can occupy a central role in the composition of a meal, other ingredients such as meat being mere complements to enhance it. In Zumbagua, the potato in some syntagms (though not in all) is clearly the dominant, the *A* factor.

In addition, the potato is defined paradigmatically, by its relation to other elements in the lexicon that can fill the same syntagmatic role: advertisements that recount the joys of substituting StoveTop Stuffing for potatoes are attempting to establish their product as belonging to the same paradigm as the potato, that is, as playing the same role in the syntagm of the nightly meal. In the Zumbaguan syntagm in which potatoes are central, white rice can be partially or totally substituted for them: they belong to the same paradigm. In the paradigmatic dimension, the potato is parallel to white rice and so, in some senses, equivalent to it. And yet it is also defined as distinct from other elements in the paradigm; as they fill the same syntagmatic role, either will help to define a culturally acceptable dish; yet simultaneously, potatoes and white rice are defined in contradistinction to each other, as being different in meaning or value.

In Zumbagua, certain foods are contrasted with other foods as being ethnically "Indian" or "white," economically "rich" or "poor." The process by which values come to be associated with foods is a complex one, and foods rarely acquire a fixed value. Their meanings normally depend to some extent on context and usage, in other words on position within a specific structure, rather than residing completely in the foods themselves as an inherent quality. These positional meanings accentuate contrast in value between items that are parallel in position (see discussion of the term "parallel" in Chapter 4). It is not easy to compare a cola with barley-mutton soup, for one is a snack and one is a main course. The contrast between serving a chicken-rice soup at a festive occasion and serving one made of *cuy* (guinea pig) and potato, however, is sharp and unmistakable. Chickens and *cuyes,* rice and potatoes are readily contrasted to one another because they are absolutely parallel. The contrast in value, in this case between ethnically "white" and ethnically indigenous, is clearest in such an example, in which the elements belong to the same paradigm.[9]

Discourse: Cooking as Metaphor

Zumbagua is changing, and younger people want to eat things their mother never cooked. These changes in people's food preferences hardly seem to constitute debates over ideology. They are not the kind of "great" ideologies we normally think of when we hear the term, the overarching political philosophies for which people have fought and died.

The obvious starting point for a study of ideological conflict in Zumbagua is not the private domain of the kitchen but the public forum of the plaza, and Chapter 2, the general description of the parish today, does indeed describe current political debates heard in the plaza. But the battle between classes, the struggle to create the power to dominate or to resist, is frequently fought on a very different terrain: not the European battlefield with flags flying and lines clearly drawn, but a guerilla warfare taking place in the interstices of unimportant incidents. "Surely it is in the coils of rumor, story, gossip, and chitchat where ideology and ideas become emotionally powerful and enter into active social circulation and meaningful existence" (Taussig 1984:494). The emergence of certain foodstuffs as topics of discussion, as rebukes, insults, punchlines, snubs, wishes, and "somedays," is the creation of an arena of conflict, but it is an arena dispersed into the atmosphere of everyday life. This discourse does not mark out a territory for itself; it remains formless and insubstantial.

Chapter 5 details the emergence of one such discourse, over white rice as an element of the Zumbaguan diet, using Bourdieu's (1979) concept of the emergence of a universe of discourse, which causes what had been *doxa,* undiscussed practice, to become defended orthodoxy or confrontational heterodoxy. When this happens, the result is not unlike Victor Turner's description of an arena: "a framework . . . which manifestly functions as a setting for antagonistic interaction aimed at arriving at a publicly recognized decision. . . . (A)n arena is an explicit frame; nothing is merely implied. Action is definite, people outspoken; the chips are down" (1974:133–134).

Turner, of course, is speaking of scenes of overt political conflict, large-scale, public events that become part of the annals of local history. But the conflicts expressed and the resolutions sought on the terrain of everyday practice do in fact constitute arenas in Turner's sense, specific loci in the ongoing, conflictual process by which change takes place. The rhetoric heard in the plaza seems far removed from the kitchens up on the hillsides outside of town, where women continue to cook, nurse their babies, pasture sheep, and work in the fields. And yet I would argue that fundamental changes are occurring as much on the hillside as in the plaza. These changes are no less than the restructuring of lives and knowledge, as the people of Zumbagua move out of their past as hacienda peons and into a new and problematic future.

There are two points to be made in reference to the role of the rural household in political change. First, images of "outside world" and "inside world," "future-oriented" and "past-oriented," while important metaphors used in the creation and maintenance of boundaries should not blind us to the actual integration of these two worlds at an economic level. The old image of "dos mundos superpuestos,"[10] in which subsistence agriculture is seen as a holdover from the past operating in its own—albeit restricted—sphere, must be replaced. Analyses such as Claude Meillassoux's (1981) show that subsistence agriculturalists in the Third World are firmly articulated with the capitalist economy and contribute to capital accumulation. This articulation alters the structure, and hence the lived experience, of the farmstead despite its apparently isolated existence.

The second point to be made about "kitchen life" is that it is in some senses prior to plaza politics, and more essential, because of its critical role in enculturation. The rhetoric of young hotheads seems to be "where it's happening," but these phenomena may be evanescent. They are especially short-lived when compared to everyday productive practices and to the reproduction of culture through the day-to-day care given to children. As is shown by the history of abortive political movements prior to the Russian Revolution, or the series of associations and political manifestations described by E. P. Thompson (1966) as contributing to the development of a British working-class consciousness, the emergence of concrete political change is a process of fits and starts. There are frequently long periods of quiescence in which no concrete moves appear to be being made.

In Turner's terms, during these periods only the social "field" is active, in other words, the abstract cultural domain where paradigms are formulated (1967:17). The paradigmatic understandings with which people face change and political conflict are regenerated in the most casual, informal, intimate domestic practices. Previous political experiences are assimilated, and the potential for renewed action is created in the discourses that have been awakened at this everyday level, here in the "coils of rumor" to which Taussig refers.

Within these coils of rumor, certain symbols crystallize as meaningful, as capable of evoking an entire field of memory and experience that can now be given a politicized valence. In Bourdieu's terms, they emerge from *doxa* into the universe of discourse. This process is critical in the making of ideologies. Henri Lefebvre points to the implicit emphasis in Marx's thought on the critical importance of language as the only access human consciousness has to the reality of praxis. "What people say derives from praxis—from the performance of tasks, from the division of labor—arises out of real actions, real struggles in the world. What they actually do, however, enters consciousness only by way of language, by being said. Ideologies mediate between praxis and consciousness (i.e., language)" (1977:261).

This notion of ideology as mediating between praxis and language can be related to Michel Foucault's analysis in *The Archaeology of Knowledge,* in which discourse mediates between language and history (1969:27). According to Marx, ideology constructs what we can say about living, and hence how we experience our lives. For Foucault, discourses—the body of actual expressions of this experience—are constructed from the interface between the abstract structures of language and the real events of history.

Lefebvre's recapitulation of Marx on these issues expresses the notion that the locus for the creation and transformation of ideologies is in precisely the kind of everyday discursive practices discussed in this book: "ideological representations find their way into language, become a permanent part of it. They supply vocabularies, formulations, turns of thought which are also turns of phrase. Social consciousness, awareness of how multifarious and contradictory social action can be, changes only in this way: by acquiring new terms and idioms to supplant obsolete linguistic structures" (1977:261).

Unlike more politicized peasants and proletarians elsewhere in the Andes, the Zumbaguans seem to be without conscious political ideology, in the conventional sense of the word, and likewise without a clear class consciousness. But, as I will argue, the people of the parish in fact have a keen understanding of their social position and of the economic and political forces that create it. The roots of this political consciousness, however, lie not in the rhetoric of activists, but in that knowledge of the world which arises from praxis. This understanding is not an ideology formulated as abstract ideas, but one closer to Marx's original conception of man's conscious existence as being inseparable from material social processes (Williams 1977:59–60).

Llama jarkuna, to pasture the sheep; *almuirzu yanuna,* to cook lunch; *trasti takshana,* to wash clothes; with these, a hundred smaller tasks: feed the pig, bathe the baby, sweep the patio, peel potatoes . . . thus a woman in Zumbagua fills her day. Each activity is constituted and surrounded by familiar tools, motions, rhythms, taking place in the well-known settings of the fields, the patio, the hearth. Pasturing the sheep involves a certain set of tools: the whip, its handle polished from many hands, and for a woman the spindle, silent and productive, just as the noisy, indolent flute will accompany a shepherd boy. (In Andean graves from before the Conquest, the box of spindles accompanies women's mummies; some Otavaleños continue this practice today.) For washing clothes the tools are different: flat rocks, cold rushing water, the heavy stick for beating stiff woven ponchos and blankets. At the hearth a woman sits on piles of straw, with their familiar smell and feel. Her experienced fingers steadily feed the fire, spreading the thin shiny grasses so that the flame catches evenly and burns hot.

Every activity is done *wawandi:* with a baby on one's back. A baby's world in Zumbagua is the movement of the muscles in his mother's back under his cheek as she wields a hoe with him tied close to her, and the smell of her cooking fire filtered through the cloth with which he is bound.

These are everyday practices, the material life from which arise knowledge, ideology, discourse. But as the baby grows into a man, he will come to see this world of his mother's and grandmother's as encapsulated within another, which distorts and oppresses it and which seems infinitely larger and more powerful than his own. Children playing in the fields stop to watch the brightly painted buses flash by on their way to places their mothers have never seen; stories are told of the marvels of Quito and Guayaquil, the huge buildings, the hundreds of cars, airplanes, and streetlights, rich women wearing makeup and high heels who hire Indians to carry their purchases.

The material presence of this world is inseparable from his mother's, though in many ways it remains alien and frightening to her. The thong of her whip is a strip of rubber cut from old tires; to wash clothes one must buy soap. The kitchen is made up of things bought, things gathered and grown and made, things traded. The straw to fuel the fire comes from the communal grazing lands, free for the taking. Wooden *bateas* (basins) and spoons are acquired through exchange with the people of

Apagua, who can get wood from the *yunga* just as the *kutana rumi* and *uchu rumi,* the great and little grinding stones, come from rocky Talatag. But the battered enamel bowls and cups and the heavy two-handled *sartén* (frying pan) were bought in the market from sharp-tongued *chola*[11] women who know how to make a *longo*[12] feel like dirt.

The life of this high valley, where agriculture is still undertaken without a plow, seems isolated from the world outside, but it is inextricably bound to the outside world by the need for money. In Zumbagua the reproduction of material life requires money: to buy laundry soap, hoe blades, tin spoons, plastic buckets.

The Zumbagua mother and child live in a situation in which two modes of production interact in a relationship of domination. According to Meillassoux, because of this relationship,

> rural communities, although in a process of change, remain qualitatively different from the capitalist mode of production. However, in the long run the general conditions of reproducing the social whole resulting from this interpenetration no longer depend on determinations inherent in the domestic mode of production, but on decisions taken in the capitalist sector. By this process, contradictory in essence, the domestic mode is simultaneously maintained and destroyed . . . [it] both exists and does not exist. (1981:95–97)

The people of Zumbagua represent their world to themselves in this way, as both real and not real. They are constantly bombarded from within and without by images of their practices as being backward and wrong. The imposition of these labels of inadequacy is a hegemonic[13] process. The subsistence economy is inevitably eroding, an overdetermined process in which ecological degradation, overpopulation, and drastic changes in the national economy have all played a part. But the erosion of people's faith in the validity of the food and clothes, language and celebrations they grew up with is also the product of a multiplicity of forces. Whereas before, exploitation of this work force was made possible by a rigid caste system in which distinctive customs preserved social boundaries, national ideologies now call for the rapid assimilation of indigenous peoples. In an isolated rural area like Zumbagua, this message filters through in small ways, but the pressure is unrelenting. It is best defined as hegemonic because it is not "expressed in directly political forms . . . by direct or effective coercion," but rather as "a complex interlocking of political forms, and 'hegemony', according to different interpretations, is either this or the active social and cultural forms which are its necessary elements. . . . What is decisive is not only the conscious system of ideas and beliefs but the whole lived social process as practically organized by specific and dominant meanings and values" (Williams 1977:108–109).

The transformation of indigenous practice occurs not only when the schoolchild is taught to salute the Ecuadorian flag, but also when his mother hesitates over what foods to serve her family, fearful that there is something inadequate in a meal of "just" homegrown foods. Even women who have little interaction with white outsiders, separated from them by the language barrier, learn the lessons of cultural and social inferiority. Children so young they have scarcely ever left the farmstead have already begun to learn them too.

The familiar world of house and field and mountain, the knowledge of which is intimately associated in the child's mind with the close warmth of his mother's body, this world that is maintained by his family's labor, by *llama jarkuna* and *jabus surcuna,* has an existence less solid than the strength of the muscles in his mother's back would suggest. Despite the evidence of a thousand perceptual memories that prove its concreteness, this experience of the world, this domestic mode of production, which is the first life the child knows, comes to seem in some senses less real than the unknown and unimaginable lives of strangers seen only through the windows of a passing bus. Because of these representations of the lived experience of being indigenous, potatoes and mutton fade before the images of white rice and chicken, bread and Cocacola.

Practice: Cooking as Transformation

I have set out to discuss cooking as structure, discourse, and practice. In thus starting from structure, from the role of foods as signs, this work seems to be taking the ultimately nonmaterialist stance of structuralism, by conceiving of semiosis as an arbitrary, given structure underlying lived experience. Rosalind Coward and John Ellis have summarized this tendency in structuralist thought, where the primacy given to "the examination of the 'sign': the relation between . . . signifier . . . and . . . signified . . . neither of which pre-exists the other or has any meaning outside their relation . . . removed any emphasis from productivity, stressing instead a pre-given meaning" (1977:3–4). The discoveries of linguistics, revealing the existence of underlying structures behind everyday speech acts, certainly caused a florescence in the study of these systems of signification. The realization that every act of speech presupposes the existence of *langue* led some theorists to give priority to *langue* in their formulations, making of *parole* simply a series of imperfect realizations. But the relation between *langue* and *parole* does not give priority to either; if there is no *parole* without *langue,* there is also no *langue* without *parole:* "a language is at the same time the product and the instrument of speech: their relationship is a genuinely dialectical one" (Barthes 1965:16).

This concept of a dialectical relation between language and speech enables analysis to meet Coward and Ellis's call for a replacement of the notion of structure with that of "the process of structuration" (1977:4; see also Giddens 1979, 1982). The structures of cuisine are not fixed and immutable, but are in a constant state of transformation. Some changes are contested, becoming arenas of discourse (as discussed in Chapter 5), but others occur without ever evoking these battles. *Doxa* itself is also constantly eroding, admitting new structures and undergoing transformations even as it is being reproduced, so that what is represented as "traditional" may at times be no less novel than the "new" ways that challenge it.

The process by which the laws of cuisine shape an act of cooking, and in turn are restructured by the form of each successive meal, is of intrinsic interest to the anthropologist because it represents the relations between the social collective and the individual. Barthes says of cooking, "broadly, it is usage, that is to say, a sort of sedimentation of many peoples' speech, which makes up the alimentary language" (1965:27).

Where cooking is concerned, this interplay of individual act and collective practice also involves another kind of interaction. The act of cooking stands at the juncture between the conceptual and the material bases of social life. Like sex, food plays an important symbolic role precisely because it has such a fundamental part to play in physical life: the reproduction of a society and its members is directly dependent on it. Cooking is not only a practice, "a particular form of productive activity by which the social formation is produced and transformed" (Coward and Ellis 1977:63); it is also specifically a part of economic practice, the "production and reproduction of the material means of subsistence" (64).

The semiotic ordering of the elements of cuisine is in fact an aspect of the material act of cooking: it is a tool that enables a woman to combine raw ingredients and prepare them for consumption. The rules of a specific cuisine, distilled as they are from the "sedimentation" of thousands of past meals, are specifically tailored to fit the material conditions of the society in question. When these conditions change, as for example with the growing scarcity of potatoes in Zumbagua, the rules of cuisine must in turn adjust to conform to the new conditions. Cuisine does not passively follow behind material practice, however: people also deploy resources and make choices according to needs and desires that have been culturally determined.

There is, then, a constant movement between conceptual framework and productive process. This movement can be portrayed as a relation between text and context (Coward and Ellis 1977:62), or between structure and history (Sahlins 1981), or, for cooking, between production and consumption: "Production is consumption; consumption is production . . . they appear as mutually connected . . . yet remaining outside of each other. Production creates the material as outward object of consumption; consumption creates the want as the inward object, the purpose of production" (Marx 1859:93). As with signifier and signified, neither process ultimately precedes the other, yet each presupposes the other at any particular moment: people grow the foods they want to eat (or buy them), but also eat the foods they can grow or buy.

In the process of unfolding Zumbagua cooking in its many social dimensions, I chose cuisine as my starting point; but in the last chapter I come full circle and discuss the everyday material practice that underlies the structures of cuisine. The rules of Zumbagua cuisine are closely intertwined with the life of the kitchen, not only in making soup but in peeling potatoes, feeding the dogs, and disposing of the garbage.

Political and Ideological Practice Within the Household

These intimate details of kitchen activity reveal a great deal about Zumbagua society and culture, not just the narrowly defined relation between economic and conceptual processes outlined above. According to Coward and Ellis (1977), the "social totality" is composed of three kinds of practice, which together "produce and reproduce real life": they are economic, political, and ideological in nature. Economic practice produces not only the means of subsistence, as in the definition given above, but also the relations of production, which in turn necessitate political practice. "[P]olitical practice produces . . . forms of social organization, and the relations of dominance and subordination between these forms" (1977:64). These relations exist not only at the macro level, in Zumbagua's relationship to the nation as a whole, but also on a very small scale, within the household. It is the social organization of the family and household that is brought to light by looking at cooking practice: the relations between mother and child, husband and wife, consanguine and affine as they share in the activities of production and

24

consumption. Their relative dominance over and subordination to one another can be seen in the labor invested in cooking, serving, and cleaning up.

The third kind of practice, ideological practice, is also interwoven into the activities of the kitchen. The term "ideology," as used by cultural Marxists, is closely related to anthropologists' use of the term "culture" (see Raymond Williams's 1977 discussion of the two terms). Coward and Ellis, following Louis Althusser, call ideology a "practice of representation" that fixes "the relationship by which the individual represents himself in his world of objects: it provides the positions from which individuals can act and represent themselves and others within the social totality.... Ideology functions, then, by putting the individual at the centre of the structure, making the subject the place where ideological meanings are realized" (1977:74–75).

This conception of ideology as a system of representations constructed by and through each individual to legitimize and interpret his or her own position within the social totality makes it possible to grasp the way that hegemony and resistance work through the infinite, unimportant incidents and objects of everyday life. Items of clothing, kinds of food, ways of speaking or cooking or organizing one's workday are the building blocks of which meaning is constructed: Althusser refers to ideology as a material force comprising "the perceived, accepted, suffered cultural objects: objects of [men's] world" (quoted in Coward and Ellis 1977:74).

This conception of ideology also shifts the focus of analysis away from the notion of "the people of Zumbagua" as a unified culture confronting choice and change. Each individual, working from a framework of understanding that represents that person's own social role, acts from his or her own system of meaning to intepret new formations as they occur. This emphasis on ideology as the construction of frameworks of meaning that though culturally overdetermined to share basic structures with other members of society, nonetheless are individual and role-specific, "alters the status of the ideological apparatuses themselves: the family assumes a greater importance . . . it becomes the arena in which the subject is produced in a certain relation to discourse, and therefore to meaning" (Coward and Ellis 1977:73–74).

The kitchen in Zumbagua is the locus of early socialization, not only through social interaction but through the sense experiences of taste, touch, and smell, the spatial orientations implicit in its architecture and the arrangement of objects, and the physical and temporal rhythms found in the work performed there. But the kitchen and the family that inhabits it also form an "arena of discourse and meaning" in the sense of being a locus of conflict. The household is not a unified "ideological apparatus"; neither do its members, according to the notion of culture or ideology presented here, share a unified interpretation of the world. The family is almost by definition composed of individuals, each of whom has a specific role not duplicated by other members. Family relationships are not built upon identical rights and duties but upon reciprocal rights and duties; these roles often involve relations of marked dominance and subordination, which allow some individuals to benefit from the labor of others.

The domain of the kitchen provides Zumbagua women with access to a specifically feminine sort of political power. In the kitchen, even more than in pasture and field, a woman exerts her control over her subordinates: mother over children, mother-in-law over daughter-in-law. A woman with recently married sons has direct control over the lives and labor of several strong, young adults and is answerable only to her husband, who considers cooking to lie outside his domain. The young women sometimes bear an onerous burden, but the passing of time will eventually bring them into the position of power. These relations in turn are supported by ideological frameworks that defend the rights of generation, gender, birth order, and consanguinity (Donham 1981; Meillassoux 1972, 1978a, 1978b).

This household-level ideological practice operates through a series of overlapping ideologies constructed around each individual through semiosis, and it is in fact intrinsic to producing the individual as a social actor. As a child, a girl looks on the stove as an instrument she will one day control and watches her mother's confident, unthinking motions there with interest, while a boy's attention is drawn elsewhere. Both children accept unquestioningly their obligation to provide household labor to their elders and know that their grandfather commands a respect and affection qualitatively greater than that rendered to the rest of the older generation.

Kitchen Practice: Ideologies of Gender and the Household Economy

As I stated earlier, ideological practice exists in close interrelation with economic and political practice, all three together constituting the social totality. The specific ideological practice found in the Zumbaguan kitchen serves to ensure the reproduction of political practice—that is to say social relations—within the household and thus to defend the family's ability to reproduce itself. This ability depends not only on relations of kinship and marriage, but on the relations of production that govern both economic activity within the household and the articulation of the household with the larger economy.

Cooking occupies a central place in the family's economic life, transforming the results of its productive activities into a consumable form. As cooks, women "stand as 'gatekeepers' between food production and consumption" (Niñez 1984:9). The cultural significance of this transformation lies in the conversion of products obtained through the household's articulation with the world beyond its walls, into the meals that are consumed within it by its members. Lévi-Strauss posited cooking as one of the core symbols of culture, the activity by which the natural world is domesticated and made social. Similarly, at the household level cooking is the means by which the family internalizes the external world. Just as, at the level of physical reproduction, the long-term survival of the family depends on bringing in people from other families through marriage, so its day-to-day survival depends on the conversion of products from outside into cooked food for household members. The hearth is the symbol of the home because it daily transforms external articulation into internal consumption. The imagery of the United States as a "melting pot" conveys this ability of cooking to transform the foreign into the domestic, the extraneous into the familiar.[14]

This ability is especially significant for Zumbagua because of the heterogeneity of household economic strategies in the parish. It is the nature of the modern peasant household to be involved in a variety of productive activities, each implying a different type of articulation with the outside world. Subsistence agriculture, wage labor, petty commodity production, buying, selling, trading: no single kind of economic practice characterizes peasants. Rather, the very multiplicity of their endeavors is what defines them.

It is not commonly a single peasant who is involved in all of these activities, but more often the peasant household as a whole. The family assigns productive roles to its members according to age and sex or other social criteria. Children may be the primary shepherds, for example, while adults concentrate on agriculture. Or, as in West Africa, women may be the exclusive agents in the petty commodities market. As a result, of the products that the household receives as the fruits of its collective labor, certain categories of things are contributed by specific family members: vegetable products from the women of the house and protein from its men, for example.

This economic practice of differentially assigning productive roles is not without political and ideological consequences. As anthropologists who study gender have been at some pains to establish, the products of these various activities are assigned value, and their producers social worth, in ways that reinforce the social structure of the household and the power relations within it. Complex ideological representations, weaving together physical and cosmological aspects of the producers' lives and bodies with the nature of the work sites and products, make their relationship seem inevitable and right. Whether it be the distaff, the frying pan, or the hoe, a woman's tools are made to seem an inseparable part of her nature, so that the tasks assigned to her appear to result from biological, not social, law.

The process of cooking itself is subject to these representations. In Zumbaguan minds, the image of the hearth is intrinsically associated with that of the woman, as mother, wife, daughter, and daughter-in-law. The whole conceptual framework I call "cuisine" is considered to be the exclusive possession of the female sex: although men in fact are perfectly competent cooks, they consider their cooking to be ad hoc improvisation attempted without the benefit of women's knowledge.

This women's domain includes serving food as well as preparing it. To proffer the prepared dish is an act laden with social significance; in Zumbagua it is never performed without a series of attendant small rituals, no matter how informal the occasion. This symbolic weight comes from the labor represented by the completed meal, from the production or acquisition of the raw materials to the processing and preparation done in the kitchen. When a woman serves a dish she has prepared, this offering of her labor for another's consumption is intrinsically an act of subordination. Thus Coward refers to a cross-culturally common symbolic association in which "the preparation of food is considered an act of servitude, the demonstration of a subordinate and servicing social position. . . . The meal is the product of woman's domestic labor, demonstrating her willingness to serve the family" (1985:12).

The act of serving food in Zumbagua is certainly intrinsic to the political and ideological role of the woman in marriage; as Gracia Clark (1985) notes for Asante market women, in Zumbagua cooking is so central to the concept of marriage that it often replaces, or serves as a euphemism for, sex as the focus of discourses about marital relations. The symbolism of serving food found in Zumbagua meals is ambiguous, however: on the surface, the formal structure of the Zumbagua meal seems to place the woman serving at the bottom of the social hierarchy. She ladles soup into bowls and hands them to her young daughter with whispered instructions that grandfather must be served first, then uncle, while she herself eats last. Despite this apparent powerlessness, the potential for "gastropolitics" afforded to those who control the serving of meals is considerable, as Arjun Appadurai has pointed out (1981). The formal structures of Zumbagua cuisine and etiquette provide delicate instruments for communicating messages about social position and relative power and even create opportunities to readjust the status quo. Far from being an unchanging mirror of family structure, this "symbol of women's subordination" provides the woman who wields the ladle the chance smugly to hand out excruciating insults while meekly proclaiming her utter lack of political power.

The economic, political, and ideological practices condensed in the meal, then, are complex and contradictory. Meals are among the most relaxing and enjoyable times the family spends together, providing the indulgence of gustatory satisfaction and the pleasure of social intercourse. But by the same token, meals often become expressions of the frustrations and conflicts endemic to family life.

For the Zumbagua household, the meal represents many things: both articulation with the outside world and the household's own internal integrity; the subordination of female to male and yet a locus of feminine power within the family; the product of work transformed into the satisfaction of desire, and the proof of the household's ability to survive and to reproduce itself.

The Household as Locus for Articulating Modes of Production

The symbolism of the meal acknowledges the economic, political, and ideological practices enmeshed within the act of cooking. It is the nature of social life that there is a constant movement between these three practices, as each, in the constant process of structuration, is changing, evolving, and reproducing itself, and in turn effecting changes in the other practices even while ensuring their reproduction. This entire process, inherently mobile, becomes even more volatile and conflictual when the economic base of the society is itself contradictory in nature, as is the case with Zumbagua.

The modern nation of Ecuador appears to be simultaneously on two very different trajectories: Quito, fueled by oil money, is expanding rapidly, while rural backwaters like Zumbagua languish in poverty. But this image of the dual economy has been under attack for some years in the economic literature (see, for example, Stavenhagen 1975; Frank 1969; Amin 1976). Alain de Janvry maintains that these forms of poverty and "backwardness," seen in much of Latin America, "are not geographically determined, exclusive, and stable structures, but are only the reflection of . . . a process whereby growth of capitalist production in the periphery feeds upon the stagnation, impoverishment, and destruction of the peasant and artisan spheres" (1981:22). According to Janvry, in areas in which the hacienda was previously the basic agrarian tenure institution, a new dominant pattern of social relations has emerged, characterized by semiproletarianization. This term aptly describes the situation in which Zumbagua men find themselves as wage laborers. Unable to support themselves on the land, they turn to the cities to find work. But the employment they find there is so sporadic, and the wages are so low, that they are unable to move their families to the cities and become full-time wage workers. Instead, they live suspended between the rural homestead and the urban workplace. Neither economy can fully support the household, so women, children, and the old eke out a meager living on the farm, with their monetary needs being partially met by the husband's wages, while he in turn is partially supported by his wages and partially by the farm.

This arrangement works to the benefit of the employer, who can attract a labor force willing to work for wages so low that a fully proletarianized family would be unable to subsist on them. When the laborer is sick, unemployed, or becomes too old to perform his job, he goes back home to the agricultural community. The employer thus escapes having to pay unemployment compensation, retirement benefits, or sick leave, or even wages high enough to permit savings. The rural area also serves as a "labor reserve," providing additional workers when the economy expands and reabsorbing the unemployed when it contracts.

These facts lead Janvry to refer to the peasant economy as "an important source of subsidies" for the modern capitalist sector where semiproletarianization occurs (1981:84). Meillassoux goes even farther, postulating that this type of temporary wage-labor migration allows the capitalist system to benefit permanently from the kind of primitive accumulation Marx had described as contributing to the birth of the Industrial Revolution (1981).

According to this argument, where only one mode of production prevails, as for example in a subsistence economy or a modern industrial economy, the economy bears the cost of the labor force's reproduction, that is, the cost of raising children. Some of the surpluses generated in production are used to supply the food eaten and the care demanded by the very young. When an economy has access to immigrants or temporary migrants who arrive as fully grown adults ready to work, by contrast, it receives labor for which it did not have to bear the costs of reproduction. Meillassoux suggests that access to this form of labor is a key aspect of the phenomenon of semiproletarianization: farming must feed not only the worker who has become old or ill, but also the next generation. When these dependent children become productive adults, their labor is diverted into another economy instead of being reinvested in the system that raised them.

According to Meillassoux, the "domestic economy," as he calls the peasant household, is especially vulnerable to this kind of exploitation because of its nature as a "collective, organised cell of production. . . . Exploitation does not operate only at the expense of an individual worker but, into the bargain, at the expense of the entire group to which he belongs" (1981:111).

The significance of Meillassoux's observations for Zumbaguan kitchen practice lies in the fact that the articulation of these two modes of production, capitalist and domestic, actually occurs at the level of the household, within each family. As Carmen Diana Deere has pointed out, this articulation occurs at the economic juncture of male and female roles, as fathers and sons hail the bus to Quito each Sunday, leaving wives and daughters in charge of the farm (1976:9). The two differing modes of production acting on the household economy are mapped onto the division of labor by sex within the family structure, resulting in a household that contains male proletarians and female subsistence farmers under one roof.

Chapter 6 details some of the consequences of this conjuncture of gender and economy. In symbolic terms, the forms of food associated with gender domains in the family and community, along with the formal aspects of the exchange of these foods between husband and wife, come to represent the contrasts between these two very different economies. The social costs of this articulation include women's impoverishment; in addition, the inadequacies of both economies place a strain on the bond between husband and wife, as each looks to the other to meet very real needs and is met only with expressions of lack. The man who comes home with handfuls of penny candies when his wife needs rice and flour and the woman who demands help with the harvest and offers only thin barley gruel in return hardly seem like loving and caring spouses. Add to these problems the growing cultural gap between the two, as their work and life experiences draw them apart, and the result is a situation in which the affective inadequacies of the marriage are exceeded only by the enormity of the economic need that binds them together.

The formation of a household made up of proletarian male and subsistence-farmer female may drive individuals apart in their political and ideological practice, but ultimately, semiproletarianization does not so much divide households as it unites economies, interlocking rural and capitalist sectors so as to permit the transfer of value from one to the other. This steady, invisible drain on the local economy of areas like Zumbagua leads to a steady impoverishment of the rural sector. The crisis in which Zumbagua finds itself, according to Janvry, "symptomizes and embodies the contradictions of peripheral capitalism" (1981:85), which inevitably causes increasing impoverishment of the rural masses. Semiproletarianization and the depression of prices for peasants' food crops provide cheap food and cheap labor for the cities, but at the cost of "ecological and demographic contradictions that cumulatively deepen the development of underdevelopment in peasant agriculture" (1981:86). Overuse of land resulting in irreparable ecological deterioration and skyrocketing population growth in rural areas are among the consequences of the system, as Janvry outlines it.

The appearance of backwardness that makes Zumbagua seem isolated from the rest of the nation is in fact the very symptom of the ties that bind it to the larger economy. Although the women of Zumbagua spend their working lives involved for the most part in the subsistence economy, they are lives in which the hours are occupied with reflections on things only money can buy. While they sift ground barley, peel potatoes, skin a *cuy*, their thoughts and discourse turn frequently to the deployment of precious Quito-earned sucres.

Every society, in whatever historical epoch, tends to feel itself beset by crises and turmoils hitherto unknown and to imagine with longing the tranquility of other times and places. But of course, stasis is unknown in history; the movement between structure and practice never stops.

> There can never be a zero point since the movement of knowledge has always already begun and includes practice as one of its terms. Reality . . . is an ever pre-given complexly structured totality, characterized by disjunctions, irregularities, uneven development and partial, fragmented movement. . . . It is the notion of contradiction, called by Lenin the kernel of the dialectic, which enables this understanding of the heterogeneous totality as being simultaneously process and structure. (Coward and Ellis 1977:86)

Both men and women in Zumbagua find themselves caught up in contradictory practices. The complex of sign, symbol, discourse, and ideology that surrounds the practice of cooking is among the aspects of everyday life that have become expressions of these conflicts. Moreover, as cooking itself combines economic, political, and ideological practices, it is one of the domains in which these processes of contradiction and transformation are actually taking place.

Notes

1. In the field of semiology and in symbolic studies in general, terms such as "sign," "symbol," "paradigm," and "system" have been defined in such a multiplicity of ways by different authors that use of this terminology is hazardous to the unwary and problematic even for the initiate. (See Roland Barthes's discussion, 1965:35–38.) In making an opposition between sign and symbol, I am basically following Barthes's (1965:38) use of the terms, though with some modification. According to Barthes, both sign and symbol "refer us to a relation between two *relata*" (35), one of which is a mental representation (38). The distinction between the two lies in the fact that "in the *symbol* the representation is analogical and inadequate (Christianity 'outruns' the cross), whereas in the *sign* the relation is unmotivated and exact" (38). I use the word "symbol" in his sense: a symbol, as Victor Turner has explained (1967), is multivocalic, condensing a wide range of sometimes contradictory meanings. In a sign, by contrast, the pair signifier/signified is evenly matched. In nonlinguistic semiotic systems, however, the relation between signifier and signified is not entirely unmotivated, and thus does not fully meet Barthes's definition of a sign. Barthes for this reason differentiates between the sign, found only in linguistic systems, and the sign-function (41), but I have found this distinction to be unnecessarily cumbersome for my purposes, and have simply referred to foods, in their role as elements in cuisine, as signs.

2. See for example Arnott 1975; Barthes 1972, 1979; Chang 1977; Clark 1975a, 1975b; Detienne 1977; Douglas 1971, 1983, 1984; Douglas and Isherwood 1979; Fortes and Fortes 1936; Fredman 1981; Goody 1982; Hammel 1967; Khare 1976a, b; Kuper 1977; Laderman 1981; Meigs 1984; Mintz 1982, 1985; Pollock 1986; Richards 1964; Simons 1967; Strathern 1977; Turner 1982; Young 1971. Fewer scholars have looked at the technical and economic aspects of cooking from an anthropological perspective, but see Goody 1982; First 1966; Bornstern-Johanssen 1975; Bruneton 1975; Lerche 1975. Social historians have also provided a wealth of excellent studies on the role of food as a symbol in social life. See for example Bonnet 1979; Forbes 1954; Forster and Ranum 1979; Hemardinquer 1979; Hilliard 1972; Mintz 1979; Revel 1982; Root and de Rochemont 1976; Sokolov 1984; Tannahill 1972. Also relevant is the work of linguists on food taxonomies. See for example Frish 1968; Lehrer 1969, 1972; Ramburger 1979; Stone 1978; Thomas 1960.

3. See for example Babb 1970; Beck 1969; Katona-Apte 1975; Ortner 1978; Turner 1984; Vogt 1976; Yalman 1969.

4. See also Firth 1966, Foster 1967, Schieffelin 1976.

5. In general, however, there are few complete studies of Andean food systems. (But see Guevara 1960a, 1960b; Mejía Xesppe 1978; Orlove 1983; Paredes de Martinez 1963; Peloso 1985; de Carvalho-Neto 1964 is also informative, and Dorfman 1984 and Orlove 1982 are interesting studies of specific Andean food symbolism in modern contexts.) More has been written on drinking

than on eating. (See for example Allen 1978; Dobyns 1965; Doughty 1971; Gomez Huaman 1966; Heath 1958, 1971; Lira 1948; Mangin 1951; Orlove 1983; Plath 1962; Vesquez 1956.) Nutritional studies (for example, Atuñez de Mayolo 1981; Mazess and Baker 1964) contain some information on dietary patterns, though most studies done in Ecuador (such as Greene 1976, Naranjo 1985; Pigott 1981; Rivadeneira 1980; Varea Teran and Varea Teran 1974) are based on growth and morbidity measures in the population, rather than on actual dietary information. An exception is Chiriboga 1985. Also informative are botanical works, especially the invaluable Gade 1975 (see also Brush 1980; Cordero 1950 [1911]; Patino 1964; Towle 1961).

6. Studies emphasizing this aspect of food and cooking include Anderson 1982; Fredman 1981; Goody 1982; Marriott 1968; and Sokolov 1984.

7. See, for example, Gade 1975:165 and elsewhere.

8. Barthes uses the terms "syntagm" and "system" (1965:59). I prefer to reserve "system" to refer to the semiotic ordering of the cuisine as a whole, and have therefore substituted the word "paradigm," following, among others, J. David Sapir's (1977) use of the term.

9. This particular contrast, chicken and rice versus *cuy* and potato, was first brought to my attention at a Zumbagua wedding where "white" guests were served the former, indigenous guests the latter foods.

10. "Two superimposed worlds" is the title of a 1973 book about Ecuador's socioeconomic problems that characterizes the country as having two completely separate societies and economies, one Indian and one white. The author, Osvaldo Hurtado, later became president of Ecuador.

11. A *chola* is culturally (and supposedly racially) part-Indian. Cholas form a distinct social group whose clothing, language, and mannerisms set them apart; they also occupy a unique economic niche as low-level, small-scale merchants, usually operating in the rotating markets of the small towns that serve large rural hinterlands. They are brokers who mediate between "Indian" and "white," between rural and urban, between integration into the cash economy, which provides their inadequate livelihood, and an unbreakable dependence on precapitalist economic activities, such as creating fictive kinships, as a buffer between themselves and always impending financial disaster.

12. An extremely derogatory epithet meaning "Indian," *longo* is commonly used by the white community to refer to their indigenous neighbors.

13. The term "hegemony" has been much in vogue among scholars on the left since the early sixties, and not surprisingly, the meanings associated with its use have proliferated alarmingly. This situation has driven some scholars to abandon it altogether (see for example Willis 1977:170 and passim), either using the concept without naming it or substituting their own terms in its stead. The further proliferation of terms, however, seems to me to have little to recommend it, and I find the concept, for all its ambiguities, to be an immensely powerful one. It offers something which Marx's own writings do not, namely a way to understand the specific forms of ascendancy of the bourgeoisie over the working class in modern stabilized capitalism. A better response to the confusion over its meaning

would seem to be its careful definition by each scholar who uses it; clarification of my own use of it in this work therefore follows.

The term is associated in most scholars' minds with the work of the Italian Marxist Antonio Gramsci, although, as Perry Anderson points out in his masterful article on the subject (1976), Gramsci is by no means the first Marxist thinker to have used it. Gramsci's writings are notoriously opaque and subject to multiple interpretations; in this opacity lie the roots of both the inherent problems and the great theoretical power of Gramsci's thought, as Anderson has eloquently demonstrated. The ambiguities in the meaning of the term, then, have a long history, through which each scholar must thread her or his own path.

My own use of the concept of hegemony originally developed out of Raymond Williams's essay on the concept (1977), from which much of the discussion of hegemony in this work is directly or indirectly taken. As I understand Williams (or as I have chosen to use his work), this kind of interpretation stems basically from what Anderson calls the "first and firmest" (1976:21) usage of the concept in Gramsci's writings. Here the emphasis is on "'the moment of consent, of cultural direction, to distinguish it from the moment of force, of constraint, of state-legislative or police intervention'" (Gramsci quoted in Anderson 1976:21).

This type of usage, with its emphasis on cultural forms rather than narrowly political and coercive ones, is of most use to anthropologists grappling with the subordinate position of ethnic minorities in neocolonial situations. It is of tremendous utility to me in accounting for the transition of forms of power in Zumbagua, where the old coercive structures of the hacienda system have been replaced by a social formation in which the bourgeois state and society of Ecuador, although largely physically absent from Zumbagua itself, nevertheless exert tremendous pressure on cultural forms within the parish, in addition to limiting economic and political opportunities.

The state in fact continues periodically to exert direct coercive power in the parish, by jailing activists, as happened while I was there, or by shooting protestors, as has happened in the recent past. But more germane to an accurate understanding of the contemporary forms of subordination that characterize Zumbagua today is an analysis like Gramsci's, in which the structures of bourgeois power in Western nations are pre-eminently a matter of the cultural ascendancy of bourgeois values, and the concomitant ideological subordination of the working class, through powerful ideological processes such as the invisible diffusion of commodity fetishism, the learning of the work routines of wage labor, and the psychologically crippling effects of racism. It is these forms and processes that I try to describe in this book, and not forms of overt coercive control.

The concept of hegemony is problematic, according to Anderson, because Gramsci wavers in his attribution of it to civil society or to the state. For Zumbagua, however, this ambiguity of interpretation reflects actual reality in a revealing way. Many of the members of white bourgeois society with whom parish residents come into contact, and who are most directly influential in imposing national ideologies over local ones, are in fact employees of the state:

schoolteachers, doctors, nurses, employees of various national agencies with jurisdiction over the parish. It is precisely the co-occurrence of bourgeois ideology and political power that renders these individuals and their cultural judgments about indigenous life so influential. At the same time, however, bosses in wage-labor, *chola* sellers in the marketplace, and religious personnel are equally powerful forces whose influence does not come from a narrowly political base. But the division of state and civil society is not very meaningful here; the indigenous population of Zumbagua harbors no illusions about the ability of these individuals to call upon the coercive power of the state if an Indian were to attempt to defy their authority, and this perceived collusion between the state and all members of other classes and races is reinforced on the plane of ideology. The ideologies and projects of bosses, marketpeople, and churchmen go hand-in-hand with those of the national government insofar as they pertain to the people of Zumbagua: all are working for greater integration of the parish into the national economy, the suppression of cultural forms deemed inimical to social and economic progress, increased participation in government projects, and in general, the pacification of a barely "civilized" and potentially hostile population into a good and productive citizenry according to bourgeois ideals.

If this problem of ambiguity in the locus of hegemonic power is not an issue in the case of Zumbagua, a second problem still remains. This is the seemingly monolithic nature of the term, as it is interpreted by some scholars. James Scott, for example, has recently written a book entitled *Weapons of the Weak: Everyday Forms of Peasant Resistance* (1985), which addresses issues and problems closely related to some of those I discuss here. But while I find the concept of hegemony to be useful for this kind of analysis, to him it suggests a greater degree of ideological control on the part of the dominant class than he (or I) find to be true of peasant societies. According to Scott, the study of the social consciousness of subordinate classes is significant precisely because it challenges the very notion of hegemony, which he sees as implying a total mystification of the subordinate class, a passivity and fatalistic acceptance on their part. For him, Marxist analysis "typically rests on the assumption that elites dominate not only the physical means of production but the symbolic means of production as well . . . By creating and disseminating a universe of discourse and the concepts that go with it, by defining the standards of what is true, beautiful, moral, fair, and legitimate, they build a symbolic climate that prevents subordinate classes from thinking their way free. In fact, for Gramsci, the proletariat is more enslaved at the level of ideas than at the level of behavior" (Scott 1985:38–39).

This type of total ideological "enslavement" would certainly be a poor description of Zumbagua, where indigenous residents freely express a well-developed hatred for members of the dominant classes and a healthy skepticism—if not utter contempt—for anything that the latter may say or believe. But Gramsci's work also permits a reading that emphasizes, not the ultimate total control which hegemonic ideologies seek to exert, but rather the constant process of ideological struggle that characterizes the relationship between classes. For example, Anderson quotes the following passage from Gramsci:

"Previously germinated ideologies become 'party,' come into conflict and confrontation, until only one of them, or at least a single combination, tends to prevail, gaining the upper hand and propagating itself throughout society. It thereby achieves not only a unison of economic and political aims, but also intellectual and moral unity, posing all questions over which the struggle rages not on a corporate but on a universal plane. It thus creates the hegemony of a fundamental social group over a series of subordinate groups." (Gramsci quoted in Anderson 1976:19)

This passage is open to multiple readings. In my own mind, although I perhaps deviate from Gramsci's original intent in offering this interpretation, hegemony exists in the constant struggle on the part of the dominant ideology to overwhelm and incorporate the ideologies of the subordinate classes, and to make its own universe the only conceivable frame of reference, to lift it, as Gramsci says, onto a seemingly universal plane. This is a struggle which the dominant class never completely wins, but in which, as long as the economic formations remain unchanged, the subordinate classes can never do more than resist. It is this dynamic tension within the cultural forms of a specific society between hegemony and resistance that I attempt to describe in this book.

The ability of competing ideological discourses to exist is perhaps greater in a society like Zumbagua's, multicultural in tradition, partially noncapitalist in economy, historically excluded from the national society, peripheral in every sense, than for those who live closer to the seats of power. But the definition of different forms of hegemony, the analysis of the precise relationships between coercion and consent, domination and hegemony, at different historical moments, is exactly the challenge that Gramsci's work offers us. What is needed to further our understanding of relationships like that of Zumbagua to the nation of Ecuador, or Latin America to the United States, is not to reject the conceptual frameworks of earlier scholars as inadequate, but rather to complete and fulfill them through specific historical analysis.

14. Since I first wrote this passage, it has been brought to my attention that the "melting pot" metaphor in fact originally referred to the industrial process of smelting, and not to the domestic cooking pot (and hence made reference to proletarianization as instrumental in cultural assimilation, an association not irrelevant to some of the arguments made here). Nonetheless, historical processes having rendered the industrial metaphor less salient in this postcapitalist era, the phrase is widely interpreted in contemporary popular thought to refer to cooking—a meaning no less culturally valid for not being the only possible one.

T W O

The Parish of Zumbagua

Anthropology studies human societies; but ethnographies are about places as well as people. Other people, other places: the people whose lives we interpret are foreign to us primarily because they inhabit distant and unknown places. Before I can explain anything about the people of Zumbagua to a North American audience,[1] I must first describe Zumbagua itself: where it is and what it is.

The location of Zumbagua is important to an understanding of its people for another reason. The people of Zumbagua are a kind of people described as Indians, Native Americans, natives, *indígenas, naturales, runas, indios, longos*. To be "Indian" in the Andes is commonly believed to be a matter of race, or, by the more enlightened, of culture: language and custom. In the Andes, however, how "white" a people have "become," how "Indian" they have "remained," has been shaped by the interaction of relations of power with the patterns of space and time. To make this statement is not to claim that ethnicity does not exist, that one can best understand a people like those of Zumbagua by reducing the category of *indígena* to that of campesino. But it is equally distorting to conceive of the "Indianness" of Zumbagua as a quality inhering in its people in some metaphysical way, as though simply through some special kind of moral character—stubbornness\ignorance\backwardness or integrity\strength-of-will\moral superiority (choose your paradigm)—they have clung to what others have lost.

Ethnicity is a product of history: before the Spanish came there were no "Indians," any more than we will think of ourselves as "Earthlings" until the Martians arrive. Since the Conquest, an "Indian" has been understood as one who conserves pre-Hispanic lifeways. But both "white" and "Indian" culture and society in the Andes are permeated with pre-Hispanic traits, while both groups also call their own many Iberian ways of thinking and behaving. Ethnicity has in fact been many things besides a racial memory or a cultural inheritance: it has been an aspect of the social relations of production, a legal and political construct, and an ideology, the content of which is constantly changing to fit the needs of new historical epochs. This Andean history of "Indian" and "white" is a process that has been in a constant dialectic with geography: the relations between the highlands, coast, and interior; within the highlands, the variation in topography, altitude, and climate that create production zones; and the relations of core to periphery, urban center to rural hinterland.

The people of Zumbagua are more "Indian" today than are most inhabitants of the Ecuadorian Sierra. The reasons for this fact cannot be completely unraveled, but certainly the history of the parish, and its location in the high *páramos*, are both factors that have influenced the cultural choices Zumbagua's people have made. Geography, both natural and sociopolitical, has to some extent been destiny for Zumbagua, as for every human society. The first part of this chapter, then, is devoted to the demography, geography, and history of Zumbagua; only after this groundwork has been laid can we turn to the economy, society, and culture of the parish today.

Demography

It is difficult to attempt even an estimate of the population, present or past, of the parish of Zumbagua. The ruggedness of the terrain, the lack of roads, and the extremely dispersed settlement pattern all militate against accurate census-taking. Four recent attempts have been made to count or estimate the number of residents in Zumbagua.

The 1974 census offers a figure of 8,759 people for the parish. At that time, the nation as a whole had some 8 million inhabitants, almost equally divided between highlands and coast and between urban and rural populations. In the province of Cotopaxi, however, with almost 280,000 inhabitants, 237,000 or 84 percent of the population lived in rural areas.

Alfredo de Costales and Piedad de Costales claim 6,783 residents for Zumbagua (1976:30), up from 5,760 in 1965 (1976:16). In 1983–1984 the figure of 10,000 inhabitants was frequently used by the parish priest, who admitted that it was simply a rough estimate. ("Se dice," he would say, "que somos ahora diez mil.")

A very careful and accurate census was taken by the district nurse of the Subcentro de Salud in 1978. As she was well known and liked in the parish, devoted a period of several months to the project, and only attempted to survey the area within a radius of one kilometer of the Subcentro, this census is probably the most successful that has been done to date. She found that within her survey area, there were 3,190 people (including the 386 residents of the *centro*). Although this area is undoubtedly the most densely populated in the parish, the fact that such a small area yielded such a high count suggests that the national census figures and the Costales's counts are low.

Population pressure in the parish is extreme; most residents consider the lack of adequate farmland to be one of the most pressing problems they face. One index of the problem's severity is the fierceness of the fighting over land inheritance; most homicides in the parish are the result of such struggles. According to the 1974 census, of 1,226 "units of agricultural production" or family farms, 806 (roughly two-thirds) are less than two hectares in size; 407 are between three and ten hectares, and thirteen are more than ten hectares in size. The latter figure, however, includes five "units" that are listed as more than one thousand hectares in size; as there are no privately owned properties this large within parish boundaries, this figure must refer to communally owned grazing lands, some of which have recently been subdivided to provide plots for cultivation to landless families.

Costales and Costales give the size of the hacienda of Zumbagua as 10,060 hectares (1976:7). According to the national census, the present-day parish is approximately the same size, 10,067 hectares. Still, it is not clear whether this latter figure includes the entire parish area or only the cultivated land within it, excluding grasslands. Based on topographic maps of the area provided by the Instituto Geográfico Militar, this figure would be approximately correct for land under cultivation, but the total parish size is probably closer to 171 square kilometers (17,100 hectares).

Taking the ten thousand population figure as the best available approximation, this estimate would suggest a population density of .58 per hectare (58 per sq km) for the parish as a whole, and 1 per hectare for the area under cultivation. In view of the approximate nature of all the data, however, any such figure must be treated with some skepticism.

Ecology[2]

Zumbagua is a land of vast spaces and immense distances. Some visitors find it an intimidating and hostile place; to others it is a place of overpowering beauty. The scale of the landscape is staggering; long vistas, encompassing heights and depths of several hundreds of meters, are commonplace.

Most human activities are enacted against the unforgettable, intrusive backdrop of this gigantic landscape. The dusty plaza where markets and fiestas take place is dominated by the hills that rise above it to the south and, to the north, by the panoramic sweep of the valley bottom with its deep gorge, crowned by the towering crater of Quilotoa rising from the valley floor some eleven kilometers away. But if the landscape seems overwhelming from the central plaza, it is much more so from the high slopes above it, where most people live. Sitting on the patio in front of a typical Zumbagua house, one can see not only the activities of all one's neighbors as they work in their fields, but also, above the fields and houses, a zone of high uncultivated grasslands crowning the hills. Rocky crags jutting out of the upper slopes are parish landmarks, and from the houses in the upper reaches, the distant snowcaps of Cotopaxi and the Illinizas come into view.

Ecologically, the entire parish of Zumbagua falls in the zone of *páramo,* or what Misael Acosta-Solís refers to as "Graminetum Microtérmico." He describes the characteristic Ecuadorian *páramo* as follows:

El Piso Vegetativo Paramal está generalmente sobre los 3.300 a los 3.500 m.s.m., a ambos lomos de las dos grandes Cordilleras. . . . La característica de los páramos es la presencia de los grandes pajonales gramínicos y por esto es que al hablar de pajonales, se supone inmediatamente a los páramos o viceversa. . . . Todas las Glumifloras de los pajonales presentan una adecuación biológica especial: hojas largas, cilíndricas o lineares, tiesas y bastante silificadas; viven formando cumulos o mechones. . . .

Asociadas al pajonal se hallan otras familias botánicas como Ciperareas, Iridaceas, Liliaceas, etc., del tipo microphilia y varias leñosas arbustivas o raquíticas. (Acosta-Solís 1968:88)[3]

But while this natural *páramo* vegetation still occurs in the parish, the ecology of the area has been altered by centuries of intensive human exploitation. Most of the landscape is filled with irregularly shaped fields that cover every slope, no matter how steep. Quadrangles of barley, fava beans, or freshly turned earth, and grass-covered fields in fallow, create sharp contrasts in color and texture at all times of the year. Scattered among the fields are houses, straw- or tin-roofed, and occasionally the bare circle of a threshing floor.

Climate

Zumbagua is not far from the equator; the southern edge of the parish is at 1° south. But despite the images of steamy heat and dense jungle that such a location evokes in North American imaginations, the high

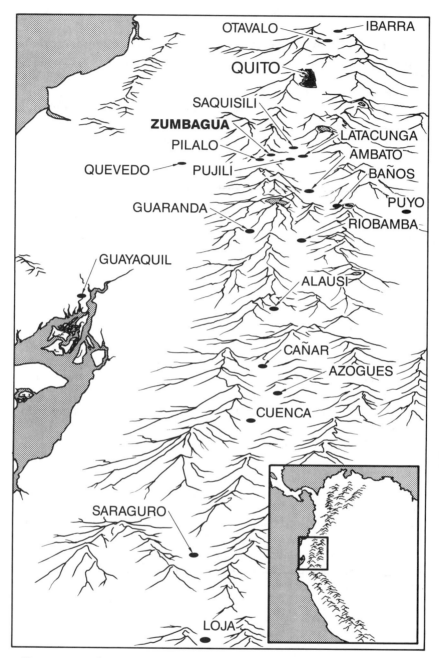

Figure 1. Northwestern South America. With a detail map of the Ecuadorian highlands, from *Republica del Ecuador: Mapa físico,* Instituto Geográfico-Militar del Ecuador, 1978. Used by permission.

altitudes of the parish give it a cold climate in which hailstorms and killing frosts are common.[4] Altitudes in the parish average 3,600–3,900 meters above sea level.[5] In the minds of most Ecuadorians, high places like Zumbagua are *puro páramo* (purely *páramo*), a zone characterized in popular stereotypes as perpetually cold, misty, and gray. Residents of Quito, for example, which at 2,850 masl has quite a different ambience, conceive of the *páramo* as an inhospitable and dreary place, as conducive to solitude and melancholia as the hot coastal lands are to extroversion, passion, and humor.[6]

The parish does experience the mysterious enveloping fogs and drifting mists for which the *páramo* is famous, as well as the gloomy skies and lowering clouds invariably captured by photographers. But there are also many days of dazzling sunlight and crystal-clear nights studded with stars. It is not an easy climate; the chilly dampness of the wet season is followed by the intense cold of the dry season, topped off by the incessant winds of bone-dry August. But neither is this climate a monotonous regimen of gray, as popular stereotypes would have it.

The agricultural cycle produces constant changes in the landscape, following the seasonal round. The gray skies of the rainy season bring with them the bright green of sprouting barley in December and January, and the cessation of the rains some months later turns the entire parish the color of ripe grain. In the months of August and September, the winds blow incessantly, and the landscape is filled with dead growth. Even the houseyards are filled with the withered black stalks of the fava beans, stacked beside the houses for use as fuel. During these months, the Andean symbolic association of wind, the dry season, and death that I had read about as a student in the United States was brought home to me as a concrete sensory experience.

Zumbagua Production Zones

The popular image of a uniform (and gloomy) ecological and climatic zone is belied not only by seasonal variation but, at all times of the year, by the internal heterogeneity of the parish. To the residents themselves, not all of the parish is *páramo*. There are two broadly defined zones, more or less determined by altitude. Lower lands, approximately 3,400–3,800 masl, are agricultural and residential, but the tops of the hills are given over to grassland.[7] There are also large expanses of land above 3,900–4,000 masl that are likewise uncultivated grasslands; some half of all parish lands fall into this category. It is these grasslands that are considered by parish residents to constitute *páramo,* not the areas in which they have their fields and houses.[8]

Utilization of the cultivated zone is characterized by monoculture and a crop-rotation system. Whereas small-scale agriculturalists at lower elevations in the Sierra, where maize predominates, utilize an intercropping system in which maize, squash, quinoa, lupines, legumes, vegetables, and herbs are all grown on the same plot, Zumbagua farmers dedicate each field to a single crop. The ideal rotational pattern is a four-year alternation between barley, fava beans, potatoes, and fallow, but ecological and economic factors frequently prevent this ideal from being realized. Nevertheless, rotation is always practiced at least to the extent that a field is never planted in the same crop two years in a row, and occasional fallow periods are observed.

The lower agricultural-residential zone is not homogeneous. Slope, shade, soils, humidity, runoff patterns, susceptibility to frost, and the wind tunnels and rain shadows created by surrounding hills and valleys are among the factors that combine to create tiny microzones. Conditions change even within the same one-hectare field. In this combination of broad, altitudinally defined zones and smaller microzones, Zumbagua is typical of Andean environments. "In the Andes, as in tropical highlands in general, profound changes in the physical environment occur over short distances up- and down-slope. On a broad scale, distinctive zones tend to be stacked, or tiered, one atop another. Within these broadly defined zones are . . . a mosaic of micro-regions" (Basile 1974:5). This mosaic of physical microzones is matched by a "crazy-quilt" of "innumerable micro-climates that prevail over short horizontal distances and lack a clearcut, orderly arrangement" (Basile 1974:19). Not only altitude but location in relation to the rainfall and wind patterns, the influences of the ocean to the west and the vast humid lowlands to the east, as well as equatorial effects, all play a part in determining local conditions throughout the Sierra.

The agricultural zone is intensively cultivated; it is a totally domesticated zone, every cubic meter of which has been worked and reworked. The *páramo,* in contrast, is uncultivated. It is known in Zumbagua as *ujsha sacha,* the grass wilderness. Nonetheless, it too is a managed ecology. Despite its apparent emptiness, it in fact supports a rather large population of grazing animals, primarily flocks of sheep intermixed with llamas and goats, but also including horses, burros, mules, and a few cattle. Although the plant cover is not sown or selected, it is controlled to a degree: the pasturage is improved by systematically burning off the grasses, which produces thick, young, green growth.

Ecological-management strategies in Zumbagua involve use of *páramo* resources to provide nutrients and energy for the lower, cultivated zone. The dominant vegetation of the zone is grasses, predominantly *Stipa ichu* but including a variety of other Graminaceae. Although the utility of this vegetation, which David Basile describes as "bunch grass vegetation, consisting largely of dead, dry stalks interspersed with low, leathery-leaved herbaceous shrubs and mosses" (1974:132), may not be immediately apparent to an observer, it is in fact used in two important ways to convert photosynthesized energy into forms accessible to humans. As Basile notes, the function of sheep in the Ecuadorian Sierra is to provide not only wool and meat but also fertilizer (1974:133). Zumbagua sheep graze in the *páramo*, but at night they are penned in the fields, where their droppings enrich the soil. Cultivation below the *páramo* thus benefits from the *páramo*'s ability to sustain vegetation, with sheep acting as the mechanisms for converting and transporting to a lower area the nutrients produced in the upper zone.

Equally indispensable is the *páramo*'s capacity to produce fuel. Studies of Andean energy conversion have tended to focus on *altiplano* use of animal dung as fuel (see, for example, Thomas 1976), but in Zumbagua the grasses themselves serve as fuel for cooking and heating. Use of wood as fuel is rare, while kerosene and gasoline use is restricted to a very few families, predominantly "white"—certainly less than one percent of the parish population. Most Zumbagua households are totally dependent on *páramo* grasses as fuels. As will be discussed in Chapter 6, *páramo* grasses or *ujsha* are ubiquitous and fundamental materials in Zumbagua kitchen management. Whether in its primary role of conversion to heat or in its many secondary uses, *ujsha* from the *páramo* fills many needs and thus frees the lower-altitude cultivated lands for use solely in the production of calories for consumption.

The *páramo*, then, is an area that superficially appears wild and untamed, when compared with the cultivated lands below, but is in fact a managed, heavily utilized resource. Nevertheless, the concept of the *páramo* as "wilderness" is of great importance in local ethnogeography and cosmology.

Production Zones Outside Zumbagua

Any discussion of the ecological base upon which life in Zumbagua is founded cannot stop with the land actually within parish boundaries. The classic depiction of human adaptation to the Andes is found in John V. Murra's concept of verticality (Murra 1975; also Brush 1977; for a discussion of the model's applicability to Ecuador see Forman 1978).

Briefly, verticality involves a single ethnic or political group directly exploiting multiple altitudinal\ecological zones. A series of political and economic changes have altered, truncated, or destroyed many Andean systems of verticality, from an initial Spanish policy of creating political entities that corresponded to ecological boundaries rather than cross-cutting them, to a twentieth-century tendency for older economic systems to give way to cash-based exchanges. Nonetheless, access to the products of multiple ecological zones remains an important strategy in many areas, Zumbagua among them.

Classic systems of verticality are characteristic of the central and southern, rather than the northern Andes. Frank Salomon postulates that in the pre-Hispanic Pichincha region, instead of the type of "archipelago" described by Murra, trade between ethnic groups may have been utilized to obtain products of neighboring ecozones (1980). But even where Murra's model is not directly applicable, Ecuador's geography makes the exploitation of multiple altitudinal zones almost inevitable in many areas. Norman E. Whitten, Jr. says of Ecuador, "Its territory, which is about the size of Oregon, encompasses contiguous, contrasting ecosystems as varied as any in the world" (1981:1).

The chain of the Andes divides Ecuador into three very different zones, coast, highlands (Sierra), and interior (Oriente). Within some three hundred kilometers west to east, altitudes range from sea level to the peak of Chimborazo, 6,310 km high, then descend again to the Amazonian rain forests of the Oriente. This ecological and climatic pattern characterizes all of western South America, but the rapid changes and contrasts are especially startling in Ecuador. The sequence of zones is highly compressed here, where the Andes are narrower than throughout most of their extension. At 1° south, the latitude of Zumbagua, the Andean chain is only 130 km wide, compared to some 450 km in parts of Bolivia and northern Chile (Basile 1974:5). In Ecuador, the salient features of any highland community's or group's location include not only the resources within its boundaries but also its proximity to other zones, especially to the eastern or western lowlands.[9] As Salomon has pointed out, these highland–lowland articulations stand as a mute challenge to the legitimacy of the national hierarchy of central places and its associated infrastructure. He says of the Quito basin area,

The little aboriginal communities ringing Quito have for at least five centuries been in both cultural orientation and economic practice, more thoroughly transAndean than any of the imperial civilizations which tried to unify forest and Sierra in a state-centralized scheme of integration. Pantropical cosmopolitans of a multitiered, multi-ethnic landscape, the Quito Runa have been, and still are, the cultural switchboard and economic depot of a transmontane integration unknown to state planners. (1981:192)

The Ecuadorian Sierra is made up of three northward-trending divisions: the two Cordilleras, Occidental and Oriental, and the Inter-Andean Valley, which lies between them. The "Quito Runa" [10] Salomon describes, living in the Inter-Andean Valley, are separated by the Cordilleras from both Amazonian and coastal lowlands, but Zumbagua, located at the western edge of the Cordillera Occidental, is clearly oriented to the littoral in terms of ecological exploitation. Although the present territorial boundaries of Zumbagua contain only high areas, just beyond the western limits of the parish there is a precipitous drop in elevation. From Apagua, the westernmost community within the parish, to Quevedo, a fairly large town to the west, is approximately seventy kilometers in distance, but Apagua is at 4,000 masl and Quevedo at 30 masl. Apagua is at the upper limits for cultivation at this latitude, while Quevedo is the center of an agricultural zone that produces lowland crops such as oranges and sugar cane.

Between Apagua and Quevedo lies a cloud-forest zone, much of which is uninhabited due to its precipitous steepness. The contrast between this zone and the *páramo* is extreme. The western slopes are forested and covered with dense, leafy vegetation, and the climate is warm and humid. Acosta-Solís's description of this zone makes clear the striking difference between this area and the treeless *páramo:*

> [E]n este gran cinturon vegetativo existe una saturada humedad ambiental debido a dos circunstancias: a la precipitación constante de lluvias, lloviznas y garúas y a la condensación de las nubes que suben desde los pisos inferiores de la Costa. . . . Estas selvas son riquísimas en especies diferentes de arboles, arbustivas y leñosas y epifitas sin fin. . . . El bosque presenta casi impenetrable por lo enmarañado de la vegetación: arboles y arbustos inclinados por las lianas que enredan por todas partes; los helechos arborescentes y epifitos no faltan nunca. (1968:67–68) [11]

Like the *páramo*, the cloud forest is considered by the residents of Zumbagua to be *sacha*, wilderness. It is also called *yunga*, a Quichua term for the western slopes ecosystem. In Spanish this region is known as *monte*. While a few Zumbagua residents own land at lower altitudes, for most people the *monte\yunga* is a wild land used for foraging. It is principally exploited as a source of wood for fuel. People who live in the western extremes of the parish exploit this zone more fully than do other Zumbagua residents. Because the western lands are among the highest areas of the parish, these families are also more heavily involved in *páramo* exploitation, especially sheep and llama pastoralism. They are thus simultaneously more dependent on zones both higher and lower than is the average Zumbagua household, and correspondingly less dependent on cultivation. There are paths that leave Apagua and plunge directly down into the *monte\yunga;* from some places in the western *páramo,* one looks out over the huge, level sea of clouds that continuously blankets the Andean slopes, hiding the *monte\yunga* from view.

Possible historical dimensions of this articulation with the *monte\ yunga* zone are discussed below, but one aspect of current Zumbagua practice that strongly suggests that access to western slope products is a well-established part of Zumbagua culture is the role accorded to foods from this area. *Yuca* (manioc), oranges, plantains, *panela* (a form of sugar), *muyu cachi* (a salt made on the coast), and *trago* (cane liquor), all of which are typical coastal products, are fully integrated into local cuisine; they do not have an image of being exotic, imported, or high-status, as do products that are grown in the Inter-Andean Valley to the east of the parish.

A comparison of Zumbagua's eastern frontiers with its western edge makes this orientation toward the west unsurprising. To the east, Zumbagua is bounded by another parish, Tigua, also in *tierra fría;* Tigua is, in fact, slightly higher in elevation than Zumbagua and has a correspondingly heavier reliance on pastoralism. It is only beyond Tigua that the descent into the Inter-Andean Valley begins, a much more gradual descent than the western one. On the western slope, Pilaló at 2,500 masl lies only seven kilometers from the parish, while in the Inter-Andean Valley to the east, Latacunga at 2,800 masl is twenty-nine kilometers distant. By bus today, Latacunga is only two hours from Zumbagua, but in living memory it was an arduous two-day trek, with a long, cold night spent in the *páramos* of Tigua.

To the north and south, the height of the Cordillera lessens somewhat. Both the region of Sigchos and Isinliví to the north and that of Anga-marca to the south have more temperate climates in which maize culti-vation is possible.[12] Zumbagua is separated from both of them by difficult terrain; roads are poor and are frequently rendered impassable by landslides, and bus and truck traffic is infrequent at best. Between Angamarca and Zumbagua lies an enormous stretch of high *páramo,* comprising hundreds of square kilometers of uninhabited land; exact boundaries between the two parishes have never even been established. The road to Sigchos and Isinliví, by contrast, after circling the exterior of Quilotoa at the parish's northern border, very gradually descends from some 3,800 masl at this point (below the 3,914 masl of the crater lip) down toward Sigchos about a thousand meters lower, at the southern edge of the Toachi River valley.

These northern and southern neighbors are not as important to Zumbagua as are the Andean slopes and Inter-Andean Valley zones to the west and east. The Inter-Andean Valley is a maize-producing region, where fruits, vegetables, and herbs of European origins are also grown; its mild, cool climates are the most amenable of any equatorial region to temperate-clime plants. Most of the foods produced in this zone are exotic or luxury goods by Zumbaguan standards; even maize, a staple for most rural inhabitants of the Ecuadorian Sierra, is consumed more by "whites" in Zumbagua than by indigenous households.

The Inter-Andean Valley, despite its relative distance from Zumbagua, is of importance to parish residents, not for its agricultural products but because it is the political and economic heart of the Sierra. The topographic structure of the Inter-Andean Valley shapes Inter-Andean Valley social organization in ways that affect Zumbagua. Basile describes the Inter-Andean Valley as "a huge graben whose fairly level floor is flanked by the two cordilleras. . . . This area is sometimes also referred to as the Interandean 'Callejon', but it is far from being the uninterrupted 'avenue' that such a term suggests, because it is broken into a sequence of fifteen basins by a series of transverse ridges joining the eastern and western cordilleras" (1974:12). The *nudos,* as these transverse ridges are called, divide the northward-trending "avenue" of the Inter-Andean Valley into discrete valleys, a separation that forms the basis for Inter-Andean Valley settlement patterns. Zumbagua is articulated to the section of the valley directly to its east, and the economic and political ties of the parish to the nation are shaped by this fact. These particular ties exist despite the lack of topographic separations parallel to the *nudos* within the Cordillera Occidental itself. To understand the significance of this articulation, we must turn to the political geography of Ecuador.

Sociopolitical Geography

The Comuna

The smallest political unit in Zumbagua is the *comuna.* A *comuna* is theoretically a political unit designed to protect the geographic integrity of indigenous communities. It has a peculiar legal status based on the supposed communal nature of indigenous social organization, including

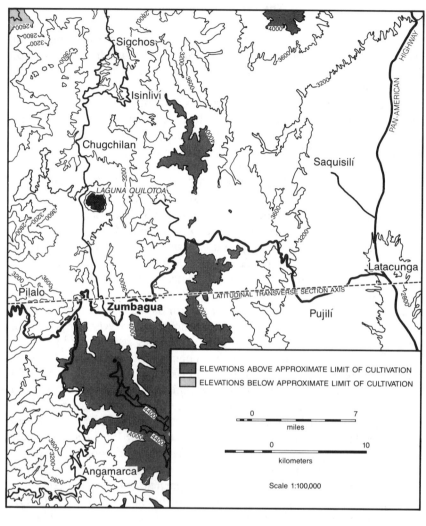

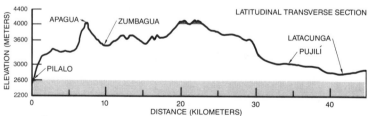

Figure 2. The region. Based on maps by the Instituto Geográfico-Militar del Ecuador, 1974. Used by permission.

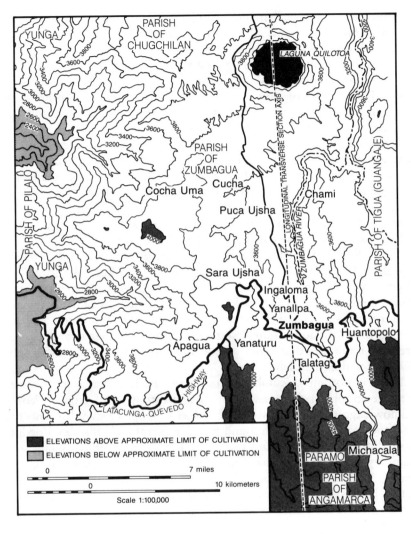

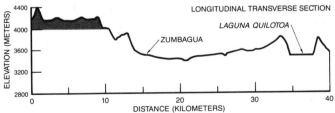

Figure 3. The parish. Based on maps made by the Instituto Geográfico-Militar del Ecuador, 1974. Used by permission.

features such as the inalienability of *comuna* land and leadership by an elected *cabildo* or council. In practice the *comuna* has taken on very different forms in different areas of Ecuador.

In Zumbagua, instead of being an alternative form of political unit to the *parroquia civil* or parish, the *comunas* actually function as subdivisions of the parish of Zumbagua. Most of the *comunas* appear to be survivals of old hacienda jurisdictions, *departmentos, lugares,* and *comunidades,* described in Costales and Costales (1976:7–10). One modern *comuna,* Apagua, was never part of the hacienda, but after centuries of independence from Zumbagua it is today a nominal subdivision of the parish. Similarly, Cucha or La Cocha previously was a *departmento* within the hacienda, comprising six subordinate *lugares* and *comunidades,* separate from the Departmento of Zumbagua. It is now legally a *comuna,* equivalent to its previous dependents and subordinate to the *caberceria* or seat of the parish, the town of Zumbagua itself.

The political life of the *comunas* is in sharp contrast to the stereotypical image of the closed corporate community in Latin America. The population of the parish lives in an extremely dispersed settlement pattern and recognizes only a very loosely defined hierarchy of named places or territorial subdivisions. The actual *comunas* correspond to some degree to these divisions, though some *comunas,* like Apagua and Cucha, are more important than others, while other *comunas* contain major subdivisions within themselves.

More importantly, Zumbagua residents seem reluctant to consider these geographical divisions as also demarcating social groups. People acknowledge their relationships to places—the place they live and the land they farm—but kinship and marriage create ties that bind people from different *comunas,* and these ties have more political significance than any that one might have to non-kin within one's *comuna* of residence. Also, households located on the edge of a *comuna* tend to form networks based on proximity, ignoring *comuna* boundaries. Even the boundaries of the parish become less important the closer to them one resides.

As is so frequently true of political boundaries, the divisions between *comunas* seem to be of significance only when they demarcate people who are hostile to one another, as is the case between residents of the *comuna* of SaraUjsha and those of Cucha and Chami, and on a larger scale between the people of Zumbagua and those of the adjacent parish of Tigua. At the same time, internal divisions within *comunas* are often more significant on a day-to-day basis than are inter-*comuna* divisions.

Although the *comunas* have *cabildos,* and organize *mingas* (communal work parties) to clear roads and build *comuna* meeting halls and school buildings, few people attend *mingas* or meetings, and many in fact express resentment at the idea that they should do so. The theoretical right of the *comuna* to fine households that do not send a family member to a *minga,* which in other indigenous areas is taken quite seriously, is unenforceable in Zumbagua.

The lack of social organization beyond the egocentered kin and *compadrazgo* networks contrasts with the classic image of the Andean community as described in the anthropological literature. It perhaps reflects the dismemberment of preexisting social forms by the hacienda, but it is also possible that the people of Zumbagua simply do not have the traditions of communal organization reported for the central Andes. The word *minga* itself evokes the forced work parties of the hacienda and the intrusive activities of government and church representatives, instead of being perceived as a tradition rooted in the community itself.

Nevertheless, some young men are interested in *comuna* politics, and the Catholic church takes an active interest in promoting local participation in the *comuna*. The church also gives small salaries, training, and support to a medical and a religious outreach person in each *comuna*. This well-intentioned practice has exacerbated some tensions within *comunas,* as some factions feel themselves excluded from these positions, and the services of these individuals are not widely sought. But the creation of such roles within the *comunas* does represent the beginnings of *comuna*-level infrastructure of sorts. As the parish moves into its third decade of autonomy, the *cabildos* may come to occupy a more significant place in Zumbaguan lives.

The Centro

The administrative seat of the parish, the town of Zumbagua, is located on the site of the old hacienda buildings, only a few of which are still standing. The modern town consists of a large, unpaved square, dusty or muddy depending on the season, surrounded by the schools, market buildings, clinic, church complex, and a series of small shops, some of which sell dry goods but most of which sell only liquor. There are a few one-block-long streets of houses.

The town, as parish seat, is something of a central place within the parish. It is popularly known as *el centro*. The *centro* is the site of the only weekly market, and the location of the Catholic church with its resident priests, nuns, and layworkers, the Colegio or secondary school, the Subcentro de Salud or clinic, and the office of the *teniente político,* the nominal political head of Zumbagua. Zumbagua *centro* is something of a vacant ceremonial center at present: perhaps half of the houses and most of the stores are locked and empty during the week. They open only on Friday nights and Saturdays, for the market.

Most full-time occupants of the *centro* are "white" families. Increasingly, however, indigenous families are building houses in the *centro,* while the "whites," frightened by the takeover of the *centro* by "Indians," almost all have plans to move out of the parish altogether, into "white" towns of the coast or the Inter-Andean Valley.

The entire town, which seems so empty and desolate, is in fact in a period of change and growth. Most of the buildings in it are less than ten years old, and new construction is under way. As indigenous residents gradually claim the *centro* as their own, and as the economic foundation of some families moves away from agriculture, the move from the *co-munas* into the *centro* becomes appealing. A house in the *centro* can serve as a storeroom for supplies used in selling in the market, as a small liquor or dry-goods store, and as a source for petty income gained by renting the whole house or space within it to *compadres* and distant kin for storage, sleeping space, or use when celebrating a wedding or a baptism. At present, however, these activities do not provide a full-time income for indigenous families or individuals: the parish is simply too poor to support much in the way of commercial enterprises. If economic conditions were to improve, the town could rapidly blossom. The framework is being laid for its burgeoning, but it is difficult to envision the circumstances in which such a change would become possible.

The Road

The road that bisects Zumbagua is the single most important means by which the parish is articulated with the rest of the nation. The highway is not a road *to* Zumbagua, but a road *through* it; for the most part parish residents know it simply as a constant reminder that the rest of the world is passing them by. Nevertheless, the road has an important impact on parish life. Though less well traveled than the Guayaquil–Quito highway, the Latacunga–Quevedo highway that crosses Zumbagua is an important artery for the nation. As one of the few roadways that links coast and Sierra, it carries a steady traffic of buses and trucks moving people and products between the two zones.

This activity has several effects on the parish. A small roadside extension of the *centro*, inhabited by "whites," makes its living selling food and liquor to passersby. In addition, a very few local men, white and indigenous, have succeeded in buying trucks or buses, from which they earn a very good income by parish standards. More significantly, the road makes travel out of the parish, either to the littoral or to the Inter-Andean Valley, relatively easy in comparison with other *páramo* areas. With patience and persistence one can almost always flag down a bus from the highway, though the white bus drivers who pass through the parish are reluctant to take "Indians" on board, forcing them to sit in the back or stand in the aisle and throwing them off at the first opportunity (courtesies that they gladly extend to *gringas* like myself who travel to "Indian" areas like Zumbagua). Once on the bus, Quito, capital of the nation, is only four hours away. The isolation of Zumbagua from the life of the nation is more apparent than real; it is economic and social rather than geographical in nature.

Parish and Canton

Zumbagua is both a civil parish and an ecclesiastical one. As a civil parish, it is one of ten rural parishes in the canton of Pujilí, Cotopaxi Province. Cotopaxi, like most highland provinces, is best described as a subdivision of the Inter-Andean Valley, basically comprising a basin of the *callejon* from *nudo* to *nudo*, along with the sections of the two Cordilleras adjacent to this basin. Within the basin lies the city of Latacunga, capital of the province, as well as several major towns, notably Saquisilí, Pujilí, and Salcedo, all of which are canton seats. Zumbagua falls within the jurisdiction of Pujilí, a market town just west of Latacunga. As seat of the canton of the same name, the town of Pujilí nominally controls an expanse of territory that stretches across the Cordillera Occidental and down into the littoral, encompassing Sierra, *páramo*, *monte*, and lowland plantation areas.

The impoverished nature of most of this territory can be deduced from the nature of the Pujilí market, held on Sundays and Wednesdays so as not to conflict with the much larger Latacunga market. In terms of foods sold, the Pujilí market is predominantly a starch market: the fruits, vegetables, herbs, and meats that more urban markets sell are all luxury goods to most Pujilí customers, who purchase only grains, legumes, tubers, and various types of flours and meals made from these products.

The starch market is a phenomenon of impoverished rural areas of the Sierra; it may appear to be the product of isolation, but lack of buying power is the real cause.

The parish of Pujilí itself lies on the interface between the Inter-Andean Valley and the eastern slope of the Cordillera Occidental. The other parishes of the canton can be divided into the western, "hot" parishes of Pilaló, La Mana, La Victoria, and Tingo, and the high, "cold" parishes of Angamarca, Chugchilan, Guangaje (Tigua), Isinliví, and Zumbagua. Zumbagua lies at the center of this latter group of parishes. Angamarca, Isinliví, and Pujilí have mixed indigenous and "white" populations, while Chugchilan, Guangaje, and Zumbagua are almost entirely indigenous. As a result, although the towns of Isinliví, Angamarca, and Pujilí are larger, more prosperous, and boast far more in the way of public works and nationally funded infrastructures than does Zumbagua, Zumbagua has de facto become a kind of second-level administrative and geographical center for the indigenous groups in the area, both for the government—as seen in the location of the secondary school and clinic in Zumbagua—and for the Catholic church, whose resident staff in Zumbagua far outnumbers that of neighboring ecclesiastical parishes.

In spite of the fact that it is functioning as an administrative center with a jurisdiction large in both area and population, the political infrastructure of the parish is almost nonexistent, and articulation with national governmental structures is fragile. There is a *teniente político*, nominal political head of the parish, but his authority is extremely limited.[13] There are no other political functionaries in the parish.

Province and Nation

To the north of the province of Cotopaxi lies the province of Pichincha, location of Quito, the capitol of Ecuador. Pichincha is the political center of the nation and a major economic hub for the Sierra as well. South of Cotopaxi is the province of Tungurahua, which is controlled by the prosperous commercial city of Ambato.

Cotopaxi itself, however, is an impoverished, sparsely populated, and predominantly rural province, and Latacunga is smaller than many provincial capitals of the Sierra. Instead of acting as a market for goods and labor produced by rural areas in the province, as both Quito and Ambato to some extent do, Latacunga instead is dependent on its rural hinterlands as a market for the goods and services it can provide. The city comprises mainly headquarters for various governmental and religious agencies active in the province; commercial enterprises that serve agriculturalists, such as feed stores and hardware shops; bus and trucking companies; and restaurants, bars, and dry-goods stores that function mainly on market days.

The nature of Latacunga's economic base is underlined by the marked periodicity of its marketplace. Unlike markets in other cities that serve a local, urban clientele that shops every day, the Latacunga market operates at full speed only on its two main market days, Tuesday and Saturday, and is almost completely inactive the rest of the week. Market women resident in Latacunga must travel to the smaller markets in the surrounding towns in order to sell every day.

Zumbagua residents use the markets of Latacunga, Pujilí, and Saquisilí to purchase items not available in Zumbagua, such as watches, radios and cassette players, tools and hardware, tin roofing materials, and some special-occasion clothing such as baptismal gowns. Women who sell cooked food in the Zumbagua market must purchase ingredients earlier in the week at one of these markets. Frequently, a large extended family sends one member, generally an adolescent fluent in Spanish, to make all their purchases. Some residents go to these towns to visit governmental offices, to see lawyers, or because they have a relative in prison. But while some parish residents are familiar with these towns and the resources they have to offer, many, primarily women, have rarely been there. For these individuals, Inter-Andean Valley towns remain part of the unknown, Spanish-speaking world beyond the parish.

Latacunga is only a place in which certain objects or services may be obtained; it is neither a potential residence nor a place of employment. But if there are no employment possibilities within Cotopaxi Province, work can be found in Quito, less than two hours away from Latacunga by bus. Young boys begin traveling to Quito between the ages of eight and twelve, so that by sixteen it is already a familiar environment. None of them take up permanent residence there; rather, they live a migratory life, shuttling back and forth between family and agricultural obligations in Zumbagua and work in Quito. Periodic unemployment finds them spending months at a time in the parish, and many middle-aged men gradually cease going to the city altogether, as they inherit land and assets within the parish from their parents. Like the *páramo*, Quito is used primarily as a zone of which the product—cash—can be invested in the cultivation of other products elsewhere, namely in the fields and family at home.

The zone of cultivation and habitation, with the network of kin and *compadres* dispersed throughout it, remains the most significant element in the life of most of the people of Zumbagua. The *páramos* above and *monte* below, the *centro* within and Quito beyond, are sources of necessary but supplementary resources to this primary, agricultural zone.

History

The history of Zumbagua is a topic worthy of a book in itself; I can provide only the most cursory overview here. I do so for two reasons. One is to dispel the image of Zumbagua as a "timeless" land, clinging to ancient ways, living isolated from the forces of history. Zumbagua is a place in which people "still" grow foods mostly for their consumption, yarn is spun on a drop spindle, flour is ground with a mortar and pestle, barley is harvested with a sickle. But the "traditionalism" of Zumbagua, far from indicating centuries of isolation from the rest of the world, is as much a product of the forces of history as are the skyscrapers of Quito.

A second reason to refer to Zumbagua's history in this introductory chapter is the recentness of its transition from hacienda to civil parish. In 1983–1984, the time of this study, the post-hacienda epoch of Zumbagua's history was not yet twenty years old, a brief episode counterbalanced by three and a half centuries of the older way of life. Instead of a tranquil and timeless world in which change comes slowly if at all, Zumbagua is a society reeling under the impact of enormous legal, political, social, and economic transformations.

In this brief summary of the parish's history, I will attempt to illuminate only a few themes. First, a long tradition of highland-lowland articulations has shaped the cultural identity of the people of Zumbagua, independent *páramo*-dwellers who have continually redefined themselves in relation to the dual influences of the "civilized" Inter-Andean Valley and the "wild" *yunga* to either side. A second theme lies in the long history of extractive institutions that steadily drained the region of its surpluses while insulating it from direct interaction with national markets, a heritage that has left it impoverished and economically disarticulated. A third, social legacy is found in the presence within "Indian" Zumbagua of a "white" community that poses as an upper class within the parish, a situation that has its roots in a previous socioeconomic system, the hacienda.

The nature of Zumbagua society earlier in this century can be illuminated by descriptions of similar haciendas in the 1940s through 1960s recorded by two observers, Basile (1974) and Crespi (1968), both of whom describe life on haciendas that had ecological settings, histories, and economies parallel to Zumbagua's. Crespi also provides information on the long history of such haciendas in previous centuries.

Before the Hacienda

The "traditionalism" of Zumbagua's subsistence practices is not the only aspect of life there that suggests cultural continuities belied by history. Many cultural traits seem autochthonous to the area but are, in fact, imported from other zones. The people of Zumbagua speak the language of the Incas and herd llamas, as do the people of the central Andes. But in Ecuador these customs are not of great antiquity; they were introduced just before, during, or shortly after the Spanish Conquest. In fact, while in language, dress, subsistence pattern, and social organization the people of Zumbagua clearly conform to the broad outlines of indigenous Andean culture, it is not clear how long ago they came to adopt this system of living. While the pattern itself has a long pre-Hispanic tradition, at the time of the Conquest the ancestors of the modern parish residents may not have been participants in it. It is possible that they were not Sierra dwellers at all, and even if they were, the degree to which the northern Andes shared a cultural identity with the conquerors from the south is not perfectly understood.

Pre-Hispanic Ecuador, as Murra observes, lay halfway between the expansive empire-building, state-level societies of the central Andes to the south and the chiefdoms of Colombia to the north (1963). According to most accounts, the northward expansion of the Inca state encountered in Ecuador a series of highland ethnic groups, generally similar in their basic subsistence patterns and level of sociocultural integration, but differentiated linguistically. These groups are conventionally described as the Pasto, Cara, Panzaleo, Puruha, Cañari, and Palta, each inhabiting a basin of the Inter-Andean Valley. According to this picture, the modern-day province of Cotopaxi would have been inhabited by the Panzaleo.

Juan Carrera Colin has fleshed out this schematic description of the Cotopaxi region in pre-Columbian times through a detailed look at documents pertaining to the *Corregimiento de Latacunga*, the Spanish jurisdiction that encompassed the area of the modern province (1981). He presents a picture of surprising ethnic diversity, partially a result of Incaic resettlement policies. Ethnic groups identified in early Spanish documents as residents of the area include the Quechua-speaking Masaquizas (Salasacas), Cañaris, Chinchasuyos, and Ingas from the south, and Pastos and Puquies-Pomasquis from the north. In addition to these immigrants, the population native to the area appears to have comprised various ethnically distinct groups. For example, the words "Sigchos" and "Angamarca," which today are place-names, are used in colonial documents to refer to specific highland ethnic groups distinct from those of the Latacunga area.

As in the present century, the societies of the Cordillera Occidental were articulated not only with the polities of the Inter-Andean Valley, but also economically with the peoples of the western slopes. Colonial tribute records reveal a flow of hot-climate goods such as cotton and capsicum linking together Niguas of the littoral, Yumbos of the cloud forest, Sigchos-Angamarcas of the *páramo,* and a succession of dominant political groups in the Inter-Andean Valley.

Of Zumbagua itself not a whisper is heard in the records of pre-Hispanic indigenous life. It is possible that the area was completely uninhabited, or that these *páramo* lands were exploited only by people who "belonged" elsewhere, perhaps in the land of the Yumbos. Pilaló, today located just beyond the western edge of Zumbagua and variously referred to as belonging to the Sierra or the *monte\yunga,* appears in the *Tasa tributaria* of 1619 as a cotton-producing *pueblo yunga;* Zumbagua could have been an upper extension of Pilaló. This dual pattern is suggested by analogy with the early history of Sigchos, which before the Spanish *reducciones* (resettlements into centralized communities) was split into cold-land and hot-land settlements called Jatunsigchos and Uchucsigchos, "Big" and "Little" Sigchos, respectively (Carrera Colin 1981:147).

It seems likely that Zumbagua, if it was inhabited at all in this period, was a rural hinterland for groups that made their living from their position on the western highland-lowland interface. Access to the *yunga* was in this period a more important resource than were the *páramo* lands themselves.

The Emergence of the Hacienda

It was with the introduction of the Spanish sheep (and the Incaic llama, possibly also introduced by the Spaniards) that the *páramos* of Zumbagua came into their own as a major productive zone. With this new economic importance came population resettlement. The creation of the hacienda economy may in fact have caused the emergence of a resident population in Zumbagua where none had previously existed. Far from having been an autochthonous society later subdued by the Spanish, Zumbagua in all probability first came into being as a result of transformations that took place under Spanish rule. Notwithstanding the

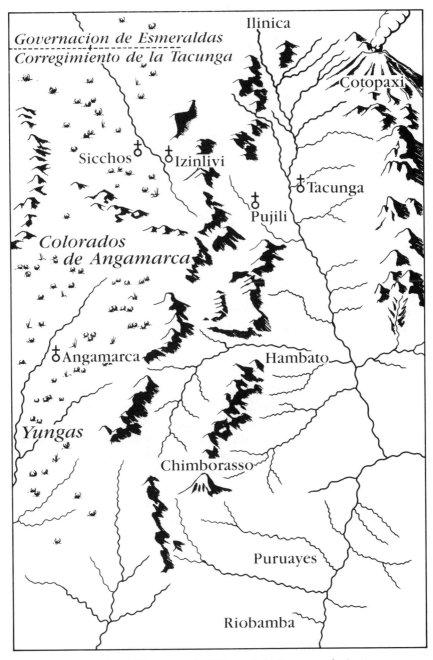

Figure 4. Adapted from detail of *Carta de la Provincia de Quito y sus Adiacentes por Don Pedro Maldonado 1750*, as reproduced by the Instituto Geográfico-Militar del Ecuador. Used by permission.

contemporary image of the "Indians" of Zumbagua as "native" to the area, their very existence as an ethnic group may be an artifact of the colonial period.

A variety of forces were at work in this period. As Basile notes, the spread of Spanish landholdings, along with ever-increasing tribute and *mita* (forced labor) demands, pushed many Indians up from lower, maize-growing lands into the *páramo* (1974:50). In the seventeenth century, however, "when the large estates physically came of age," even *páramo* lands increasingly fell under Spanish control (Crespi 1968:40). Previously existing landholdings were expanded, and new estates came into being. Zumbagua appears in a list of properties dated 1600 simply as "Hato de vacas que llama Laujua de Zumbagua," which suggests that the place name was initially associated with a mere resting-place for herders caring for cattle in the *páramo;* but it soon came to figure in documents as a property of worth. Documents relating to the sale of Zumbagua to the Augustinians, in whose hands the property was to remain for several centuries, are dated 1639. Nearby, other great estates, in Apagua, Tigua, Mocata, Chugchilan, and elsewhere, also took shape. The history of land tenure in what later became Canton Pujilí was probably similar to that described by Muriel Crespi for a northern *páramo* area of Ecuador:

> During this period, La Merced Monastery enjoyed mounting success as an economic institution. . . . Its holdings expanded by purchase and . . . [because] well-wishers of the Church commonly provided it with gifts of land. . . . Like other estates, . . . Pesillo had been undergoing marked physical growth . . . throughout the 17th century. . . . By the end of the 18th century estates of different religious orders virtually monopolized all of what is today Canton Cayambe. Little if any vacant land intervened between neighboring haciendas. (1968:41–48)

In the area around Zumbagua, a few "free" communities, such as Apagua, survived into the twentieth century, but throughout the Sierra residents of such "free" communities were drawn into the orbits of the haciendas as laborers, so that their position ultimately differed little from that of the hacienda Indians.

The expansion of the great landed estates, coupled with urban Spanish populations that were on the increase while the rural indigenous population was decimated by epidemics, created an acute labor crisis in the rural Sierra. The cities needed food, but the estates lacked the manpower to produce it. The crown responded to the problem by increasing the forced-labor drafts or *repartimientos*.

In the seventeenth-century form of the *repartimiento*, a labor system began to emerge that was to endure, under various forms, well into the twentieth century. The *mita* or *repartimiento* theoretically lasted only for one-year periods, but in fact the development of a debt peonage system quickly placed the *mitayos* under permanent obligation. Bound by debt to the landowner, indigenous families began to live out their entire lives on the hacienda. A nucleus of permanent hacienda residents began to form.

Again, Crespi's information on Cayambe provides insight into the process:

> La Merced utilized the available institutions for procuring laborers to attend Pesillos' increasing herds and expanding physical and natural resources. In 1616, the local Crown authorities were advised that Pesillo's sheep alone totalled 17,000. For lack of sufficient shepherds, it was claimed that animals were going astray and that *mitayos* were urgently needed. . . . There is little reason to suppose that the fate of these *mitayos* differed greatly from that of many others throughout the sierra haciendas. They were undoubtedly incorporated into the indigenous hamlet . . . and adjusted to permanent residence within the hacienda community. (1968:44)

A document of 1639 records a similar request for laborers to work as shepherds in Zumbagua. During the succeeding decades, Zumbagua became a major wool producer; in 1780, it produced ninety thousand pounds of wool (Carrera Colin 1981:155). With production at this level, the shepherds mentioned a century earlier had presumably been augmented by a considerable additional labor force. The hacienda had become not only an economic institution, but a society.

At the same time, several economic features of the hacienda had emerged that were also to be of long duration. First, the hacienda was capital-poor but land-rich. Labor had to be acquired without cash investment; hence the establishment of a system whereby the hacienda could exchange land for labor. Legal sanctions that kept peons on the land, plus a social system that provided them with few alternatives, served as additional reinforcements.

Under successive governments, this labor system took on different names: the *repartimiento* gave way to *concertaje*, *concertaje* to the *huasipungo*. Under all of these systems, land for cultivation and pasture was exchanged for labor. The hacienda, though a commercial operation, functioned almost completely without the use of wages.

At a larger level, the church-run hacienda did not receive cash payment for its products. For the most part they were not sold, but were used within the larger economic system of the religious order. Crespi describes colonial Pesillo as follows:

> Economically Pesillo tended to be self-sufficient. . . . But the hacienda was not producing for its own needs alone. Pesillo was one unit in the larger church organization, and its produce was distributed and consumed . . . throughout the larger domain of the Order of La Merced. . . . This redistribution was usually contained within the realm of La Merced, but occasionally Pesillo's produce reached a market external to the Order and was exchanged for cash. Some profits were returned to Pesillo for the maintenance and enlargement of hacienda buildings. . . . More often, cash profits were returned to the central office in Quito. (1968:55)

Zumbagua, though of tremendous economic significance to the Augustinians, likewise did not directly exchange its products for cash. The primary purpose of the hacienda was to provide wool for the great *obraje* at Callo, near Latacunga, as well as to other workshops in the province of León (Costales and Costales 1976:4). Like many Sierra haciendas, Zumbagua was thus in the position of being simultaneously a productive enterprise the surpluses of which were siphoned off and reinvested elsewhere—hence clearly a profit-making enterprise—and an enterprise that was not establishing for itself a role in a market economy.

The Hacienda in the Republic of Ecuador

In 1930 Ecuador became a republic, but this change must have had little immediate effect in Zumbagua. Debt peonage continued to bind more and more of the indigenous population to the haciendas during the nineteenth century. By the beginning of the twentieth century, however, a threat to this system had emerged. The coast, which had been transformed into a cash-oriented plantation and export economy, had spawned a liberal reform movement, which in 1895 gained national power under the leadership of Eloy Álfaro. Despite the fears of Sierra landowners, however, Álfaro's government reinforced the laws supporting hacienda labor arrangements. As was to happen again in the 1960s, a reform movement that initially threatened the existing economic system in the end transferred its attention from reform of the entire highland agricultural economy to an attack on institutionally owned haciendas. The Álfaro government concentrated on the expropriation of ecclesiastical estates, enacting in 1908 the *Ley de Beneficencia* or "Manos Muertos." The expropriated properties were to be leased out to individuals, and proceeds from this arrangement were to be used to fund the newly created Asistencia Social, a public welfare agency with programs benefiting the urban poor.

Zumbagua changed hands as a result, passing from the Augustinians to a series of temporary landlords. The socioeconomic structure of the hacienda itself and the nature of its articulation with the larger society and economy remained relatively unaltered. The surpluses it produced, as in previous centuries, generated profits destined to benefit the urban centers of the nation.

As a result, Asistencia Social haciendas remained undercapitalized. Basile reports that in the 1940s, Ecuadorian haciendas in general suffered from poorly trained, badly paid, and overworked managerial staffs, absentee ownership, and antiquated equipment. He notes that the situation was especially acute on haciendas owned by the Asistencia Social (1974:130), and that the situation had not improved by the 1960s. He describes an Asistencia-owned hacienda in Pichincha Province as having "a run-down appearance, eroded and exhausted soils, equipment that was inadequate in amount, efficiency, and state of repair, and agricultural and social practices reminiscent of the feudal age" (1974:125).

The source of this state of affairs lay in the nature of the Asistencia Social itself. Crespi describes the agency's operation in the early 1960s as follows:

> The Asistencia . . . is nearly autonomous financially and is expected to support itself and its endeavours largely from the returns of the 77 haciendas under its control. . . . Rental fees and returns from the direct management of the estates are collected by the Asistencia and then apportioned to a number of dependent public institutions—schools, orphanages, hospitals and asylums for mendicants. . . . These . . . are fully dependent upon the Asistencia for operating funds. . . .
>
> Despite incomes from 77 haciendas, the institutional patron of Pesillo is cash-poor. Continual financial drain by dependent agencies . . . keeps the patron constantly in arrears for even the smallest debts. (1968:143)

In the twentieth century, then, haciendas such as Pesillo and Zumbagua still operated under a tremendous shortage of capital. Land remained the only asset. As in previous centuries, indigenous labor remained essential to the hacienda but had to be obtained through nonmonetary means. "The hacienda . . . acquires a labor pool and satisfies other needs by engaging in an asymmetrical exchange of resources. . . . The utility of the system is clear. In lieu of a full cash wage the patron grants access to natural resources . . . unsuitable for commercial exploitation or excess for present needs. Such an arrangement is not unattractive to landless and powerless peasants. In the absence of subsistence alternatives, their own labor is a surplus resource" (Crespi 1968:142–147) Scarce capital and abundant land were constants; labor, so scarce in the colonial period, by the twentieth century had become overabundant. According to Crespi (1968:68–69) and Mercedes Prieto (1980:106), by the 1960s population pressure within hacienda boundaries had created a new class of landless younger families within the indigenous population. *Huasipungueros,* those who had been granted a plot of land in return for a permanent labor obligation, actually constituted a privileged group among peons (Crespi 1968:68–69).

In Zumbagua as well, Costales and Costales (1976:4–5) report that the 1960s found almost 10 percent of indigenous hacienda residents without land. They were bound to the hacienda through a variety of other labor arrangements, primarily the *yanapa.* Basile defines a *yanapero* as one who receives only foraging rights on communal lands as a return for his labor (1974:55). Internal differentiation among *huasipungo* holders also existed: the true *huasipunguero* received wages in addition to his plot, but almost as many were *arrimados* who received no wage; in addition, the size of the *huasipungo* varied from two to twenty-nine hectares (Costales and Costales 1976:4–5, 14).

Schematic description of labor and land-use arrangements under the hacienda masks the complexities of the system in operation. In addition to contractual relations with the hacienda, residents also entered into labor and tenure agreements with one another. Basile describes a four-hectare *huasipungo* on which "one-fourth of the area of the *huasipungo* was used with five different sharecroppers, some of whom brought in additional sharecroppers of their own" (1974:127).

Within this century, then, the available evidence suggests that considerable economic differentiation existed within the indigenous work force. Even at the upper end of the scale, however, the livelihood provided by the *páramo* haciendas of the Asistencia Social was scarcely adequate. Basile concludes his description of the *huasipungo* as follows:

The produce from the four hectares of *huasipungo* and the income from labor on the hacienda provided only enough food for two meals a day and little more than the clothes on their backs. Yet this *huasipungo* was one of the larger holdings and its occupants were considered among the more fortunate members of the hacienda labor force. Most of the other *huasipungos* on the hacienda were so much smaller that often *huasipungueros* sold their future crops . . . in advance. . . . [E]ven if they had been able to keep all of their harvest for their own use, it still would not have been sufficient to meet their needs. (Ibid.)

Highland-Lowland Articulation Under the Hacienda

The hacienda of Zumbagua owned land on the western slopes and maintained a sugar mill there. This property was located some distance away; the children of white hacienda employees remember the arduous trips associated with managing these properties. Indigenous residents of the parish old enough to have worked for the hacienda recall the assignment to spend a period of time working in the *yunga* as the most dreaded of all tasks. According to possibly apocryphal tales, death and disease were to be found there, and horrible injuries occurred to peons operating the mill machinery. Neverthless, this aspect of hacienda life kept alive the precolonial articulation of *páramo* and *yunga*, as well as the image of the cloud-forest ecosystem in Zumbagua minds.

In addition to working in the lowlands for the Zumbagua administration, some hacienda residents went to the *yunga* on their own. Young men unable to secure contracts with the hacienda sought work on small *fincas* (farms) on the western slopes. This practice continued after the hacienda era and still exists today.

Finally, there is evidence of *páramo* dwellers farming their own lands on the slopes. According to Cisneros Cisneros, the people of Apagua, then a "free" community, utilized the *yunga* lands heavily. "El grupo indígena . . . de *Apahua* (4.100 m) . . . al N.O. de Zumbagua, . . . ha constituido una Comunidad Agraria en tierras de uso común. . . . En las secciones medias y altas cultivan cebada, frejol, arveja y lentaje; dada la extensión incluye secciones bajas subtropicales ('yunga') donde tambíen se cultivan plátano, caña, café, papa china, patatas, etc." (1948:219).[14]

The total picture of *yunga* exploitation at this time remains unclear, but these data suggest that there were at least three kinds of involvement between the *páramo* and the *yunga* during the twentieth-century hacienda period: exploitation by the hacienda itself, using indigenous males as laborers; temporary male migration for wage labor on an individual level; and, in the case of Apagua at least, cultivation of family-owned plots.

The Death of the Hacienda

In the early 1960s, a wave of liberal reform again threatened to remove the legal underpinnings of the hacienda labor system. The movement to break up large estates and redistribute land to the peasant farmers, thus putting an end to the latifundia-minifundia land-use pattern that has characterized the continent, spread throughout much of Latin America during these years. In addition to the influence of revolutionary movements, the idea of agrarian reform was in part spurred by fear that the Cuban Revolution might spread (Janvry 1981), and, in Ecuador, by economic pressures internal to the Sierra, which dictated the replacement of the extensive, low-capital hacienda system with smaller, more capital-intensive operations (Barsky 1980).

As had been the case for the previous century's liberal reform, the Ecuadorian Agrarian Reform, when it actually came to pass, primarily affected institutionally held rather than individually held estates. Whitten summarizes the effects of the reforms that initially took effect in 1964 as follows: "In this 'revolutionary' reorganization the state mainly changed state haciendas into cooperatives where previously 'bound' peasants were allowed to lay claim to unused or underutilized land. On the private haciendas such bound peasants were often given no more than formal title to their traditional meager holdings" (Whitten 1981:12). There was also an attempt to relieve the demand for land without disturbing large private holdings, through colonization of the lowlands and promotion of cattle ranching and dairy farming, enterprises believed to be more lucrative than traditional forms of agriculture and pastoralism.

However ineffectual the Agrarian Reform was in altering the socioeconomic structure of the Sierra as a whole, for Zumbagua the immediate effects were overwhelming. Centuries of hated oppression had come to an end. The exact sequence of events is unclear, but the ruins of the hacienda buildings in the *centro* give mute testimony to one initial reaction by the freed peons. Buildings and trees belonging to the administrative center of the estate were razed in an outpouring of emotion at the removal of the despised *patrón*.

The actual division of land appears to have been a somewhat chaotic process that resulted in wide disparities in the size of landholdings. *Arrimados* and *yanaperos,* who together constituted almost half the households in the parish, were not entitled to receive lands, while white ex-employees of the hacienda presumably were able to take advantage of existing debts and cash shortages on the part of *huasipungueros* to buy up properties quickly, thus amassing respectable landholdings for themselves.

Despite these inequalities and the economic problems that have beset the parish since 1965, the people of Zumbagua have no regrets about the passing of the hacienda. Although there is conflict over what form the new Zumbagua should take, there is no question that the chance for political and social self-determination has been eagerly welcomed by all indigenous residents and is a source of fierce pride among them.

The Legacies of the Hacienda

The Cultural Legacy of Violence

Relations between white *patrón* and Indian laborer were idealized as a father-son relationship of mutual if asymmetrical dependence and great affection. The *patrón* cared for and protected "his" Indians, and they responded with undying loyalty. As Eugene Genovese has masterfully shown for black-white relations on North American slave plantations, the emotional realities of such relationships are complex and contradictory (1974). In the Andes, both sides certainly relied on the father-child ideology when attempting to manipulate each other, but its use was not always hypocritical.

Nevertheless, in reality the Indian-white relationship was more often characterized by brutal exploitation answered by barely contained hostility than it was by sentiment. Jorge Icaza's classic novel *Huasipungo* (1953) depicts the brutality of the hacienda system in Ecuador. Crespi's description of Pesillo, an Asistencia Social hacienda like Zumbagua, also provides a vivid picture of work relationships:

What is never relaxed is the rank distinction between peons and señores. On horseback and equipped with whips, symbols of their status, the mayordomos and mayorales regulate all the day's activities. The threat of the whip, usually snapped at their legs, urges the peons on to work. The peons are warned of the approaching mayordomos by the stream of obscene and angry insults from the supervisors and, as in some dance drama, they usually artfully leap away from the cracking whip. All the while they . . . engage in verbal interplay with their supervisors. . . . A kind of oral battle ensues wherein insults, frequently disguised as jokes in order to avoid open hostility, are hurled between peons and overseers. (1968:194)

Older residents of Zumbagua describe similarly hostile relations with white overseers.

Tales of verbal abuse are lent credence by the nature of the Spanish loanwords that have entered Zumbagua Quichua. Visitors to my house were always startled to hear Quichua-speaking women, when addressing a recalcitrant animal or disobedient child, suddenly launch into a stream of Spanish obscenities.

If whippings and curses characterized white-Indian relations at their best, it is not surprising that conflicts, when they arose, were marked by naked violence. The deaths of whites at the hands of Indians, such as occurred in Pesillo at the turn of the century (Crespi 1968:61–62), and more recently in Salasaca (Diaz 1963), are everywhere remembered, while the deaths of rebellious Indians from the colonial period to the present are too numerous to be recorded. The people of Zumbagua remember that political turmoil has often led to indigenous deaths at the hands of white authorities, both before and after the end of the hacienda.

For the most part, fear of reprisals created an internal pressure within the indigenous community that prevented the outbreak of violence (or, rather, prevented direct response to the institutionalized violence of the hacienda system). But the history of the Andes has been a history of indigenous revolts, small and large, and white fear of the Indians was a day-to-day reality of hacienda life, even when no open rebellion occurred. Crespi says of Pesillo in the last days of the hacienda, "Ideally, peons have no power of any kind. . . . Nevertheless, every administrator fears a sudden eruption of violence from the numerically overwhelming Indian labor force. . . . In Pesillo, labor problems have never ceased since at least the turn of the century when the Indians killed the first administrator. Nothing equal to the bloodshed reported for this time has ever recurred, but no patron has ever forgotten the potential for its occurrence" (1968:173, 184). Twentieth-century *patróns* of the hacienda at Zumbagua never spent the night at the hacienda, out of fear that they would be murdered as they slept by the "wild" indigenous peons (María del Carmen Molestina Zaldumbide, personal communication).

In modern Zumbagua, as in Salasaca, Cañar, and other indigenous areas of the Sierra, this potential for sudden death has not been forgotten. "If you had come here in the old days," some Zumbagua men would remark pleasantly upon meeting me, "they would have found your body at the bottom of a *quebrada*." Even those who appeared more welcoming made me uneasy with their constant, unsolicited assurances that "Nothing would happen to me" because "It's not like the old days," assurances that sounded too much like warnings.

In the parish today, civil servants and ecclesiastical functionaries on one side, and the people of Zumbagua on the other, struggle to define a system of political articulation that will not replicate the abuses of the past. Impeding this process is a mutual fear that the violence of the past will be repeated. An unspoken threat, the memory of Indian violence and white reprisals lies between the two sides like a sword, a ready weapon for either to use against the other in justifying mistrust or hostility.

The Social Legacy: Zumbagua Whites

Although Zumbagua is primarily indigenous, like every indigenous area it has a small nucleus of "white" families that dominate the life of the *centro*. They are for the most part descendants of hacienda employees, although several individuals are outsiders who married "white" residents of the parish or simply "happened" to come to Zumbagua and, making a niche for themselves, never left. Unlike indigenous residents, Zumbagua "whites" lament the passing of the hacienda. From their perspective, a system that assured them social, political, and economic superiority within the parish has been superceded by a more fluid society in which their position, no longer institutionalized, must be constantly re-consolidated through informal structures.

Asymmetrical *compadrazgo*, as Crespi notes, was an important social corollary to the rigidly stratified relations within the workplace. "[P]ersonalized ties . . . lend support to the formal organizations by indebting less favored persons to more powerful or influential ones. These are also self-perpetuating systems since in order to maintain their prestige positions with regard to subordinate persons, those with power or influence must continually validate their roles by interceding on behalf of others" (1968:170).

Under the hacienda system, an overt power structure dictated the nature and amount of direct control and financial advantage residents had over one another. Personalized relationships between "white" employees and "Indian" peons merely supported and expanded these rights. Since the mid-1960s, however, when parish "whites" lost the legitimacy conferred on them by the hacienda, asymmetrical fictive kin relations have become increasingly important as a mechanism by which "whites" maintain economic and social control in the parish.

"White" economic control in the parish centers around female shop-keeping, male bus and truck driving, and an interlocking series of asymmetrical relationships with indigenous residents. All of these strategies have their roots in hacienda life.

The role of "white" men in transportation has been a feature of Sierran society since colonial times, when lower-class Spaniards found work in the New World as muleteers. Also, organizing transportation and communication between the isolated estate and the outside world, as well as within the hacienda's sprawling territory, was an important aspect of day-to-day hacienda management.

Shopkeeping is likewise a traditionally "white" role, especially for women, that has persisted into the present day. This role has historically been associated with abuses and exploitation (see, for example, descriptions of the shopkeeper-Indian relationship in Burgos 1970 or Parsons 1945). Crespi (1968:133) describes shopkeeping as a typical employment of hacienda employees' wives.

Not only aspects of the modern economic structure of the parish, but also certain features of its geographical layout can be traced back to hacienda Indian–white relations. Although it is changing slowly, the *centro* remains primarily a "white" stronghold, which "Indians" use only on market and fiesta days. This pattern dates back to the pre-1965 role of the *centro* as an all-white nucleus that served both as nerve center for the estate and symbol of the hacienda's power. Crespi says of the *centro* at Pesillo:

> For upper-echelon staff, all non-Indians, the administrative compound is a work and recreational center as well as a residential area. Indians live dispersed over the hillsides. This residence pattern is clear-cut and never violated; only non-Indians may live within the administrative compound. For Pesillo *llacta* the nucleated compound serves as a special sort of community center. Residents congregate here for work, to receive pay, for recreational and ritual observances and in order to use the limited educational and transportation facilities. (1968:126–127)

The other cluster of "white" inhabitants in the parish is located just above the *centro*, clinging to the highway. This community originates not from hacienda employees but from another hacienda phenomenon, the *apegados*, poor whites who clung to the fringes of the large estates, eking out a living by providing services to their residents and administration (see, for example, Crespi 1968:57–58).

In mentioning the history of this roadside community, it is perhaps also worth referring to the historical significance of the road itself, which, though travelers were not impressed with either the road or the towns it passed, nevertheless served as an important means of access between coast and Sierra. Teodoro Wolf at one point refers to it as a "bridle path" (1892:227), but also comments, "It is noteworthy that the road (rather bad) which leads from Quevedo to Latacunga is the last which communicates the interior of the Republic with the inhabited littoral region; for all the rest toward the North . . . there exist nothing but very bad and very little-travelled foot paths" (1892:147–148). Of the towns the road passes, he says of Latacunga that it is "a regular city," though "somewhat gloomy" in appearance; Pujilí he describes only as "without special recommendation," while Zumbagua is one of a series of "miserable towns or villages of a few houses" (1892:569).

The Economic Legacy: Poverty and Disarticulation

The legal freedom conferred by the Agrarian Reform of 1964 did not release the people of Zumbagua from their grinding poverty. The economic structure of the nation as a whole remained intact, and this fact in itself insured the continued poverty of the region.

Unlike the capital-intensive, high-productivity, export-oriented plantations of the coast, the Sierra haciendas had evolved into systems designed to minimize investments rather than maximize returns. For the Augustinians, Zumbagua products were never intended for the market, but only for use within the Order; thus the forces typically operating in commodity production did not directly affect the estate. Under the Asistencia, Zumbagua products were sold, but the impoverished nature of the organization dictated that low costs remain the primary goal in the organization of production. In addition, as with the Augustinians, profits were reinvested in the urban arm of the system, instead of being used to improve rural production.

The legacy these practices left for the parish of Zumbagua is not only one of exhausted soils and archaic technology, but also one of the absence of an established means of profit producing within the national economy. The traditional role of Sierra products as low-prestige goods destined for internal consumption by a cash-poor social stratum continues to cripple parish farmers.

The nature of the hacienda as an economic system left another legacy that contributes to Zumbagua's poverty today. Cash is so scarce in the parish that it has a value far higher than its "market" worth. This situation is not the result of a subsistence economy, in the sense of one that has never participated in a national economy, as is sometimes assumed. Rather, the lack of both capital and ready cash in the parish is the artifact of a long evolution within the hacienda of an economic system in which goods, services, and land could be exchanged without the use of money. Scarce capital could thus be concentrated in those parts of the system which lay outside estate boundaries.

The death of the hacienda brought an end to many of the structures that had enabled hacienda peons to satisfy their needs without cash. Yet they were also left without the wherewithal to enter the cash economy fully. They have neither capital to invest nor a market for their goods that would enable them to turn a profit from their labor.

The Parish Today: Ethnicity, Power, and Wealth

Although Ecuador is a nation of incredible ethnic diversity (Whitten 1965, 1974, 1976, 1981, 1985; Naranjo 1978; Stutzman 1981), the people of Zumbagua have only a scanty and distorted awareness of many other groups, especially blacks and Amazonian peoples. But even in the *páramo*, other ethnic groups are not entirely unknown. The fiesta of Corpus Christi brings the Salasacas to town in their distinctive black ponchos, for example, and the bilingual school has an Otavaleño teacher with white trousers and glossy braid; some of the variation in clothing and dialect within highland indigenous groups is thus familiar to parish residents.

It is during the Saturday market that Zumbagua residents are exposed to some of the contrasts among nonindigenous Ecuadorians. Each kind of food has a characteristic kind of seller. The cholas wear bell-bottomed trousers, big butchers' aprons, and baseball caps or round sailor's hats. Their hats are emblazoned with "Los Pitufos" (the Smurfs), Budweiser emblems, or the Christlike face of Che Guevara. Like Indian women, they wear earrings and necklaces, but of a characteristically chola type.

Even within the cholas there is a heterogeneity that seems to sort itself out according to specialization. The round shiny-faced women who preside over mountains of breads are a slightly different breed from those selling dry goods. The latter are middle-aged women whose businesses are fairly prosperous and require a substantial initial investment. They are imposing and self-important people, quick to anger and to verbal abuse. "Indians" approach them timidly and are frequently rebuffed. The goods for sale here—rice, cooking oil, sardines—are associated in the minds of indigenous buyers with the ethnic whiteness and superior class status of the seller.

The women who sell herbs are also middle-aged cholas, knowledgeable about the pharmaceutical, magical, and gastronomical properties of their wares. For them, an indigenous market such as Zumbagua is the least desirable place to sell. "Indians" use few of their wares and are relatively ignorant of the "white" cosmology\pharmacology that underlies their use. The herb women are at their happiest giving motherly advice to young middle-class urban women: this type of sales increases the seller's prestige, while selling to "Indians" decreases it.

Some of the younger cholas with less capital to invest sell cooked treats of various kinds; other small-time enterprises include selling candies, cookies, matches, and packaged seasonings. These enterprises are marginal at best, run by young teenagers with nothing more than a few hundred sucres worth of merchandise and a cloth to display it on.

The cholas seem like a brash, magpie group until the *costeño* men come to sell raw fish, brought by truck from the sea. Miserable in the unaccustomed cold, the fish sellers yell and shout at passersby, scorning them for dummies, cajoling, threatening, begging, and teasing them to buy. They keep up a constant loud sales pitch and try with their boisterous, irrepressible sallies to get a retort from the soft-spoken "Indians" they despise. In their presence even the sassiest chola seems restrained and circumspect, a typical highlander.

The market is a dazzling display of people and goods alike; not only are the botanical products of Ecuador's ecological zones to be seen there, but the contrasts between highlander and lowlander, urban chola and rural *runa*. Among those who live in the parish, however, this national diversity gives way to a one-dimensional ethnicity: people are either "Indian" or "white".[15]

Although there is blurring at the intersection of the two, there is no room for a third term. "Cholo," "mestizo," and *misti* (all terms referring to persons of mixed Indian and white identity or race) are words infrequently heard in the parish, and then only to refer to market sellers who come from outside. The only exception to the dual categorization of parish residents is the term "gringo," used to refer to the religious community and the clinic staff, thus identifying them as "foreign" to the parish and so outside its social hierarchy.

Racial or phenotypic whiteness has little to do with social whiteness in Zumbagua. The centuries of forced miscegenation associated with hacienda living have left a sprinkling of fair hair, green eyes, and pale, freckled skin among the "Indians" of the parish, while the "white" community includes not only people of purely "Indian" appearance but even a three-generation family of blacks. By national standards the Zumbagua elite are neither rich nor white, but within parish boundaries they are both.

Ethnicity in the parish is primarily marked by clothing or by language. "Indians" speak Quichua, "whites" speak Spanish. "Indian" clothing is unconstructed; it consists of lengths of cloth that can be wrapped or folded about the body to form ponchos, shirts, shawls, sashes, and carrying cloths (Robinson 1968). The more tightly fitting and tailored a person's clothing, the "whiter" he or she is. Also, "Indian" clothing, whether handwoven or purchased, is heavy and thick and worn in many layers as protection against the cold. "Whites" wear thin polyester clothing, though they may don heavy "Indian" ponchos at night. This thin clothing represents the fact that "whites" typically spend their days indoors in shops or buses, while "Indians" work out-of-doors, unprotected from the elements.

In general, there is a parallel between the distinction made between Indian and white and the social dimensions of wealth, gender, and age. Each category in Zumbagua exhibits a polarized form in which, on the surface at least, one pole is marked for prestige and power, the other not: white over Indian, man over woman, rich over poor, "savvy" post-hacienda generation over "backward" pre-hacienda generation. The relations between these polarities can be seen in the overlap between them in symbolic representations. Wealth, and especially the possession of cash, is associated with whiteness. Ambitious indigenous people frequently can be identified by their eagerness to master "white" behavior and dressing styles.

"Whites" of both sexes speak Spanish, but in "Indian" households, men speak both Spanish and Quichua while women typically speak only Quichua. "Indian" children speak Spanish to a far greater degree than do their elders, while in "white" households, adults are bilingual but the young know no Quichua at all.

Dressing styles also correlate youth, masculinity, whiteness, and wealth. Young people's clothing is more "white" than that of their elders, while Indian male dress becomes part of the lexicon of "white" female dress. "White" women and cholas wear trousers, and when a "white" woman is cold, she dons not an Indian shawl but rather the masculine poncho.

Some women who are ambiguously placed between Indian and white roles in the parish have ambiguous gender as well: they may be unmarried, may even be rumored to be lesbian. An indigenous man commonly takes on some white traits without losing his indigenous identity or his masculinity, but an indigenous woman who nears the ethnic boundary seems to blur several categories at once.

According to the stereotypes of modern life in rural areas of the Sierra, the strength of a place like Zumbagua does lie with youth and the move toward cultural whiteness:

> The designation *blanco,* white in terms of national standards, is inextricably linked with high status, wealth, power, national culture, civilization, Christianity, urbanity, and development; its opposites are *indio,* Indian, and *negro,* black. The false resolution of the opposites is found in the doctrine of *mestizaje,* the ideology of racial mixture implying *blanqueamiento,* whitening. *Stereotypically,* the . . . Sierra is divided between whites and Indians, the former progressive, the latter backward. . . . [P]oor Indians are poor *because* they are Indians. (Whitten 1981:16–17)

In Zumbagua, where social whiteness is not based on physical appearance and where there is no mestizo category, the emphasis on *blanqueamiento* as the only road to success is even clearer than in national ideologies. According to this way of thinking, the future belongs to those of Zumbagua's young men who are oriented toward the urban centers, speak Spanish, have some money, and take an interest in national affairs.

Controversy in the *Centro*

And, in fact, young men who want to push Zumbagua to become more like the Inter-Andean Valley, more politically and socially participatory in the life of the nation, do form a distinct force in the parish today. There is a groundswell of protest at the lack of infrastructure in the parish by some residents, especially men who have worked in Quito. Comparisons are often made with the town of Pujilí, which—like most Inter-Andean Valley towns—has paved roads, electricity, running water, street lamps, plazas with gardens and walkways, and telephone, telegraph, and mail service.

Zumbagua does have a few of these services in the main plaza. There is electricity most evenings for a few hours; the first streetlamps were installed while I was living in the parish. There are wells that supposedly provide *agua potable* (safe drinking water) in the plaza and in a few of the outlying *comunas.* Many of these services are maintained by the Catholic church and were put in place under church direction, though the funds are largely governmental in origin. Because the state maintains no administrative offices in Zumbagua, and the church has been the only stable institutional presence in the parish, most government programs have been administrated under its auspices. In recent years this practice has caused resentment among some of the ambitious young men in the parish, who are anxious for political power but are without any established route by which to seek it. They blame their frustrations on the church, which they see as usurping all political power in the parish.

There is also a very recent attempt on the part of the Ecuadorian government to construct and maintain public schools throughout the parish of Zumbagua. These schools are for the most part staffed by underpaid and unenthusiastic "white" teachers who commute daily from Pujilí and Latacunga and who tend to consider the climate of Zumbagua intolerable and its inhabitants uncivilized and uneducable. Absenteeism on the part of both teachers and pupils is high, and the level of education achieved is minimal.

The schools in Zumbagua *centro*, elementary and secondary, are much better. The "white" residents of Zumbagua send their children to these schools, as do those indigenous families who consider literacy and fluency in Spanish to be important skills and who live close enough to the *centro* for their children to walk to the school there. The basic skills learned in these schools include attitudes and behaviors that will enable these children to hide their rural, indigenous background to some extent when they seek jobs in the cities. The teaching materials used present indigenous lifeways as inferior and backward, but Zumbagua parents see these lessons not as demeaning, but as necessary in order to learn how to think like, and so compete with, nonindigenous Ecuadorians.

This public school system coexists with a church-run program that emphasizes Quichua literacy and indigenous culture. This program is resented by many of the younger parents, who see it not as an effort to teach children pride in their own heritage, but rather as designed to keep them in their place by denying them the knowledge necessary to compete with whites. In their minds, pressing worries about economic survival override the threat to cultural survival perceived by the clergy.

The Catholic priests' use of Quichua, the lack of public works, and the close interrelation of church and state had all become highly charged issues in the parish by 1983. My arrival in the parish coincided with a period of tremendous political ferment. A new organization had made itself felt in the parish, its membership consisting primarily of young landless men whose experience since preadolescence has been that of wage labor in Quito. The emergence of this group as a unified force

marked the beginning of a new era for the parish. Their goals were unclear; the association was rumored to be Communist, to be Evangelical
Protestant, to be part of a nationwide movement, to be nothing but a
pathetic fantasy on the part of its leaders. Like the people of Zumbagua
in general, the group was unpoliticized in the sense of having no clear
understanding of the spectrum of national political ideologies. Their
speeches and discussions were salted with fragments of discourses from
wildly disparate sources, Communist and right-wing, soothing pallia-
tives of government officials and indigenists' invective.

Night after night, *centro* residents lay awake listening to loud songs,
speeches, and occasional rifle shots fired into the air, originating from the
movement's headquarters. Tense weeks passed in which the apparent
lack of a coherent message in these disjointed rhetorical phrases prevented many people from taking sides. Finally, both the movement and
its opposition coalesced. In a classic Turnerian scene, a distinct arena of
conflict emerged, which demanded a decisive resolution: the group of
young men and some women moved to expel the priests from the community. This arena, once defined, was henceforth referred to as the *problema*. As it is commonly used throughout the Sierra to refer to political
crises, in fact, this word glosses in much the same way as Turner's
"arena."

But even when the arena was most clearly drawn, as individuals took
sides and the conflict was clearly marked out in the space of the *centro*
with enemy camps and a demilitarized zone in between, the discourse
remained opaque. The group's complaints and demands were contradictory, and many of their accusations against the priests were blatantly
untrue.

Nevertheless, two central issues could be defined: the ecclesiastical
programs to protect and foster the Quichua language and the disburse-
ment of government funds for development projects through the church.
These issues reflect a desire to reject the church, the old institution for a
mediated articulation with the outside world and for material help and
ideological guidance, in favor of direct interaction with state bureaucra-
cies. The help of the fathers as friendly and powerful protectors is no
longer sought. These young men, who have grown up since the era of the
hacienda, are eager to compete directly, as citizens and as equals, with
white townspeople of the Inter-Andean Valley for government resources.

The location of the struggle itself, in the *centro*, is another index of the
changing times. The *problema*, at least in one of its dimensions, could be
translated into kin, neighbor, and *comuna* problems in the area of Chami
and PucaUjsha. Yet it was not fought there, but in the *centro,* among the

ruins of the hacienda buildings, within the new town that is springing up. Not only the subject of the conflict, but the very place in which it was enacted signified new formations in the parish.

The reaction of most of the parish to the move to expel the priests was extremely negative. The essential integrity of the Catholic workers was widely recognized, as was the fact that they represent powerful national forces that would not take kindly to their mistreatment. Threatening them with violence was seen as antithetical to the group's general aims of achieving greater national participation for the parish.

The *problema* was brought to an end by a combination of pressures. A very few and very frightened rural military police were stationed at the church; various officials came to the parish to attempt to "reason" with the rebels. It was obvious that more decisive action on the part of the government would follow if the situation continued. At the same time, popular opinion within the parish was becoming more and more vociferously disgusted with the movement, which had degenerated into drunken nighttime forays against the homes of supposed church loyalists. The movement had reached a dead end. The *problema* ended when several of its more visible leaders were carted off to the Inter-Andean Valley and incarcerated. The organization then settled down to quietly challenging the church for control of various enterprises funded by the government in the parish. Their most notable success was a cooperative dry-goods store operating in competition with the government-subsidized, church-supported store.

There is no doubt that the movement's decision to confront the Catholic establishment in Zumbagua did little to enhance its credibility. But the backlash of public opinion in the parish was not simply over the organization's poor choice of adversaries. The perceived long-term goal of emulating "white" and Inter-Andean Valley forms of social organization is not universally accepted in Zumbagua.

For some parish residents, the general lack of governmental and white "interference" in Zumbagua life is welcomed, and especially the absence of coercive institutions. The lack of police or prisons in the area is a matter of pride to many residents, who consider their absence to be a tacit acknowledgment by the state that the parish is autonomous and beyond national control. It is also considered proof that whites and outsiders are afraid of the people of Zumbagua, and of indigenous people in general.

White fear is sometimes perceived by Zumbagua residents as an obstacle to obtaining economic and social parity and at other times as a good thing, a needed defense in a hostile world. This ambiguous response to the increasing penetration of Zumbagua by the state can be demonstrated by another incident that occurred in the *centro*. The occasion was the 1985 fiesta of Corpus Christi, almost two years after the *problema* described before. The fiesta of that year featured new elements added by the people of the *centro* to make it more like the fiestas of the Inter-Andean Valley towns. There was a Saturday night dance and a beauty contest; as the main event, an important official from the provincial government of Cotopaxi put in an appearance. He and his wife watched some of the bullfighting and the costumed dancers, and then, during a lull in the performance, the couple descended to the ring and began to promenade around it, waving and smiling in the time-honored way of politicians.

At this point it became apparent that not everyone in the parish shared the enthusiasm over these new, more "civic" aspects of the fiesta. Those who had been complaining that neither white customs nor white politicians should play a part in a Zumbagua fiesta saw their chance to protest. By a mysterious "accident," all of the bulls penned outside the ring were stampeded into it, and the politician and his high-heeled wife had to flee for their lives, scrambling over the barricades in a quite undignified fashion.

This incident brings to light the other side of political opinion in Zumbagua. Not only is the possible growth of a political infrastructure roundly rejected by many, but there is a strong isolationist and antiwhite sentiment in the parish as well. The hacienda remains a hated symbol of white presence in the parish, its end the opportunity for a totally indigenous and self-sufficient Zumbagua. According to this line of thinking, to invite white institutions back into the parish after finally gaining freedom from them is a kind of foolishness only those too young to remember the bad old days could espouse.

The image of the oppressive hacienda is ambiguous, however. Among the freedoms denied the peons of the hacienda was the right to adopt white ways. Indigenous culture provided protection and indigenous social structure a safety net for the people of Zumbagua, but the dual categories of Indian and white also served to crystallize the rigid class structure of the Sierra. The ethnic markers of clothing, language, and custom curtailed social mobility. Indigenous people were routinely stigmatized, exploited, and abused for being "Indians," but they were simultaneously denied the chance to become anything else.[16]

Freedom from the hacienda, then, might be interpreted as the freedom to leave behind the stigmatized language and clothing of the "Indian" and so enjoy material and social privileges previously withheld. Yet the young men who come back from the cities wearing "white" clothing complain of being derided as *lluchuj*, naked, by their fathers and brothers who still wear the poncho. These incidents, along with the movement's failure to arouse general support and the setting loose of the bulls, all suggest that the parish as a whole remains unconvinced that acquiring the trappings of modernity and "whiteness" are desirable ends. There are threads running through the questions of ethnic identity, of isolationism and integrationism, that reveal an economic and social reality subversive to many of the assumptions fundamental to the political and ethnic discourses heard in the *centro*.

Indigenous Wealth

Superficially, young men often seem to be better off than their parents. Not only do they speak Spanish and converse easily of the big cities and current affairs of the nation, topics of which their elders profess ignorance, but they have jobs and money, wear shoes and wristwatches, live in tin-roofed houses, travel around the parish by bus. Their parents meanwhile trudge barefooted back and forth from their fields to thatched huts. Young men also seem to have long periods of leisure, while their fathers leave home before dawn to work in the fields.

According to indigenous ways of thinking, however, neither idle hours nor small change for bus fares counts as wealth. Wealth consists of land, livestock, and access to labor. These things the old have and the young do not. Land and animals are acquired very gradually during a parent's lifetime, in the form of small gifts given at puberty, marriage, or the birth of a child; and by inheritance at the parents' death.

Even slower to accumulate are the lifelong partnerships of the *compadrazgo* system, which provide one with business partners, loan services, and agricultural labor, in differing amounts according to the degree of symmetry in the relationship. Young people begin with only *padrinos* to whom they owe labor; they will gradually acquire *compadres* with whom they can exchange services, but it will be many years before they will become *padrinos* themselves.

The middle-aged individuals who work hard all day do so simply because they have a lot to do; being occupied in itself is an indication of a kind of wealth. They have land to be farmed, animals to look after, social commitments to meet. Their life is spent in fields and pastures and in the homes of kin and *compadres*. The political life of the *centro*, with its orientation toward power structures outside parish boundaries, is peripheral to their world. In their eyes, many of the affectations of their adult children are marks of poverty, not of wealth. Young men wear cheap polyester clothing and machine-made ponchos not only for reasons of style but because they own only one handmade poncho, a gift from their father. Only older people own the sheep to provide the wool for a poncho, and the *compadrazgo* ties to have it spun, dyed, and woven.

The money that young men earn is enough to buy some of the trappings of whiteness: a cassette tape player, a radio. It is not enough, however, to buy land or livestock, and they do not earn enough to live on purchased foodstuffs like a true proletarian. The young remain dependent on their parents for their daily sustenance, and for their long-term survival as well, through the eventual inheritance of property.

At the same time, the young cannot afford to invest in an agricultural future either. Ecuador's explosive population growth has not left the *páramos* untouched; there are often half a dozen siblings waiting to divide a meager landholding. Even people who take pride in indigenous ways themselves are raising their children to lead other lives, knowing that their land will support only one or two.

Behind the outbursts of conflict in the *centro* lie more than one interpretation of the surface values of old and new, white and Indian, rich and poor. Each image contains contradictory valences and holds more than one truth. The young men showing off their Spanish competency, arguing politics in the plaza of an afternoon, dismissing the ignorance and conservatism of the old, are to some extent flaunting an independence they do not have. As long as their wages remain too low and unpredictable to do more than supplement the subsistence provided by the family farm, plaza politics will remain a hollow threat to the stability of *comuna* lifeways. But families struggling to live on tiny and overutilized farms are also partially dependent on their young wage earners.

The controversy over how best to survive in the decades to come can be heard behind the rhetoric of the plaza, but it finds expression on the farmstead as well. The debates heard in the *centro* serve as an introduction to the problems of identity and choice confronting the people of Zumbagua today, but the position taken in this work is that the roots of resistance are not to be found in overtly political rhetoric. "[I]deology is not a slogan under which political and economic interest of a class presents itself. It is the way in which the individual actively lives his or her role within the social totality" (Coward and Ellis 1977:67). In Zumbagua, the hundred conversations of everyday life about how much to spend, what to wear, what to cook, and what to eat are political decisions; they form part of the ongoing debate on the meanings of ethnicity, wealth, age, and gender. The chapters that follow explore how the practice of cooking, in particular, expresses the contradictory position of the modern Zumbagua household in its economic, social, and cultural life.

Notes

1. It may seem ethnocentric to write so explicitly to a North American audience, but it seems to me to be a more straightforward approach than to write to an unidentified group of readers. It is an inescapable aspect of the ethnographic project that the writer assumes an audience, "us," which implicitly does not include the people being described, "them." As an American reader of British and French social scientists, I know too well that when the topic is everyday practices such as eating, the implicit assumption of the writer as to the audience's shared cultural knowledge is crystal clear to any reader who does not share the author's ethnic origins. The assumption of "usness" in these circumstances seems presumptuous and arrogant. Far better, then, to admit my own identity from the start, without any pretense to some sort of scholarly omnipotence that places me above national boundaries. A Midwesterner writing at a Midwestern state university, I must assume that, like myself, most of my readers grew up spending July in the swimming pool and January building snowmen, eating cornflakes for breakfast and peanut butter at noon. I hope that those who did not will consider this assumption to be laughable provincialism rather than cultural imperialism.

At this juncture, the people about whom this work is written are unable to read it; one can only hope that someday this will not be the case. If someone from Zumbagua ever reads these pages, I can only hope that she or he, too, will find my profound ignorance about so much of Zumbagua life humorous rather than offensive.

2. The best brief description of the modern nation of Ecuador is found in Whitten 1981. Classic references on geography, ecology, and climate include Wolf 1892, Acosta-Solís 1968, and Ferdon 1950. Salomon 1980 has a useful summary, and Basile 1974 contains the best brief, complete discussion of other authors' work on these topics. For a more detailed description of the topography and hydrography of Zumbagua itself, see Wolf 1892:77–78, 227, 375–377, and 663. Cisneros Cisneros 1948:1–10 and Costales and Costales 1976:1–10 also contain less detailed descriptions.

3. "The *Páramo* Vegetative Zone is generally found at about 3,300 to 3,500 masl [meters above sea level], on both slopes of the two great Cordilleras. . . . The presence of large graminaceous grasslands is characteristic of the *páramos;* hence, when speaking of grasslands, one immediately assumes *páramos* and vice versa. . . . All the Glumifloras [sic] of the grasslands feature a special biological adaptation: large leaves, cylindrical or linear, stiff and highly silicified; they live in the form of clumps or pillows. . . . Associated with the grasslands are found other botanical families such as Ciperaceae, Iridaceae, Liliaceae, etc., of the *microfilia* [sic] type, and various woody, stunted shrubs."

4. According to Costales and Costales, "en las parroquias de Guangaje y Zumbagua, . . . la temperatura media fluctua entre los 6 y los 12 grados C" ("in the parishes of Guangaje and Zumbagua, . . . the median temperature fluctuates between 6 and 12 degrees C"; 1976:36). Edwin Ferdon lists the yearly average temperature of a station on the slopes of Cotopaxi, standing at 3,590 masl, as 7.5° C, while Cruz Loma in Pichincha Province, at 3,950 masl, averaged 6.3° C (1950:73).

5. The town plaza in Zumbagua is at 3,480 masl, somewhat below the average elevations in the parish as a whole. The lowest point in the parish is at approximately 3,200 masl, while high elevations consistently exceed 4,400 masl. Minimum and maximum elevations of sample *comunas* are as follows: Puca-Ujsha, 3,460–3,660; Yanatoro, 3,580–4,140; Huantopolo, 3,640–4,446; Michacala, 3,900–4,340. The plaza of Apagua, on the western edge of the parish, is at 4,000 masl.

6. These stereotypes have crept into scholarly descriptions of the *páramo* as well. David Basile, for example, in his description of climate types, describes the *páramo* as follows: "[Below the Perpetual Snow] zone is the *Páramo* (ET) to approximately the 11,000 foot (3,360 meter) contour; this is a cold, humid area, that is subject to frequent frosts. The *Páramo*, generally overcast and hidden from view by mists and rain . . . is an area avoided whenever possible. The fine drizzle that is characteristic of overcast conditions is itself often referred to as *páramo*" (1974:23).

7. In thus limiting the use of the term *páramo* to areas predominantly grassland, parish residents are in accordance with Acosta-Solís, who notes that "El término PÁRAMO no es solo un piso altitudinal, como muchos creen o dicen. El PÁRAMO es una formación altiandina florística típica, dominada generalmente por el 'pajonal'" ("The term *páramo* is not solely an altitudinal zone, as many believe or say. The *páramo* is a typical high-Andean floral formation, dominated typically by grassland"; 1968:135).

8. The limits of these zones, as Enrique Mayer has demonstrated for Peru (1985), are determined by patterns of human use. Whereas the ecologist's or geographer's *páramo* is an ecological zone, Zumbaguan usage of the term designates a production zone. The division of land into two discrete zones is not the result of ecological restraint, but rather is created by the deliberate deployment of resources into two distinct land-use patterns: cultivation and usage for pasture, forage, and fuel. This fact is readily acknowledged by parish residents; in fact, a major debate in some *comunas* concerns the possibility of raising the lower limits of the *páramo* to give landless young men fields to cultivate.

9. Other modern indigenous highland groups described in the literature as exploiting adjacent lowlands include the Saraguros (L. Belote 1978; J. Belote 1984); Pomeroy 1986 describes a Bolívar Province group involved in *monte* cattle farming. Other highland peoples, including indigenous inhabitants of Imbabura, Chimborazo, and Azuar provinces, also exploit lowland areas.

10. The word "Runa" as used by Salomon, Whitten, and other authors is a descriptive term for indigenous Andean peoples that connotes self-determination

and cultural autonomy. In Zumbagua, as in many parts of the Andes, these connotations of the words are unknown; *runa* is simply a derogatory term equivalent to the North American "nigger." In this work, use of the capitalized "Runa" indicates the former meanings, while the lowercase *runa* stands for the word as used in Zumbagua.

11. "In this large vegetative belt, a saturated atmospheric humidity exists, due to two circumstances: the constant precipitation of rains, drizzles, and fogs and the condensation of the clouds that rise from the lower zones of the coast. . . . These forests are extremely rich in different species of trees, shrubs, woody plants, and epiphytes without end. . . . The forest seems almost impenetrable because it is a sea of vegetation: trees and shrubs bent by the lianas entangled on all sides, treelike ferns and epiphytes are present everywhere."

12. The climates of both of these areas are also moderated by their being located in valleys that open toward the west, in contrast to Zumbagua, which is rimmed on all sides by the highest ridges of the Cordillera. Angamarca, at 3,000 masl, has valley lands below 2,600 masl, while Sigchos and Isinliví, at 2,800 masl, are at the southeastern extremity of the Toachi River valley, which ultimately empties into the ocean.

13. From the perspective of residents of the outlying *comunas,* the primary if not the only purpose of the *teniente político* is dispute settlement. There is, however, a very lively political scene operative among white residents of the *centro,* church employees, and a very small number of other indigenous individuals involved in *centro* life. This activity is of only peripheral interest to most parish residents, however, and I remained largely uninvolved in it myself.

14. "The indigenous group of *Apahua* (4,100 m) . . . to the northwest of Zumbagua . . . is formed as an agrarian community on communally used lands. . . . On the middle and high sections they cultivate barley, peas, and lentils; because the territory also includes low subtropical (*yunga*) sections, they also cultivate banana, sugar cane, coffee, *papa china* [*xanthosoma,* an edible tuber native to the *yunga*], potatoes, etc."

15. In Zumbagua, this bipolar ethnic scale, with its overtly racist symbolism, is matched by actual cultural differences. In many areas of highland Cotopaxi, however, communities are divided into a "Indian" and a "white" class even though the two people are identical culturally and cannot be distinguished by an outsider. The discrimination against the "Indian" members of these communities reveals the class nature of this distinction in much of the Ecuadorian Sierra.

16. Orlove 1983:46 notes that, earlier in this century, mestizo elites punished indigenous peoples of the Lake Titicaca region who affected "white" traits such as the wearing of shirts or the use of sheet-metal roofs, and he speculates that some modern uses of these items may represent "a break with the old Indian way of life, the adoption of some formerly prohibited mestizo traits" (47).

1. Palm Sunday: The image of Christ being carried in procession.

2. Barley harvest

3. Corpus Christi: Procession in honor of the fiesta sponsor.
(The woman carrying the staff is the sponsor of the day's festivities.)

4. Corpus Christi: The bullfight.

5. Easter Sunday: Calling the bulls from the *páramo* with the bocinos.

6. Man and his son in the *páramo*.

7. Woman resting in front of her *compadres'* house.

8. Zumbagua *centro*.

9. Market day: Local woman selling soup with toasted maize.

10. Market day: Buying bread.

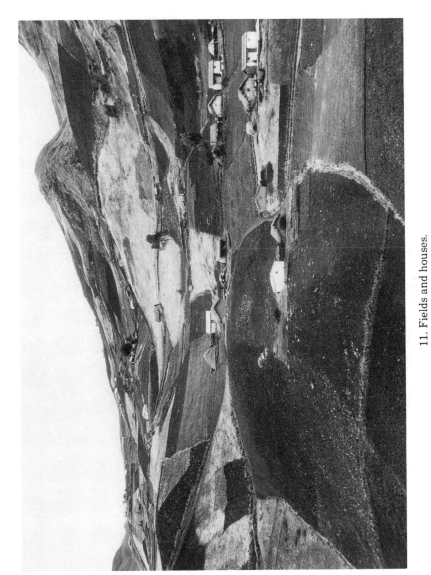

11. Fields and houses.

THREE

The Diet of Zumbagua: Basic Vocabulary

Diet and Cuisine

If the ends of cooking are material, so too are the means. A language is made of sounds, a cuisine of foods. The elements that fill the categories of Zumbagua cuisine are the starches, meats, and vegetables that constitute the diet of the parish.

For the purposes of this work, I establish a distinction between two conceptions of food and cooking: diet and cuisine. Diet is simply what people eat: the list of what foods are eaten and in what proportions, as well as their nutritional values. The basic, everyday composition of the parish diet was clear to me long before I grasped the rules of cuisine that underlay the making of meals. I could observe the starchiness of the food, the proportion of barley to potatoes, the frequent use of onions.

Cuisine is a separate consideration. Cuisine refers to the cultural construction of meals, the structures that organize knowledge about foods, and the pattern of their preparation and combination. After many meals and many conversations I learned to group foods as belonging to categories of Zumbagua cuisine. For example, large peeled potatoes are equivalent to rice, while small potatoes cooked in the skin belong with fava beans. At the same time, I learned that foods within the same category may have different values. *Yuca* may substitute for *papas*, chicken for *cuy*, but although the treatment of the ingredient is the same, the value of the finished product is quite different.

One difference between diet and cuisine is the importance of interhousehold variation in analysis. In studying diet, interhousehold differences are a consideration. Differences in wealth, for example, affect diet. Zumbagua people are not forthcoming in talking about relative economic status, but one begins to notice that some households have fresh fruit and others do not, and to recognize the meal of plain barley gruel as the mark of hard times. Variations are also caused by other factors, such as relative dependence on subsistence agriculture and access to different ecological zones. In view of the variety of economic strategies utilized by the people of Zumbagua, success at activating a wide personal network is also important, because it can substitute for direct access to resource zones (for example, having a high-*comuna* compadre who gives you onions, or receiving half-rotten fruit from a truck owner who wholesales fruit brought up from the *monte*).

In the discussion of cuisine, interhousehold variation is not an issue, as it is in diet. A poor woman cooking barley and water and a rich woman whose cooking pot contains barley, mutton, carrots, and onions are utilizing the same structure in their cooking; one prepares a minimal and impoverished, the other a maximal, full-blown version of the same culturally correct dish.

There are other interhousehold differences, however, that are matters of cuisine, as well as of diet. They could be called questions of style, but in Zumbagua they are regarded as being ethnic in nature: certain ingredients, techniques, and combinations are "white," others "Indian." These pattern differences are not without correspondences to interhousehold differences in diet that result from economic stratification. "Whiteness" and wealth, "Indianness" and poverty tend to go hand in hand. Ethnicity in Ecuador is, among other things, a language for expressing ideologies of class. But the correspondences among diet, economic stratification, social class, and the expression of ethnicity through cuisine are by no means absolute. Their interrelationship is a topic to which I will return repeatedly in the pages that follow.

Zumbagua Diet

The diet of the parish is the material base underlying all of these usages and practices. This chapter is a discussion of Table 1, a listing of the foods most commonly eaten in the parish. Custom and meaning do enter into this discussion, but it is only in the following chapter, on meals, combinations of foods, and foods for special occasions, that the cuisine itself is primarily considered. Diet may be said to precede cuisine; just as I had to learn the former before I could study the latter, the structure of cuisine is easier to express once the basic materials from which it is constructed have been described.

Table 1. The Diet of Zumbagua

I. STARCHES

A. LOCALLY GROWN STARCHES

papa\papa	potatoes
cebada\sibada	barley
haba\jabus	fava beans

B. PURCHASED STARCHES

fideo\pidiu	noodles
avena\"quaker"	oatmeal
harina\pulvu	wheat flour
harina de habas\jabus pulvu	fava-bean flour
verde\virdi	green plantains
yuca\yuca	manioc
maíz\sara	maize
morocho\muruchu	hard maize

C. LESS COMMONLY USED STARCHES (*grown or purchased*)

lenteja\lintija	lentils
chocho\tarwi	lupines
arveja\urbijus	starchy peas
zambo\quitu	squash
quinua\quinua	quinoa
trigo\trigu	wheat

II. COMPLEMENTS

A. MEAT

1. Locally raised meat

borrego\llama	sheep
llama, llamingu\llamingu, runa llama	llama
chivo\chibu	goat
chancho\cuchi	pig
cuy\cuy	guinea pig
pollo\atallpa	chicken
conejo\kuniju	rabbit
ganado\wagra	cattle

2. Products of local animals

manteca\wira	fat
huevo\lulun	eggs
leche\lichi	milk

3. Purchased meats and meat products

sheep, llama, cow, or pig meat; chickens	
pescado	fish
manteca\wira	processed vegetable shortening

Table 1. The Diet of Zumbagua (*continued*)

sardinas	sardines
atún	tuna

B. VEGETABLES

cebolla\sibulla	onion
zanahoria\sanurya	carrot
tomate\tomati	tomato
zambo\quitu	squash
col\col	cabbage
nabos\nabus	wild mustard

C. OTHER SEASONINGS

1. *de sal (used frequently)*

ají\uchu	hot pepper
sal\cachi	salt
sal\muyu cachi	raw salt
sabor\mishqui	packaged flavorings, mostly monosodium glutamate
culur\achiote	annatto seed (*Bixa orellana*)

2. *de sal (used infrequently \ "white")*

ajo	garlic
apio	celery
cilantro	coriander (leaves)
orégano de sal	oregano
(others)	

3. *de dulce (used frequently)*

panela\rapadura, mishqui	raw sugar
azúcar\mishqui	processed sugar
limón\limón	lemon/lime

4. *de dulce (used infrequently \ "white")*

arrayán	myrtle
canela	cinnamon
hoja de naranja	orange leaf
orégano de dulce	sweet oregano
(others)	

III. WANLLA

A. BREAD

pan\tanda	bread
huahuas de pan\tanda huahua-kuna	bread babies

B. FRUITS

1. *common*

orito	small, sweet banana

Table 1. The Diet of Zumbagua (*continued*)

capulí	native fruit similar to a cherry
mandarina	mandarin orange
naranja	large orange

   2. *uncommon\"white"*

piña	pineapple
mora	raspberry
others	

C. SWEETS

galletas	cookies
caramelos	candies
colas	soft drinks
gelatina	glasses of flavored gelatin drink

D. COOKED FOODS FROM THE MARKET (SOME EXAMPLES)

   1. *meats*

hornado\cuchi aycha	roast pork
fritada\cuchi aycha	fried pork
cuero\cara	pork skins
pescado	fried fish
huevo duro\(yanush') lulun	hard-boiled egg

   2. *starches*

mote\muti	hominy
chochos\tarwi	lupines
papas con aji\cariuchu?	potatoes with hot sauce
a variety of fried patties (potato with cheese, flour with egg, flour with egg and cheese)	
chilenos	doughnut holes
pasteles	sweet fried breads
queso con miel\mishqui tanda?	whey or soft cheese with sugar syrup

Starches

The importance of starches in the Zumbagua diet cannot be over-emphasized. Starches predominate in every meal. They are by far the most important part of both diet and cuisine. This preponderance is so pronounced that in my presentation of Zumbagua foods I have reduced all other foods to two categories: complements—that is, ingredients that may be added to a dish to improve its flavor, color, and consistency, or to make it "fancier"—and *wanlla*—snacks or treats—foods that are never, properly speaking, part of a meal. At some seasons of the year, certain vegetables are added to meals in a large enough proportion to make them more than simply flavorings or complements, but these occasions are rare. Starches make a meal; other ingredients are secondary.

A subsistence pattern based mainly on starchy vegetable foods is characteristic of most peasant diets and indeed of the diets of many horticultural and agricultural peoples both today and in the past:

> Most . . . sedentary civilizations have been built on the cultivation of a particular complex carbohydrate, such as maize or potatoes or rice or millet or wheat. In these starch-based societies . . . people are nourished by their bodily conversion of the complex carbohydrates, either grains or tubers, into body sugars. Other plant foods, oils, flesh, fish, fowl, fruits, nuts, and seasonings—many of the ingredients of which are nutritionally essential—will also be consumed, but the users themselves usually view them as secondary, even if necessary, additions to the main starch. This fitting together of core complex carbohydrates and flavor-fringe supplement is a fundamental feature of the human diet . . . [throughout much of] our history. (Mintz 1985:9)

Potatoes

The potato is renowned as the mainstay of the indigenous Andean diet. According to local people's exegesis, the potato is the king of Zumbagua foods, the staple, the validator. During the time that I was there, however, almost no potatoes were grown in the parish.

I arrived in September 1983, just after the harvests. It was a hard time for the people of Zumbagua. Heavy rains of disaster proportions, part of the general El Niño phenomenon that had devastated Ecuador in 1982–1983, had ruined the potato crop completely and severely damaged the other crops. Even stored potatoes had rotted in the straw from the humidity. People said that "not even the pigs would eat them."

The results of this disaster reached beyond that year itself. Because precious seed stores were gone, seed potatoes for the next year's planting had to be purchased. For households already reaching into scarce cash funds to buy potatoes to eat, it was an onerous burden. The crisis was aggravated as the prices of both seed and eating potatoes skyrocketed beyond what they had ever been in living memory. Also, planting potatoes seemed risky. Many Zumbagua farmers were skeptical that the rains had really stopped; opinions diverged sharply as to whether the phenomenon was just a freak or signaled a permanent change in the zone's climate. Few families planted potatoes the first year I was there, and no one planted a great many.

Of those who did plant, many discovered in the months to come that the plants did not thrive: few reached maturity, and those that did never flowered. This lack of success was attributed to the fact that the seed was purchased and came from another region. Buying seed goes against local custom, and it is indeed possible that the purchased varieties could not adapt to the altitude of the parish, unusually high for Ecuador.

Mysteriously, a few families did have luscious, healthy fields of potatoes, and they were much envied for it. Trips with my landlady to visit her natal *comuna* were always punctuated by a brief stop to admire a potato field passed en route. "Lindo, lindo"[1] she would breathe and then lapse into a few minutes' silent staring. For her, the immediate experience seemed to be one of intense aesthetic enjoyment at the sight of the dark, healthy green leaves, rather than of economic calculation or envy per se.

When the potatoes did not come up, households were faced with a new dilemma: they still had to buy potatoes to eat and, having lost the investment of seed (and in some cases fertilizer) as well, did they dare to invest in seed again? Responses to the problem varied. The next year, 1985, drought struck, and not only were there few or no potatoes, but even the favas and barley scarcely produced. Yields were the worst I had seen.

This third harvest made me question whether the El Niño year had been as cataclysmic is is widely assumed. When I had originally asked about that harvest, informants had frequently told me that it was part of a sequence of six or seven years of bad luck. Knowing that the effects of that year's rains had been unlike anything Ecuador had seen in fifty years, I discounted these statements. Now I began to wonder whether potatoes had in fact been the most important staple prior to 1983. Perhaps they never had been, or perhaps there was a gradual trend away from potato growing, as overcrowding and overuse degraded the soils.

Although farmers might attribute poor harvests to fluctuations in the weather, yields might never return to what they had been. The latter possibility was independently suggested to me in a personal communication by Enrique Mayer, who stated that it has been his opinion for some time now that one of the first indicators of degradation in Andean soils is the shift from dependence on the potato to planting mostly barley.

Whatever the long-term trend, several facts are clear. One is that there has been an almost total impoverishment of the potato gene pool in the Zumbagua area. All adults and adolescents of the area could reel off the names of a dozen or more varieties of potatoes that used to be grown in the area. Today, only purchased varieties, primarily *leonas,* are grown.

There is also an apparent diminution in the use of other tubers (*oca, melloco*), though informants stated that these types had never had any great primacy in the diet.

At the same time, it is clear that potatoes are important to people. All households diverted any funds available for buying food to the purchase of potatoes as soon as the prices became reasonable. I was repeatedly told that in good years, when people had their own potatoes to eat, other starches such as maize and *morocho* ("hard maize") were purchased with money now being spent on potatoes. The current situation was emphatically seen as an unusual and unpleasant state of affairs.

Nevertheless, the primary staple food in the parish today is not potatoes but barley, especially in the more impoverished families. Among better-off families, potatoes and barley may play more or less equal roles in the diet, and there are some meals eaten during the week that contain potatoes without barley or fava beans. But in my opinion the ability to eat such meals has become a sign of a household's economic success. While more than half of Zumbagua households occasionally eat such meals, there are some families who go through weeks and months in which they are unable to do so.

Barley

At the other extreme from the diet of the well-to-do, who occasionally eat entire meals that contain no barley and might perhaps go an entire day without eating it, is the monotonous diet of the extremely poor. In some households, day follows day without anything being cooked and eaten in the kitchen except barley gruel. In fortunate households, the potage may be flavored with sugar or salt or a lump of fat. A chopped onion or a few small potatoes might be added; in season, the leaves of adventives can be stewed together with the grain.[2] But I have frequently shared meals that consisted solely of ground barley and water.

While most children in the parish do not appear to suffer from malnutrition, in these households there are periods of extremely inadequate diet. Nevertheless, this stone-ground barley meal is far superior to its equivalent among poor Ecuadorians who are severed from an agrarian base: babies in the cities eat white-flour gruel and drink sugar water. In Zumbagua, nutritionally inadequate meals (I have never seen a meal in which there was an insufficient *amount* of food; it is only the full nutritional complement that is sometimes missing) are typically a sporadic occurrence. The seasonality of the agricultural diet is partially to blame, but so is the intermittent nature of the help that poor families receive from kin and neighbors. More salient, in most cases, is the nature of the marital bond between peasant wife and proletarian husband, a subject that I will discuss in Chapter 6.

The importance of barley in household diets, then, varies widely according to economic status. Poor indigenous families depend heavily on barley, "white" families on rice. White families seldom if ever eat barley, while indigenous households of all economic levels always have it on hand. Between these extremes is the well-to-do indigenous household,[3] in which dependence on barley and potatoes is balanced, and rice is eaten too.[4] As will be discussed subsequently, days typically begin and often end with barley, and, depending on the time of year, midday meals often contain barley as well.

Barley is prepared in two different ways: heavily toasted, twice ground, and sifted to a consistency as fine as corn starch (*máchica\ mashca*); or lightly toasted and coarsely ground (*arroz de cebada\ arrus*). These two foods, *máchica* and *arroz de cebada,* form the foundation on which both diet and cuisine rest.

Fava beans[5]

The place of fava beans in the diet varies widely according to the season. From Semana Santa to Corpus (approximately April to June), they are eaten fresh (*habas tiernas\llullu jabus*). During this period, many meals center around *jabus;* they become the staple starch for the parish as a whole. Even when other dishes are prepared, handfuls of *llullu jabus* are added. When used this way, *jabus* come close to filling the role of "vegetable" as we know it in our own cooking, in other words, they are fresh, green vegetable foods present in amounts greater than a complement but less than a main course or main ingredient. In these months, fava beans are a staple food, playing a major part in most meals and some part in every meal.

The rest of the year, dried fava beans are toasted, or boiled and toasted, as a snack. They are also ground into a flour used to make thick soups (*coladas*). The frequency of use varies according to household, and it varies from year to year, depending on the quality of the harvest. The fava-bean harvest is not as reliable as the barley harvest, as it is prone to frost damage, blight, and disease. In this regard, households with higher-altitude lands do better, because frost damage is more severe in lower parts of the parish due to the tendency of cold, wet air to settle at night. Frost damage is extremely specific, however, frequently touching part of a field and leaving other parts unhurt. Higher-altitude lands also produce fava beans until later in the year.

In my experience, fava-bean flour was not much eaten, but informants claim that I was never there in a good year. Not only were fava-bean harvests small, but many households chose to sell favas in order to buy potatoes.

Purchased staples

Noodles, oatmeal, and wheat flour are three commonly purchased processed staples. Households with a cuisine that is extremely indigenous will choose these items when buying purchased foods: they are fully integrated into indigenous foodways. Noodles are sometimes used as the main ingredient of a clear soup (*caldo*) and sometimes as a complement or supplement added to another main starch, potatoes and/or rice (see below).

Oatmeal is eaten only after it has been strained. Only the liquid is retained, the rest being given to the pigs (see Chapter 6). The liquid is used as a thickening agent for soups or beverages, in which it is the main ingredient, with other flavorings, sweet or "salty," added. It is basically used as a substitute for *máchica*.

Oatmeal is also the most commonly chosen starch for the production of *chicha\aswa*, or fermented alcoholic beverages. Throughout the Andes, *chicha\aswa* is most commonly made of maize, though many other types are known. In the lowlands, a manioc *chicha\aswa* of extremely low alcoholic content is the mainstay of the diet in many areas.

Chicha\aswa is disappearing, in Zumbagua and in the entire Andean region. In Zumbagua, it is always mentioned as a necessary component of celebrations, especially weddings. Despite being among the first things mentioned when I was eliciting idealized descriptions of a wedding, in actual practice—as consultants are quick to point out—many weddings do not have *aswa*. On the occasions when it is made, Quaker *aswa* (pronounced "kwacker"), fermented strained oatmeal, is the most common form. Pineapple was most frequently mentioned when I asked for alternative *aswas*, but it seems to me that the expense would be prohibitive, and I never heard of an actual wedding at which *piña aswa* was served.

Wheat flour is used as a substitute for *máchica*. It can play a significant part in the diet of those who have no land, because it is very cheap. It is more frequently eaten in the hard period before Pascua, when supplies from last year's harvests are low and this year's harvest is still several months away.

Plantains

Plantains, a lowland crop, are sold both ripe (*maduro*) and unripe (*verde*). The *maduros* are for frying; this technique is seldom used in the indigenous kitchen, so they are not purchased by most households. *Verdes*, which are boiled, are occasionally used in the Zumbaguan kitchens as an additional starch. They are most commonly eaten together with *llullu jabus* in that season, and play a part in the local version of *fanesca*, the traditional Ecuadorian Easter soup.

Manioc

If I had not arrived in Zumbagua after the disastrous rains of 1983, I would never have guessed the role of *yuca* in Zumbagua diet. It is sold in the market every Saturday, along with other western-slope products such as *muyu cachi, rapadura,* and plantains. Only poor families normally buy it; it is very cheap. It is usually eaten mixed with potatoes in a soup and is considered an inferior substitute for the more costly potato.

It is in this guise of a substitute for potatoes that I first encountered *yucas* in the parish. During the months when the price of potatoes was so incredibly high, everyone, even wealthy white households, purchased manioc instead, and everyone, "white" and indigenous alike, complained bitterly about having to eat *yuca*. It was experienced as a very real hardship.

Manioc, then, serves as a much disliked substitute staple in famine or crisis years. It is probably extremely suitable for this role, for the climate of the zones in which it is grown is so extremely different from that of the Sierra that droughts or blights that affect Zumbagua crops would be unlikely also to strike manioc. At the same time, some of these zones lie very close to Zumbagua geographically, and patterns of exchange between these areas and the parish are well established.

Maize and hard maize (Sara *and* morocho)

Like the potato, maize appears to be lessening in importance in the Zumbagua diet. The first year I was in Zumbagua, no maize of any kind was purchased except as the very occasional cooked-food treat, usually in the form of *mote\muti*. Informants insisted, however, that in good years the money being used to buy potatoes would have gone to buy maize and especially *morocho* (a hard maize used to make flours and meals). And, in fact, after the improved harvest of 1984, *morocho* did appear in the diets of several households, not all of them well-to-do. It was ground and used like *arroz de cebada*. Sweet corn (*choclo*) also made an appearance among more monied families, though less commonly. Older residents are emphatic that maize should be a part of the diet, but younger families seem accustomed to its absence.

It is interesting to note that, while farmers from lower-altitude communities in the province who grow maize categorize *morocho* as a separate crop, not reducible to a larger category of maize-in-general, in Zumbaguan minds *morocho* is definitely a kind of *sara*.[6]

Other starches

Lentils, peas, lupines,[7] and quinoa[8] are enjoyed by the people of Zumbagua. They play a very small part in the overall diet and are regarded primarily as adding variety to the basic fare. They most commonly show up in *fanesca*. Their purchase, along with fish if possible, is part of the Pascua food expenditures.

When describing an ideal existence, people mention that they would like to plant small amounts of these crops in addition to their staples. And in fact, several households did so during my stay. Most people, however, seemed to feel that they were living too close to disaster not to plant all their land in barley and fava beans, and expressed envy of those who did have small harvests of these other, nonessential crops.

Squash

The only variety of squash I have seen eaten in the parish is a large, round, hard squash, bright orange like a pumpkin on the inside. It is cut up and cooked in soups along with other ingredients, the skin and seeds being left on and then spat out when eaten. It plays a very small part in the diet.

Complements

Meat and vegetables play a very peripheral role in most Zumbagua meals. It is perfectly acceptable in Zumbagua society to eat a meal consisting of a single starch, barley or potatoes. There are many additions that would, it is agreed, improve such a meal, but it violates no cultural norms to serve it as is. This fact is in itself a strong indication of the centrality of starches and the peripheral or "optional" quality of other foods.

It is also important to note that, while in the majority of households onions at least are present in every meal, and proteins and other vegetables are included more often than not, the quantities are often small, regardless of availability. Three onion stalks are normally thought to be an appropriate amount for a soup that will feed seven people, three dogs, and the pig. Meat is frequently present more as a flavoring than as a significant ingredient; individual servings contain broth, but the pieces of meat are often bone and gristle to be sucked, rather than actual morsels.

There are occasional meals in which meat plays a much larger part, though always subordinate to the starch. The same is not true of onions or the other vegetables mentioned here; more are not used if available.

Meat and meat products

Sheep. Mutton is the most commonly eaten meat in the parish. An extended family will butcher one of its own sheep, dividing the meat among the various households belonging to it. They do so when an animal dies of natural causes, for special occasions (both calendrical and life-crisis), or simply when it is felt that there has been too little meat for too long. There is an extremely wide variation in the frequency of meat consumption among families of the parish. Traditionally based families who are not suffering from a shortage of land probably eat the most animal protein, especially if they have easy access to high grazing lands.

Sick people and women during confinement are always given a great deal of meat. The only meals in which meat and meat broth are the main ingredient are those served to the sick or at houses in which a baby is being or has been born. They are served not only to the patient but to visitors as well, except in the case of a lingering illness, when household resources have been strained for some time: then the meat is reserved for the sick. Illness and childbirth are thus occasions for butchering, a fact that no doubt contributes to the eagerness of friends and family to visit new mothers. If there are no animals available for butchering on such occasions, or if the illness is prolonged, meat will be purchased and prepared exclusively for the sick person.

Preference is given to the youngest child, and to children in general, in dividing meat. At mealtimes, men are served more meat than women, and older adults before younger ones. Nonetheless, distribution of protein by gender may actually favor women despite appearances to the contrary, because women frequently cook themselves tidbits of meat while making a meal.

The butchering of animals leads to a pattern of occasional, comparatively heavy protein consumption interspersed with meatless periods. This tendency is offset by several practices. It is mitigated by the sharing of meat between households of the extended family. In addition, small gifts of cooked food from the celebrations of other families—weddings, baptisms, house raisings—may arrive at the house.

The cold climate, which inhibits rotting, so that meat can be kept for several days, is another factor. Generally, the blood and internal organs are consumed on the day of butchering itself, followed by the head and feet. The ribs and legs are kept for later consumption. Hanging on a wire strung from the rafters, in the smoke from the fire but above its heat, the meat becomes partially desiccated and will keep for some time. Last to be eaten are strips of fat suspended in this manner, used to flavor soups long after the rest of the meat is gone. The last strip of fat may be eaten some ten days to two weeks after the butchering, several meatless (or at least muttonless) days having intervened.

Mutton is also sold in the market. It is divided for sale in the following manner. The largest portion that can be purchased is a "half," comprising half of the neck, ribs, and one fore and one hind leg. A separate package is made of the internal organs: lungs, liver, and heart. The four feet and the head comprise a third package. The stomach, intestines, and blood may be bought, but are usually kept by the butcher. Frequently a woman of his family uses them in the preparation of cooked food for sale. There seems to be a tacit understanding that, while men usually butcher, the blood, stomach, and testicles are immediately the concern of the woman or women doing the cooking. (It is not at all unusual for a woman to butcher. As with most tasks, there is a tendency for butchering to be assigned to one sex, but no stigma is attached to the other sex doing the job. In marriages in which a high-*comuna* woman marries a low-*comuna* man, he or his family may ask her to butcher when the need arises, knowing that she grew up having more familiarity with such tasks. Still, while female butchers are a familiar sight in larger markets, women do not butcher in the Zumbagua market.)

Llamas and goats. Llamas are eaten more rarely than sheep, being less common and more valuable. But they are butchered both in households and in the market. The process resembles that of butchering a sheep. Goats are infrequently eaten; they are less valuable and less common than llamas.

Pigs. Pigs are extremely valuable. Every household tries to raise at least one pig, and piglets are highly prized, for they can be sold for a substantial price. Unlike the other foods a household produces, the pig is not intended for household consumption. Pigs are raised as a financial enterprise: they transform waste products from the kitchen into a readily convertible asset. The death of a pig is a great calamity, because it marks the loss of an initial investment and of one of the family's largest assets, the one most easily converted to cash during unexpected crises. One measure of the economic importance of the family pig is the intensity of the conflicts that can arise from accusations of blame for a pig's illness. Public mourning at the death of a pig is by no means unheard of, though those not affected by the loss find such behavior rather humorous.

Pork is rarely eaten by people of the parish, because it is so expensive. When it is eaten at all, it is usually bought already cooked in the market, either in small portions for immediate consumption or in large pieces to be taken home and eaten with other food. Even when a pig dies unexpectedly and is butchered by its owners, a great effort is frequently made to sell the meat rather than eat it. The wealthiest household of the extended family or a wealthy compadre may be put under tremendous pressure to buy the meat under these circumstances.

Guinea pigs, chickens, rabbits. These animals will be discussed together in terms of their place in the diet, despite significant differences in their roles in the cuisine. These animals are raised within the household. In the case of the guinea pig or *cuy,* this statement is quite literally true; they are raised inside the house, as their delicate constitutions cannot stand the cold.[9]

Home life in Zumbagua is permeated with the presence of the *cuyes,* shy, darkness-loving creatures who hide in the corners of the house and under the beds. Nighttime inside the house is filled with their noises, and the retelling of dream omens frequently begins with the *cuyes:* "all of the *cuyes* suddenly became silent" or "all of the *cuyes* suddenly began making noise at once." Chickens supposedly live in the patio, though in my experience they tend to be inside the house whenever humans are. Rabbits are raised in pens in the patio.

While few families raise chickens and fewer still rabbits, it is a rare household that does not have *cuyes.* Some stigma is attached to the sale of *cuyes,* and people are reluctant to admit that such sales take place. Ideally they should only be given (extremely conservative families also feel this way about sheep and llamas). Chickens are bought in the market, but they are very expensive.

The meat of all of these animals is used for special-occasion meals, as discussed subsequently. Normally, they are not eaten on an everyday basis. But the grassy adventives fed to the *cuyes* become very meager during the dry season, and most of the males and older females may be killed and eaten at this time, to give the rest a better chance for survival.

Beef. Very few families own cattle, and those who do utilize them as milk producers and, like pigs, as "walking banks." Cattle are not butchered in the Zumbagua market, though beef is readily available in Inter-Andean Valley markets and is comparatively inexpensive. Unlike chicken, beef would never be chosen as a special-occasion meat in Zumbagua; unlike pork, it is not featured as a market-day taste treat. Neither do Zumbagua cooks purchase cow's feet, tripe, or other cheap parts to cook: the famous Ecuadorian *caldo de pata*, cow's-foot broth with *mote*, is unknown here. In sum, beef plays an extremely insignificant part in the diet of the parish, though I have known households to purchase a pound or less to make special meals for invalids or new mothers.

Animal fats. Animal fat is a highly prized substance. Its basic use is to flavor soups. *Manteca "Porky,"* cheap processed vegetable shortening, is most often used in its place, but a lump of animal fat is the ideal.

Wira is also considered to have a variety of medicinal purposes. Prudent housekeepers store a small amount of *llama wira* (sheep fat) or *llamingu wira* (llama fat) to use as an unguent for applying to wounds. I have seen a lamb's broken leg set with an ingenious flexible splint that was put in place only after liberal amounts of *llama wira* had been massaged into the injured limb; local nurses despair of the unsanitary practice of rubbing animal fat onto a newborn infant's navel, then firmly binding the belly with cloth. Great healing powers are attributed to *cuy wira*, no doubt proportionate to its great scarcity.[10]

Eggs. Few indigenous families eat eggs on a day-to-day basis. The rare family that owns a laying hen will cook those eggs not sold or used in redistributive\reciprocal networks as follows. An egg is broken into a bowl and beaten well. An equal amount of liquid from the soup is added into the bowl, and the mixture is beaten again. The liquid is then stirred rapidly into the pot. The egg thus completely disappears into the soup broth. Although theoretically the addition of an egg can change the consistency of broth (as in Greek and Chinese egg soups), in actual practice in Zumbagua the amount of liquid, and the presence of starches, usually renders the egg unnoticeable. Nevertheless, it is a welcome addition to the pot.

The most prominent usage of eggs, however, is not as a minor nutritional supplement to everyday meals. Like *cuyes,* eggs function as symbolically marked special-occasion foods.[11] They are the only appropriate gifts on certain occasions, especially when favors are asked. This type of windfall is only likely to come the way of the well-to-do, as their help is more likely to be wanted. White families in the parish often receive large numbers of eggs, *cuyes,* and other food gifts, because Indians frequently come asking favors.

An indigenous household may thus suddenly acquire a great number of eggs on very rare occasions. Then they are eaten with abandon, usually hard-boiled, as a form of treat or *wanlla,* rather than as part of a meal. The "white" custom of eating a boiled egg with bread and coffee is not practiced.

Milk. Unlike fat or eggs, milk occupies no special place in Zumbagua theories of healing,[12] neither is it a special-occasion food. Nevertheless, it is both rare and valuable. A continual complaint about the neighboring haciendas, which are dairy farms, is that they sell all of their milk directly to large milk-processing plants along the Pan-American Highway, which in turn sell directly to the cities. No milk is sold in the Zumbagua market. Because of the scarcity of cows, cows' milk is almost unknown in the parish. But women from the high *comunas* milk their sheep; the small amounts produced are added to soup in the manner described above for eggs, providing a small protein supplement.

Purchased meats. The purchasing of meat was discussed previously. I will just briefly comment here on meats purchased in the markets of the Inter-Andean Valley. An advantage to buying beef, pork, or mutton from these markets is that it is sold by the pound, so that small amounts can be purchased. These products are occasionally available in Zumbagua, but only as a special favor conferred by the butcher. It is hence expensive not only in terms of the money charged, which is higher than usual, but also because of the implied debt incurred, which the butcher may cash in by demanding some unexpected, expensive, or troublesome favor at a later date. (The same is true for purchases of locally grown staples in amounts less than a quintal; it was a continual problem for me until I had built up enough of a personal network to be able to "borrow" a few pounds of potatoes from neighboring households, to be repaid with "loans" of costly cooking oil or bread.)

The most usual occasion for this type of small purchase of meat is for an invalid or a woman giving birth. The purchase of chickens is a different matter. It may be done for a special-occasion meal among status-conscious families who wish to avoid the "Indian" *cuy,* or to serve to white compadres who disdain *cuy*. Women who have a market stall usually buy several chickens from the Inter-Andean Valley markets earlier in the week, often sending another extended family member or a trusted friend to make the purchase. The fowl are used to make a watery chicken-and-rice soup, which is a mainstay of the menu at "Indian" booths. As the entire extended family and its network of compadres are served gratis at the stall, food bought "strictly" for market sales in fact contributes to family diet as well.

"Porky." Processed vegetable shortening is purchased by many households, if they have any money at all for nonnecessities. Along with packets of *sabor,* a spoonful of "Porky" is added to soups as a flavoring in home cooking. It is omitted if there is meat in the soup.

On rare occasions, a piece of meat may be fried in Porky. Another use is in toppings or sauces made of onions and tomatoes, chopped fine and fried in Porky, made to serve with rice and/or potatoes. This kind of cooking is considered "white," and associated with coastal cuisine. The amount of fat in the Zumbaguan diet is negligible, as most food is boiled and/or toasted.

Pig fat is also for sale in the market. Deep orange in color, filled with crumbs of bacon and cracklings, with a rich, smoky smell, it is considered to be delicious but prohibitively expensive. As it is sold weekly in the Zumbagua market, someone must purchase it, but I have never seen anyone other than "white" women cook with it. It is believed to be too "dirty" for medicinal use, though a spoonful of it in the food of people who have lost weight through illness is thought to be beneficial once they are on the road to recovery.

Fish. Fish is occasionally purchased raw at the market. The fish are small, strong tasting, and full of bones, but local people like them very much. They are cooked fried in a skillet to eat with rice, or stewed to make *fanesca* at Easter time. Both dishes are expensive and rather special, though they would not qualify as appropriate "special-occasion" dishes. Households that have small ponds on their land try (rather unsuccessfully) to raise fish in them, just as people occasionally attempt to grow plants that are not suited to the altitude.

Tuna and sardines. These products are available in cans. They are bought only for special-occasion meals, when they are mashed up, sometimes mixed with onions, and used as a sauce or topping for potatoes, rice, or noodles. They may also be mixed with noodles, which are then used as a sauce for rice and/or potatoes. The sardines commonly sold in Ecuador are canned in a tomato sauce, which is appreciated as adding flavor to a sauce made using sardines.[13]

Vegetables

Onions. The onion is the single most important vegetable in the Zumbagua diet. In almost every household, onions are eaten every day. Only in the poorest households or at times of direst poverty are there no onions.

The onions grown and eaten in the parish are a high-altitude variety unknown in the United States. They produce a very small bulb; only the greens are used in cooking, but they are quite strong. The sweet, red *paiteña* beloved of Ecuadorian cooks is not used in Zumbagua.

The amount of onion used in a meal is controlled by a strong cultural preference that onions should be present but not overwhelmingly so. Soups have the stalks of at most three onions added. Sauces or toppings made of finely chopped onion and other ingredients fried in shortening are served in small quantities, not more than a tablespoon. Hot sauce made of chopped onion, hot pepper, and salt is used in even smaller amounts.

Carrots and tomatoes. These two vegetables are used like onions, but less frequently, because they must be purchased. Amounts are usually very small, and they are chopped very fine. They are never eaten raw when prepared at home, though they are sometimes ingredients in the uncooked, marinated toppings added to *chochos* and *mote* sold by cholas in the market.

Cabbage and mustard greens. Cabbage is purchased, and therefore is seldom eaten. Because it is very inexpensive, it appears in Zumbagua cooking pots somewhat more frequently than other purchased vegetables, but it is still not ordinarily used. When cooked, large pieces of it are added to soups in fairly large quantities. It is most commonly added to thick barley soups.

Nabus or mustard greens (*Brassica campestris* L.), which grow in the parish, are cooked like cabbage. Not being purchased, they provide a rare leafy vegetable for poorer families, albeit a seasonal one (see Gade 1975:159).

Other Seasonings

The seasonings used in the parish can be divided according to familiarity. Within Zumbagua cuisine, while some seasonings are central to indigenous cuisine and are an unsurprising, usual ingredient in any family's meal, others are alien, familiar only to women who have had some experience with life outside the parish. Older people or women who have never left the parish may be utterly unfamiliar with them; Quichua names for them are not known in the parish. Most of these seasonings are familiar to the "white" women of the parish, though they do not cook with them on a daily basis. An indigenous woman cooking with these seasonings might be accused of "trying to be white."

Another division of seasonings is savory/sweet, *de sal/de dulce*. Savory seasonings will be discussed first and then sweet.

Hot pepper. Capsicum, red pepper, is a seasoning of some symbolic importance in Andean culture. Its actual dietary significance in Zumbagua is minimal, however; it certainly does not approach Frank Salomon's description of the role of *ají\uchu* for the area around Quito in pre-Hispanic times: "no solo universal, sino el mínimo absoluto de comodidad" (1980:144–145). His statement that "la capacidad de las unidades de familia, y de parentesco no-político, para garantizar estos mínimos de comodidad, era un símbolo de suficiencia económica, y por consecuencia, su escasez, como un signo de debilidad y de deterioro de la autonomía" (1980:145)[14] could not be taken to apply to *uchu\ají* in Zumbagua today. The line between the "socially acceptable" diet and bare subsistence, as he phrases it, could perhaps better be drawn today by the presence or absence of potatoes or a steady supply of bread.

Still, if his description is interpreted as meaning that *uchu* was a luxury, but one with which every household was familiar, then modern Zumbagua usage does not differ from this description. Like other purchased vegetables, it is seldom bought; its absence is more frequent than its presence in the typical kitchen. Unlike carrots and tomatoes, both introduced to Ecuador by the Spaniards, however, the use of this Andean native is fully integrated into local cuisine. The scarcity of *uchu* could be a recent phenomenon; Appleby (cited in Orlove 1983:25) found for the Departamento de Puno in Peru that *uchu,* at one time ubiquitous in the area, had become an expensive luxury and was almost eliminated from the rural diet as the Peruvian economy worsened. The dietary significance of *uchu* would seem to be minimal, though its extremely high vitamin content may make it significant nutritionally, especially because, unlike other vegetables, it is never cooked.

Salts. Two types of salt are used in the parish. One is purchased, commercially processed salt, bought in plastic bags from the white merchants who sell other manufactured goods. The other is raw or rock salt brought up from the salt mines on the coast. Trucks piled full of the mineral are at the Zumbaguan market every Saturday. Men and women who sell it stand in the truck with a shovel and dump chunks of salt into whatever container—usually a cloth or a scrap of paper—purchasers provide. This strong-tasting, reddish salt, called *muyu cachi,* is popular with local people.

Salt has a history and significance in the Andes similar to that of *uchu.* As described before, in Zumbagua it is frequently combined with *uchu,* and in some respects the use of *muyu cachi* parallels that of *uchu.* A small amount of *muyu cachi* may be balanced on the side of the plate to be eaten with certain foods, especially *llullu jabus* and/or small potatoes cooked in the skin, much the way a man eats *uchu.* Unlike *uchu,* however, *cachi* is eaten in this way by both men and women.

Salt is also used when cooking. It is added to soups, rice, or the water in which large peeled potatoes are cooked, along with other seasonings: *sabor,* fat or shortening; chopped onion. For this purpose either *muyu cachi* or purchased salt may be used. The only occasion on which *muyu cachi* is not appropriate is when meats or toppings are fried, for it does not dissolve when added to the skillet. This type of cooking is not common, however, and has "white" connotations.

Packaged flavorings. These tiny packages of flavorings are locally called *sabor* in Spanish but also referred to as *mishqui,* a generic term that usually means "sweet" but also glosses as "tasty." They are extremely inexpensive. *Sabor* is used freely by Zumbaguan women. There are households so poor that they must do without it, but women who can do so use it in every pot of soup. The standard set of seasonings for any soup is salt, *sabor, wira,* and onions. Although *sabor* is a purchased complement, it enjoys a status different from other "imported" goods, such as tomatoes and carrots or the various herbs commonly used by "white" women.

Achiote. The bright red *achiote* or annatto seed (*Bixa orellana*), locally known as *culur* in reference to its use as a coloring agent, is native to the South American lowlands, where it is widely used as a dye and as face and body paint. In the highlands its use is exclusively culinary. In cooking, as in the decorative arts, *achiote*'s bright red color is important. Like paprika in U.S. cuisine, *achiote* adds more color than flavor to foods; Gade describes its precolonial and modern purpose in Peru as being "to color food" (1975:189).

In order to use achiote, the inedible seeds must be placed in a hot liquid, which absorbs their color. This liquid is then drained off, using a special implement manufactured from an empty sardine can, the lid of which is still partially attached and punctured several times at the end opposite the opening. The seeds are inserted in the can together with a lump of *wira.* The can is left near the fire until the *wira* melts and then tipped over the cooking pot so that the melted *wira,* now bright red, can drain out the punctured end, leaving the seeds behind. The seeds are retained for future use.

Achiote is not used in everyday cooking in Zumbagua. Its classic use is in the preparation of *boda\buda,* a dish that is an absolute must for special-occasion meals. *Buda* is always spoken of with such delight that I was amazed, when I actually ate some, to discover that it was simply a plain barley gruel brightly colored with *achiote.* I am told that a much more elaborate *buda* can be prepared, using eggs, cheese, and other ingredients, but even at the special meals of fairly wealthy people I have only seen colored gruel. People prefer to spend their money on meat, rice, coffee, bread, and other foods for the meal instead of making a more elaborate *buda.* The *achiote* alone is what makes it *buda:* the bright red color marks the occasion as festive.

Achiote is also used to color\flavor other dishes. It may be added to any "salty" dish but is especially used for sauces and toppings. The commonly prepared noodle or noodle-and-sardine sauce for rice and\or potatoes is usually colored with *achiote.*

Infrequently used\"white." Garlic, celery, and cilantro are almost never used in indigenous households of the parish, though cilantro is used in the preparation of chicken soup for sale in the market. *Orégano de sal* is occasionally purchased, usually for preparing *aguitas* (herbal teas), for medicinal purposes. *Orégano de dulce* (sweet oregano) is preferred for this purpose, however. To my knowledge, other "salty" herbs are not used for culinary purposes in the parish, but they may be occasionally bought for medicinal purposes.

Sugars. Sugar is a food of some importance in the diet, and its significance is growing. Inadequate meals are "bolstered" by the addition of white sugar in poor households, while men who cannot afford to bring home bread and noodles from the city bring candies instead. Landless households with some access to cash—hence, households in which the adult members are young—tend to rely more heavily on sugar. For example, the young married women who live in a house in the *centro,* held for their extended family's use, and who have some cash income through their absentee husbands, consume high amounts of sugar compared to other women. In contrast, for a landed, established couple to substitute sweetened gruels for "real" soups, as some do, is considered a sign of improvidence and immaturity.

As with salts, there are two types of sugar used in the parish. One is white processed sugar, purchased from the white merchants who sell various kinds of dry goods. Another type of sweetener, *panela\rapadura,*[15] is a less processed form of sugar, made in smaller family-owned mills in cane-growing country and sold by merchants who specialize only in this item. *Rapadura* is more expensive than white sugar and therefore is disappearing from the diets of most households, except as an occasional luxury. Older people and more traditional families insist on its presence in the diet, however.

Rapadura is unlike either brown or white sugar. Refined white sugar has been separated from molasses. "Brown" sugar is white sugar that is then remixed with some molasses to add flavor; the darkness of the sugar depends on the amount of molasses added. *Rapadura* is sugar from which molasses has not been separated; it is made by simply boiling sugarcane juice to evaporate the water content. It is somewhat reminiscent of a very dark brown sugar, but it has a richer, heavier flavor and is moister and less granular. It is formed into hard cakes, most commonly in the form of heavy, round discs with convex sides, about the diameter of a large dinner plate and some ten centimeters thick. They are sold in pairs, tightly wrapped in a protective covering of dry leaves or husks from the sugarcane plant.

Unlike white sugar, *rapadura* has a distinctive taste, somewhat similar to maple-syrup candy. It is used by Ecuadorians of all classes and races as a flavoring for certain dishes, most notably the famous national beverage, the *canelazo* (hot water, *panela*, and *trago*). In Zumbagua, it is most commonly used to make a hot, sweet beverage, called *café* even though it contains no coffee. It is also used in the preparation of sweet gruels and drinks of all sorts.

A liquid form of *rapadura* called *miel* (literally "honey") is also known in the parish. The classic use of *miel* is in the preparation of a special dish eaten at weddings, in which pieces of bread and cheese are floated in a bowl of *miel*. Versions of this dish are offered for sale in the Zumbagua market every Saturday.

Limón. The *limón*, halfway between a lime and a lemon, is used for medicinal purposes in Zumbagua. Any type of inflammation, congestion, or infection of the head, throat, or lungs is first and most frequently treated with hot water in which *limón* has been immersed. This preparation is drunk frequently enough to be a regular part of the diet, especially for the elderly, among households that can afford it.

Infrequently used\"white" sweet seasonings. Of the vast array of "sweet" herbs commonly used in the Ecuadorian kitchen, such as *arrayán, hoja de naranja, canela, clavel, manzanilla, hierba buena, toronjíl,* few ever enter the indigenous Zumbagua kitchen. I have occasionally been served an *aguita* of *orégano de dulce* in the evening at young couples' homes, and some women buy a variety of sweet herbs to flavor the *colada morada* made for Finados (although to do so is a conspicuous imitation of whites, and women who prepare for Finados in this way comment that they know the "right" way to do things, in contrast to their "ignorant" neighbors). For the most part, however, such herbs are only purchased for medicinal purposes, and even then most households prefer either locally grown herbs prescribed by knowledgeable local people, or packaged pills, powders, and bottled liquids prescribed by local shopowners, to purchased herbs bought from market cholas.

Wanlla

Wanlla is anything that is not part of a meal. In this sense, it could be translated as "snack," "treat," "junk food," or "dessert food," and *wanlla* can be all of these things. But use of these terms obscures the fact that for most households *wanlla* is an important part of the diet and provides some nutritional elements not provided by meals. Fruits are the primary example, and *wanlla* such as gelatin, fried fish, bits of pork, and hard-boiled egg provide protein. Some starches not grown or cooked in the home may be eaten as *wanlla,* especially maize and lupines, and wheat in the form of bread. Much *wanlla,* however, consists primarily of empty calories. Sweet breads and cookies, soft drinks, and hard candies are all popular *wanllas,* and consumption of this type of food appears to be on the upswing in the parish. *Wanlla* foods fall into four basic categories: breads, fruits, sweets, and cooked foods bought in the market.

Bread

Bread is the *wanlla* par excellence. It is the universally appropriate gift, the favorite treat. The distribution of bread is critically important in many social and ceremonial contexts. Large amounts of bread are necessary for certain formal gift-giving exchanges: between bride's and groom's families at weddings, for the dead on Finados, when asking a formal favor. Bread received in this way is redistributed to the extended family.

In Zumbagua minds, bread has none of the qualities of a staple. It is truly a *golosina,* a treat, a luxury. More so than perhaps any other food, consumption of bread is directly dependent on a family's disposable cash income. It is the one special food that everyone would like to have on hand all the time, while at the same time it is recognized that no one ever "needs" bread. Potatoes and barley are necessities; bread is for enjoyment.

Although breads, like other *wanlla,* are usually handed out as snacks unrelated to any meal, there are two ways in which they may be served in a more structured manner. (In Zumbagua, loaves of bread are not commonly seen. Most bread is sold in the form of small rolls, and thus, like bananas, form small, self-contained, ready-to-eat food items. Its closest parallel is probably the banana.) One way is with *café,* as will be discussed in more detail in Chapter 5. The other is as part of a special "substitute meal" eaten in those extraordinary situations in which one cannot get cooked food and has cash. This meal consists of a soft drink and two breads. On the streets of Quito, it is an everyday sight to see "Indian" workmen buying this meal at small corner stores. On one occasion in Zumbagua this "meal" was served to people helping to plant a field, as it was far from the field owner's home and close to town. It was served with some solemnity, as befitting an unusually large expenditure, and was received with mixed emotions. It was at once very thrilling to receive such expensive and luxurious fare and yet very unsatisfying as fuel for exhausted bodies.

Although people express greed for bread, it is regarded as something of which one eats a small amount at a time, not as something to satisfy hunger. To eat six or seven pieces of bread at once would be as odd and greedy as to eat several desserts in our own society. Two breads is the normal amount eaten at one time, and one is considered quite sufficient; in fact, mothers frequently divide one bread among several children.

Common Fruits

The fruits that are eaten all the time in the parish include bananas, most commonly the small, sweet *orito,* and several varieties of oranges. They are somewhat expensive by parish standards; few households can afford to buy them on a regular basis, but most probably buy them at least once or twice a month. Households in which one or more males work in the *monte* have access to this type of fruit whenever the men come home, and their extended families may sporadically receive fruit also. The few families in which a member owns a truck or bus that travels to the *monte,* or works for the owner of one, have large supplies of these fruits, usually those bruised or damaged in transport.

Capulí. This fruit is native to the New World, though it was probably not known in Ecuador until after the Conquest (Gade 1975:161). It is very similar to a cherry. During the *capulí* season, the Zumbagua market, like all of the highland markets, is full of *capulíes.* Every household has them. Because fruit is a longed-for luxury, this season is one of pure delight. People revel in the abundance of the fruit: men coming home to the parish on the buses carry huge, overflowing containers full of it; children's hands are stained with the juice; every sweet *colada* has *capulies* in it.

Uncommon\"white" fruits. Ecuador, a tropical nation, has an abundance of fruits. Most of them are seldom eaten in Zumbagua. Many are simply unknown to most residents of the parish. Pineapples are occasionally brought home from the outside as a great treat by someone who feels exceptionally wealthy. They are enormously enjoyed by those who receive them. Other fruits, such as strawberries, papayas, avocados, cherimoyas, and so on, are scarcely ever seen.

Sweets

Inexpensive sweets are an important part of social interchanges, so they have some importance in the diet. They are eaten primarily by women and children.

Cooked food from the market

The cooked-food sellers do a lively business. Husbands who work in the city make a point of buying cooked food for themselves and their wives; any sale made at the market is celebrated with purchased food and with *trago;* the *trago* sellers buy food, the cholos all have to eat, the cooked-food sellers buy from one another. Food that is bought in the market is seen more as *wanlla* than as an actual meal, even when it is similar to food that is eaten at home. Many people bring cooked food from home to eat at the market, being unable to afford to buy lunch there.

Chicken soup, the most expensive and "elite" food offered for sale, must be consumed on the spot. But most of the cooked foods offered for sale can be wrapped up and taken home or taken to another part of the market to be shared with a companion. Little bags of *mote* or lupines topped with chopped vegetables, toasted maize, bacon bits, and hot sauce; fried fish; portions of pork; sweet breads; even cooked potatoes with hot sauce are wrapped up in scraps of cloth, paper, or plastic and taken home as *wanlla* for household members who stayed home to care for animals and children.

These kinds of treats obviously have a function more social than purely dietary. The whole category of *wanlla*, in fact, is defined by the social uses to which the foods within it are put, whether those foods be animal or vegetable, expensive or cheap. The fact that Zumbagua diet involves use of such a sociocultural definition reveals the close connection between diet and cuisine, the cultural ordering of foods and cooking. Now that the basic vocabulary of Zumbagua foods has been established, we can turn our attention to the question of cuisine.

Notes

1. *Lindo,* Spanish "beautiful," is a loanword that has entered Zumbagua Quichua with the same meaning. *Suamj,* Quichua "beautiful," is not commonly used, as it is in other Quichua dialects. In Zumbagua Quichua, *lindo* contrasts with *kwila,* "cute" or "pretty." Like *sumaj, lindo* can also be used to describe beauty other than appearances (e.g., beautiful ideas or actions); see Whitten and Whitten 1985.

2. According to Daniel Gade,

Adventives (Anderson 1939:364–365) include both those plants unintentionally grown by man in his fields and gardens (weeds) and those pioneers that spread into habitats created by humans . . . (ruderals). . . . Many useful weeds and ruderals are allowed to maintain themselves up to a point because they have some value to man. Some weeds, such as *Amaranthus quitensis, Chenopodium petiolare* and *Brassica campestris,* are highly valued as human food, particularly the very young leaves. *Brassica campestris* may eventually be domesticated if present practices continue as many depend so much on these weedy potherbs that they may intentionally select them. Domesticated animals . . . eat many more adventives. . . . In a folk society such as that of the Vilcanota Valley most elements of the adventive flora have some compensating value, and few plants are totally objectionable. (1975:68–69)

3. Well-to-do by parish standards. No one living in the parish is well-to-do by national standards (except possibly a very famous shaman), and Zumbagua is poor even in comparison with other indigenous areas.

4. The diet of well-off households is good only as long as they are involved in both cash enterprises and agriculture. Benjamin Orlove suggests that for the Andean area as a whole, "the replacing of locally-produced native foods with the purchase of Western foods [is] accompanied by a decline in nutritional status" (1983:2). In Ecuador, it certainly seems that a complete move into the cash economy, unless it be accompanied by an enormous upward move in economic status, is generally accompanied by a corresponding sharp decline in overall nutritional profile. Cheap processed foods are substituted for the grains and vegetables of the agrarian diet. In the case of Zumbagua, "city" meals substitute soft drinks, sweet, eggless white breads, and unenriched noodles for stone-ground barley, onions, and fava beans.

5. Gade says of the *haba,*

> *Vicia faba L, haba* or broad bean, is one of the most important crops in the
> [Vilcanota] Valley. . . . Introduced from Spain in the sixteenth century
> (COBO I:409), the broad bean is perhaps the only European food carrying
> the stigma of being "Indian food". In Spain the broad bean served primarily
> as livestock feed and was food for humans only when other food sources
> were scarce (ALONSO DE HERRERA I:156). When the lowly Spaniard came to
> the New World, his social status automatically elevated, he stopped eating
> the broad bean. However, the Indians quickly found it better than their
> native tarwi, and began growing it in large quantities in areas above 3,300
> m. Today it is the most widely grown leguminous seed plant in the upper
> valley . . . and is an essential staple food for many country people.
> (1975:164–165)

6. Gade explains that "An essential distinction that goes back to Inca times
is the classification of maize into "hard" and "soft" types. GARCILASO DE LA
VEGA (1960:36) noted two kinds of maize in Cuzco: *muruchu* (or *morocho*), a
hard flinty maize, and *capia,* a soft presumably floury type of maize. COBO
(I:160) used *morocho* to designate the hard maize of the lowlands that the Spaniards fed to their horses, and this term is still current" (1975:113).

7. Gade describes the history of the lupine as follows:

> *Lupinus mutabilis Sweet, tarwi,* is a native domesticate grown for its edible
> seeds. It is an erect herbaceous annual with blue flowers. . . . [T]arwi seeds
> are flatter, smaller and more rectangular than the seeds of the common kid-
> ney bean. Tarwi very probably was domesticated in Peru. . . . The Spaniards
> first called it *altramuz* after *Lupinus albus* which was cultivated in Spain at
> that time, also for its edible seeds. In the Vilcanota Valley, tarwi is clearly a
> relict crop. . . . Solid fields of tarwi are rare and usually it is planted in a
> corner of a maize field or on the periphery of another field to act as a bar-
> rier. . . .
> The great amount of work involved in processing the tarwi for consump-
> tion may partly explain its decline and its replacement by broad beans which
> resist equally well the low temperatures but which do not require this pro-
> cessing. (1975:168)

8. Gade: "*chenopodium Quinoa Wild, quinoa,* is a domesticated herbaceous
plant. . . . In no place in the Vilcanota Valley is it grown as a basic crop, occu-
pying unmixed fields. . . . [Q]uinoa is often sown as a living fence around a maize
field" (1975:152–155).

9. The inability of *cuyes* to withstand cold is frequently used as an excuse for
the following situation: young couples desirous of upward ethnic\class mobility
frequently choose to build cement-block houses with tin roofs instead of using
traditional materials (straw, adobe, wattle and daub). The new houses are much
colder, for neither roofs nor walls hold heat. In addition, the tin roof does not
permit smoke to leave the room, so that if straw fires are used for cooking, the

room becomes unbearably smoky. If an expensive gasoline stove is used instead, the atmosphere improves but the house becomes colder still, having lost its only source of heat with the removal of the fire.

For these reasons, although many couples stick it out, one often finds that after a few months the new home stands abandoned. The couple has taken up residence in a straw hut behind it. The reason given is always the same: the *cuyes* were dying from the cold. The discomfort of the human beings involved is never mentioned as a factor, so that one is left with the rather humorous picture of a human family being forced to light fires, cook, and sleep in their *cuyes'* straw hut, abandoning their own fine new home.

10. The significance of *wira* for healing is related to the general Andean theory of wellness, in which *wira, tullu, yawar* (fat, bones, blood) are seen as three basic bodily principles (Bastien 1978:54; Weismantel 1983). Although I did not specifically study curing in Zumbagua, I was aware of the prevalence of these ideas in the parish. Illnesses were frequently explained as loss of *wira*, for example, and the beliefs tht have been reported elsewhere in the Andes about whites eating *runa wira* (see, for example, Allen 1978; Casaverde Rojas 1970) are found in Zumbagua as well.

11. The parallel between eggs and *cuyes* extends into curing as well. The well-known practice of "cleansing" a patient or diagnosing illness, which is the stock-in-trade of even the most amateurish Andean curer, is classically done with a *cuy* (see, for example, Parsons 1945:64–67; Sharon 1978:19, 75; Gillin 1947:125–126) but may be done with an egg (see Parsons 1945:64–67), or, in Zumbagua at least, less effectively with a candle. The egg or *cuy* is passed over the patient's body, and the illness then passes into the egg or into the body of the *cuy,* which dies during the process. While somewhat beneficial, this practice usually cannot effect a complete cure in itself, as the *cuy* or egg is "too small" to hold all the sickness found within the ailing human body. A more important function is diagnosis: the healer opens the egg, or the *cuy*'s body, and can see the nature of the illness through the effects it has had on the egg yolk or on the *cuy*'s internal organs.

12. An exception is human breast milk. I have seen a woman bathe her husband's head with her own breast milk, when he was ill from drinking, and give it to him to drink. On another occasion, within a different extended family, it was suggested that a woman similarly overcome by *trago* be given milk from her sister's breast, but 7Up was substituted. Like the breast milk, it was used both to bathe the head and as a drink.

13. A rather amusing incident occurred when the antichurch organization began their dry-goods cooperative. One of the young leaders purchased a supply of sardines from the United States, which he sold to local people assuring them that these were *de lujo* (of especially high quality, fancy). When people returned to their homes and opened the cans, they found that the sardines were packed in oil. This discovery occasioned great outrage: they had been cheated out of their tomato sauce. In Zumbaguan eyes, these sardines were not *de lujo* at all, but were of quite inferior quality.

14. "The capacity of the family units, and of nonpolitical kinship, to guarantee these minimums of comfort, was a symbol of economic self-sufficiency, and consequently, its scarcity was a sign of weakness and loss of autonomy."

15. The word *rapadura* comes from the Spanish *raspadura,* another word for *panela.* Through a process that occurs in many dialects of Quichua, however, locally *rapadura* has come to be identified as the Quichua word for this type of sugar, while only *panela* is recognized as a Spanish term. Sidney Mintz notes that Haitian creole also uses a word *rapadou,* derived from Spanish *raspadura* (1985:xxii).

FOUR

The Cuisine of Zumbagua: Underlying Structures

The Place of Food in Zumbagua Life: Time and Space

In a rural society like Zumbagua, in which the major activity is the production of food and most of what is grown is for internal consumption, food does not hide in the kitchen. The landscape is filled with it; all activities have to do with it; the place, Zumbagua, is colored and formed by the foods it produces just as the bodies of its people are made out of the food the land gives them.

In Zumbagua both time and space take on forms determined by food crops. Work time revolves around crops and animals, all destined to be eaten. Larger time, the calendar year, is shaped by the agricultural cycle. There are times of stubbly, empty fields, times of gleaming, newly exposed black earth waiting for seed, times of bright young green, of golden yellow, and finally the times that the earth is overloaded with food ready to be brought from field to patio and finally to the kitchen.

These times are not only ultimately but also intimately related to cooking and eating. The seasons shape diet and cuisine: the changing colors and smells of the land are linked to periods of plenty and of scarcity in the life of the kitchen. When the new fava beans color the fields a dense, dark green, the kitchen too is invaded by a plentitude of green, fresh-tasting beans. Later, as the dry gold of ripe barley overwhelms the eye when out-of-doors, the same color fills the kitchen as well. Piles of barley stalks lie by the stove for fuel, and cascades of pale gold fill the air as the grain is sifted. Its smell permeates the kitchen. Later come periods of empty fields. In the kitchen, each meal is counted in terms of the dwindling stockpile in the storeroom.

In the Zumbagua diet, starches predominate. This pattern is written not only into the structure of meals, but into the landscape itself. All three of the main cultigens—barley, potatoes, and fava beans—are starches.[1] Even when a small amount of a more unusual crop is planted, it is usually another kind of starchy food: lentils, peas (far more starchy than sweet), lupines, quinoa, Andean tubers.

The predominance of starches is written on another kind of Zumbaguan space as well: the market. To an outsider, the Zumbaguan market makes a rather dismal showing compared with other regional markets of the highlands. The selection of goods, especially foodstuffs, is very small, and prices are high. In contrast to most Ecuadorian markets, there are almost no fresh vegetables to be found—it takes a practiced eye to ferret out the few dried-out carrots, the tiny pile of wrinkled tomatoes. Locally grown onions are the only exception. Fruits are somewhat better represented: there are always some citrus fruits and bananas—but for the most part it is a starch market. The lower half of the plaza is dedicated to the sale of local products: potatoes, barley, and fava beans, sold only by the quintal (hundredweight). Farther up, trucks from the lowlands sell plantains and *yuca* (manioc), as well as raw salt sold by the shovelful. Up with the manufactured goods such as clothes and aluminum pots are the processed foods sold by cholas from the Inter-Andean Valley. Cooking oil, vegetable shortening, and white sugar are here, but again, starches prevail: flours of various sorts (wheat, corn, bean, barley), noodles, oatmeal, white rice.

Other cholas sell breads near the cooked-food section of the market. The butchers are busy killing and skinning sheep and the occasional llama, but raw eggs are hard to come by, and milk is not for sale. Of course, an entire hidden market deals in "precious" commodities such as eggs, milk, and tomatoes—commodities as common as any others in the markets of the Inter-Andean Valley, two hours away and a thousand meters below. Those (primarily "white") women lucky enough to have comadres from outside get personal deliveries of such special foodstuffs, carried out in utmost secrecy. The ability to obtain these goods without leaving the parish is a mark of superior status among the "white" society of the plaza, the structure of which is determined as much by (real or fictitious) relations with the outside world as by internal relations among its members.

The cooked-food sellers are busy, most of them local women who earn a small amount of cash this way. They sell special foods that are rarely cooked at home: watery chicken soup, small plates of rice with a scanty topping of shortening, *achiote*, onion, and tomato. Hard-boiled eggs, glasses of gelatin, and soft drinks are also sold. Other women sell frybreads with coarse sugar sprinkled on them, in competition with the white adolescent boys from the Inter-Andean Valley who have a machine for making *chilenos*, round, doughy, doughnut-like treats.

The marketplace is a clearly defined and internally structured space, in which different kinds of things are sold in different areas. The division of space is partly by origin of the things being sold—coastal, highland, local—and partly by type—condiments and cooking utensils, starches, meats; clothing versus food, cooked versus raw. Each specialty has its own space, some marked out in rectangular blocks, others stretched out all along one thoroughfare of the market, so that a plan of the market would look rather like the scheme for a large garden.

These structures are permanent and fixed: the positions of onion sellers, volleyball players, potato wholesalers never change. It is an environment that has a characteristic, unforgettable quality of noise, color, movement, and above all of restricted spaces: one is repeatedly trapped in narrow aisles and tiny booths, overwhelmed by piles of food, mountains of salt, rows of shiny clothing, walls of plastic boots.

In Zumbagua, however, as in many rural areas, the market is a space with a peculiar relationship to time. Despite the fixity of its internal structure, the market itself is utterly ephemeral. The sun comes up Saturday morning to find it fully in existence, pulsing with activity, but the next dawn reveals only windswept and empty plazas, in startling contrast to the divided and overloaded spaces of the day before. Starving dogs and stray sows snuffle at the remaining scraps of garbage; even the holes where the posts were inserted to erect the stalls are lost in the blowing dust of the dry season or the *invierno* mud. Each week the marketplace is reconstructed. The big empty spaces at the heart of the town fill up with people and things.

Local Systems and National Systems

Zumbagua Cuisine Within the National Cuisine of Ecuador

The Saturday market is filled with the sight and smell of foods that many Zumbagua women never cook at home: fried fish from the coast, *mote* from the Inter-Andean Valley. The people selling these foods, however, do eat them every day. For a *costeño* not to eat fish, or a chola to go without *mote,* would be as unthinkable as for a Zumbagua household to start off its day without *máchica*. The people of Zumbagua recognize that other people have other diets and other cuisines, and they borrow elements from them as exotica with which to enrich their own fare.

As these examples show, the Zumbagua semiotic system is filled with elements that also belong to other systems, the systems of people who, for the most part, are richer and whiter than those who live in the parish. For heuristic purposes, it would be possible to study Zumbagua foods in isolation from the other semiotic systems that surround them, but the parish has never existed in such isolation. Zumbagua cuisine has evolved as a system that, like its people, exists in a certain ethnic and class relation to other cuisines. Just as position defines meaning within a semiotic system, so the system itself exists in structured relation to other systems.

Not only does the system as a whole then become a symbol in a meta-language about the relations between styles and the groups that use them,[2] but the form of the system itself is to some extent shaped by its position in this larger system of signs. As long as distinctions such as highland/lowland, north/central/south, urban/rural, province/capital continue to be meaningful in Ecuadorian life, elements existing within semiotic systems that belong solely to one side of these pairs will be defined not only in contrast to elements within their own system, but also in contrast to elements of other systems. A *papa* (potato) is one of the three main foods grown in Zumbagua, and therefore is partially defined as not-barley and not-*habas*. But it is also not-*yuca*: it is highland, not lowland food.

The people of Zumbagua are poor, rural, indigenous, and they live in the Sierra. In addition, they live above the zone of maize cultivation. Self-evident comments, perhaps: but all of these facts about them are reflected in their cuisine; in fact, as the next chapter will show, at times one food, *máchica*, symbolizes all of these facts within its fan of referential meanings (Turner 1967).

Not only the diet of Zumbagua but its cuisine differs from that of the nation as a whole. Zumbagua people eat "Indian" foods in "Indian" ways: not only elements and techniques but the very syntagmatic chains by which they are combined into meals are not the same as even the "typical" highland Ecuadorian cuisine. This difference is significant: it signifies not simply a particular way of life but one that is stigmatized.

National Cuisines

The cover of a popular Ecuadorian cookbook, *Doña Juanita* ("Doña Juanita" n.d.), displays a brightly colored photograph of a plate of food. The meat, potatoes, and vegetables on the plate are accompanied by a mound of white rice and topped with a fried egg. This kind of dish is referred to in Ecuador as a *seco*. In the typical *seco*, the plate holds a piece of meat (beef, chicken, goat) cooked using one of a rather limited repertoire of techniques, condiments, and vegetables. At the side are perhaps some fried potatoes and another vegetable, or a relish of marinated, finely sliced onions and tomatoes with *limón* and cilantro. The dominant element on the plate, however, is the large unseasoned pile of white rice.

In the full *almuerzo*, the *seco* is flanked by a preceding soup and terminal sweet *colada*, dishes that evoke a meal structure descended from pre-Hispanic patterns. But as *caldo de pata* and other Ecuadorian soups are increasingly replaced by imports like "Cream of Mushroom," and fruit *coladas* by a glass of cola or a dish of canned peaches, the earlier heritage becomes less visible even though the sequence of courses still bears its mark.

In using the photograph of a traditional *seco* for the cover of her book, "Doña Juanita" has a particular message in mind for Quito housewives who might wish to buy it. The significance of this picture goes beyond the messages, "This book is about food" and "The recipe for this dish is inside this book." Like Roland Barthes's photograph of a soldier (1957:116–119), this photograph also carries a nationalistic message. The presence of rice and egg pronounce that here are to be found the traditional foods of Ecuador, the *platos típicos* which symbolize the country's heritage. Here are no recipes for pizzas or for sandwiches made of Wonder Bread, American cheese, and bologna (*pan de miga, queso americano y pastel mexicano*), the glamorous fast foods, processed foods, and snack foods that are *de moda* among the young and the nouveaux riches, students, and professional classes. *Platos típicos* are substantial, solid: bland and starchy, they reach their full flower in the traditional *almuerzo,* the heavy midday meal at which the entire family gathers. *Platos típicos* stand for the strength of the family, that primary virtue of traditional Ecuadorian society.

The situation in Quito, where *platos típicos* and fast foods vie with one another for primacy in the food consciousness of the city, is not unusual. Cuisine is not always a matter that is taken for granted. Tensions build and arguments break out over what to eat, and how, and when. The existence of competing cuisines make visible cleavages between social roles, bringing out the differences between old and young, man and woman, rich and poor.

Among the urban middle-class of Quito, disagreements about what to eat have ideological valences which can expose schisms between class, generation, and gender. A well-to-do hotel owner delights in taking North American tourists out to lunch at restaurants that have "real Ecuadorian" food, holding forth over the table about the decadence of Europe, visible in its cuisine as well as its sexual mores. What a contrast to the respectable and family-oriented life of conservative Quito, he points out, where food is a daytime, family affair, and nighttimes are for light, restrained eating and early bed.

But: "My children only want hamburgers and pizzas" the middle-aged women of Quito confess to one another, appalled. Like rock music and fast cars, such meals are signposts on the road to perdition as far as many parents are concerned. For other Ecuadorians, the threat implicit in fast-food cuisine is not to the family but to the nation. Kentucky Fried Chicken and Tina Turner are part of the cultural invasion from the north, attacking Ecuador's integrity as a nation and her people's self-identity as possessors of a unique culture. As a result, one finds young leftists conscientiously listening to *cúmbia* and eating ceviche in an attempt to preserve some ideological and cultural purity.

The ideological importance of *platos típicos* for Ecuador is problematic, however, in a way that characterizes a dilemma Ecuadorians face in seeking an autonomous identity through emphasizing their nation's cultural heritage. For *platos típicos* carry other messages besides "family" and "nation." They also stand for the poor, the ignorant, and the non-white: people with whom the elite, for the most part, do not wish to identify.

This opposition between the full *almuerzo* and the fast-food snack, though real, obscures a more complex hierarchy of cuisines. Shrimp ceviches and tropical fruits like grenadilla and cherimoya certainly stand on the Ecuadorian side of the two rival American cuisines, U.S. and national, found in Quito today. But although "Ecuadorian cuisine" appears as a unified entity when opposed to sandwiches or pizzas, Ecuador in fact contains many cuisines. For example, the long-standing rivalry between highlands and coast is symbolized by potatoes versus rice, by *locros* (stews) versus *secos* (dry meals), by blandness versus spiciness. This separation exists even though the *seco* made with rice is found throughout Ecuador. As its prominence on the cover of *Doña Juanita* shows, the *seco* dominates Ecuadorian cuisine; this dominance reflects a certain historical relation between coast and Sierra.

Platos típicos of all sorts also evoke the provinces rather than the capital city. In small towns and even provincial capitals, the restaurants all serve the same fare: *churrascos* and *apanados, pollo dorado, seco de chivo* (all of which are types of *secos*) appear on every menu, and all are assembled on the plate in the same way. But while for Quiteños such dishes signify provincialism and a native heritage being left behind by the modern world, to the people of Zumbagua the same menu represents that outside, urban, modern world from which they feel disenfranchised.

The Place of National Cuisines Within Zumbagua Cuisine

Like the sophisticated Ecuadorian confronted with emblems of popular culture from the United States, the people of Zumbagua view dishes such as the restaurant *seco* with both hatred and desire. White rice, fried foods, large quantities of meat, vegetables that do not grow at parish altitudes are all objects of unsatisfied yearning.

The *secos* contrast with everyday meals in Zumbagua not only in ingredients but in other ways, including aesthetic principles about color, texture, temperature, and consistency. In the parish, it is held that to be appealing food should be liquid, thick, uniform, and barely lukewarm. It is this ideal for which women strive in their cooking. The *seco* by its very nature as a nonsoup contrasts with this norm.

Differences in cuisine go beyond such generalized aesthetic preferences, however. Cuisines also consist of underlying rules for assembling ingredients into a meal, rules of exclusion and inclusion that are based on constituent syntagmatic and paradigmatic axes. Zumbaguan cuisine differs from "white" cuisine along these dimensions as well, though there are similarities that betray the common heritages they share. Just as Ecuadorian Spanish is colored by Quichua and Zumbagua Quichua is peppered with Spanish (Guevara 1972; Salomon 1984), so the elements and fragments of the two cuisines are interpenetrated. If the boundary between the two is permeable, it is real nonetheless. Each household in the parish makes its own decisions as to what "white" elements it will incorporate into its own idiocuisine, and the small everyday arguments that arise over these choices mark small individual stances on issues that are ultimately ideological. "White" usages exist at the edges of what is considered usual or acceptable. Some are simply elements within a particular paradigm that carry a value of "whiteness"; others are actual alterations in the syntagm itself. "Whiteness" is frequently associated with expensive foods, but the correlation is not absolute.

Meals and the Cuisine of Zumbagua

From the many meals I witnessed and shared in Zumbagua, it was possible to abstract a basic semiotic system. Figures 5 through 9 show the basic structures that order the production of meals in Zumbagua. This is the *langue* of Zumbagua cooking: these diagrams contain rules for the composition of possible meals, instead of describing any meal in particular. Because Zumbagua cuisine is a simple and limited system, it was possible to include in each paradigm all of the possible elements of the set. This abstract representation of Zumbagua cuisine demonstrates the existence of an underlying system at the bedrock of cooking practice. It is a set of rules governing the relations between elements, from which a large but finite number of meals can be generated.

The construction of these diagrams is primarily based on Barthes's analysis of the semiosis of food:

> Let us now take another signifying system: food. We shall find there without difficulty Saussure's distinction. The alimentary language is made of i) rules of exclusion (alimentary taboos) ii) signifying oppositions of units . . . (for instance the type *savoury/sweet*); iii) rules of association, either simultaneous (at the level of a dish) or successive (at the level of a menu); iv) rituals of use which function, perhaps, as a kind of alimentary *rhetoric*. (1964:27–28)

This chapter is devoted primarily to discussing the *langue* of Zumbaguan cuisine: the rules of exclusion and association presented in the diagrams, the associations and signifying oppositions discussed below, as well as some of the rituals of use that form such an important part of family life. These formal patterns are significant in themselves, in that they constitute a rich cultural domain, one that structures the experiences of emotional attachments, the passage of time, physical longings and satisfactions. But they also form the basis for what Barthes calls "alimentary speech, which is very rich" (1964:28).

In describing Zumbagua cuisine, I use terms—*sopa* and *seco, caldo* and *colada*—that come from Ecuadorian national cuisine but are here applied to categories used within the parish. They are not words that people of the parish themselves use. Although more acculturated and Spanish-speaking residents of the parish may use these terms to apply to Zumbaguan dishes, monolingual Quichua speakers do not. Soups are commonly referred to simply as *almuirzu*, from the Spanish *almuerzo*, lunch. To some extent, ingredients define dishes, so that to say *arrus*, meaning *arroz de cebada*, coarsely ground barley, in itself implies a barley-meal-based *colada*, to which whatever other appropriate ingredients available will have been added; the same would be true of *jabus pulvu*, and so forth. The categories I am using are implicit categories used by Zumbagua women when cooking: they refer to specific types of syntagmatic chains I discovered in their practice. I use the Ecuadorian Spanish terms because they most closely approximate native categories—not surprisingly, considering the common cultural roots, European and Native American, of both cuisines—and to avoid meanings implicit in English cooking terminology.

In these discussions, and elsewhere in this work, I have used two terms, parallel and validator, that need to be explained. I derive both of these concepts from the rules underlying cuisine. When two foods are referred to as parallel in usage, the implication is that they stand as substitutes for one another in certain categories of cuisine. (In Figures 6 through 9, parallel elements are to be found in the same column, connected by either a V or a <u>V</u> symbol. Figure 5 explains the symbols used in the subsequent diagrams.) It does not mean that the two foods are necessarily parallel to one another in all aspects of the cuisine; for example, *llullu jabus* (fresh fava beans) and *carawan papakuna* (potatoes cooked in the skin) stand in parallel relation to each other in the type 2 *seco* (Figure 8), but potatoes cooked in their skins could not substitute for *llullu jabus* in a *sopa* (Figure 5), and in fact they would not be found in a *sopa* at all.

A second critical concept is that of the validator, an ingredient that is so central to the composition of a dish or a meal that its presence defines the meal or dish as such. White rice is the validator of a meal in "white" cuisine, and bread is the validator of *café*. According to popular Ecuadorian stereotypes, potatoes are the validator of meals within indigenous cuisine in the Sierra, playing the same role that rice plays in other national cuisines. In Zumbagua, however, potatoes have become too scarce to perform such a function, if they ever did so.

The diagrams detail the internal relationships among foods within various meals and dishes. I will not comment in detail on elements or relationships at this level, except in passing to illustrate certain aspects of Zumbagua cuisine.

What the diagrams do not explain are the relationships of each of these patterns to one another and how the pattern of every day, the passing of the seasons, and the coming of special occasions are all reflected and created through the making of meals. The following sections, though they discuss each diagram in turn, are directed toward elucidating these larger relationships. This discussion is based on the structures of cuisine as presented in the diagrams and serves to comment on contrasts between the various syntagms: *sopas* versus *secos*, raw preparations contrasted to cooked ones. But in making clear the role of meals and foods in marking the seasons and occasions of Zumbagua life, connotative meaning as well as denotative roles come into play.

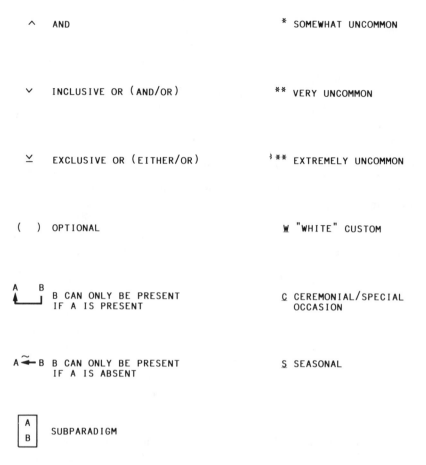

∧   AND

∨   INCLUSIVE OR (AND/OR)

⩽   EXCLUSIVE OR (EITHER/OR)

( )   OPTIONAL

A   B
└─┘   B CAN ONLY BE PRESENT
      IF A IS PRESENT

A ⇜ B   B CAN ONLY BE PRESENT
        IF A IS ABSENT

⎡A⎤
⎣B⎦   SUBPARADIGM

*   SOMEWHAT UNCOMMON

**   VERY UNCOMMON

³**   EXTREMELY UNCOMMON

W̲   "WHITE" CUSTOM

C̲   CEREMONIAL/SPECIAL
    OCCASION

S̲   SEASONAL

VERTICAL READINGS (COLUMNS) REPRESENT SYNTAGMATIC CHAINS OF ASSOCIATION.

HORIZONTAL READINGS (ROWS) REPRESENT SYSTEMIC (PARADIGMATIC) CHAINS OF ASSOCIATION.

ITEMS ARE ARRANGED LEFT TO RIGHT FROM MOST ESSENTIAL TO LEAST ESSENTIAL.

ITEMS ARE ARRANGED TOP TO BOTTOM FROM MOST COMMON TO LEAST COMMON.

THE UPPERMOST ROW REPRESENTS THE MOST BASIC CATEGORIES: SUBDIVISIONS ARE BELOW.

(SYMBOLS ADAPTED FROM RUBINSTEIN 1975:53–56.)

Figure 5. Explanation of symbols used in Figures 6 through 9.

The Basic Structure: The *Sopa*

In Zumbagua, despite the general centrality of starches and the peripheral position of other ingredients, there is no one starch that must preside over every combination of foods in order for them to be recognized as constituting a meal, as there is in so many agricultural diets around the world (Mintz 1985:8–9). A lack of strict validators in fact typifies the cuisine of the parish, despite the extremely small total number of ingredients familiar to Zumbagua cooks. For those who can afford it, there may be flour-thickened potato-and-cabbage soup one day, barley soup the next, and rice with fried fish the third. Even the poor experience a seasonal variation from barley gruels to fresh fava beans and back again.

Validation occurs not through the presence of a particular element but through the use of a familiar pattern in the composition of the meal. Mary Douglas speaks of the pleasure with which people react to being served a familiar dish as "the flash of recognition and confidence which welcomes an ordered pattern" (1971:80).

In Zumbagua cuisine, like that of white Sierrans, there are two basic categories of dishes, *sopas* and *secos*. But in contrast to the white *almuerzo*, in which *sopa* and *colada* flank a central, validating *seco*, in Zumbagua the *sopa* has a clear predominance. If there is no single type of food that marks the *almuirzu* as a meal, there is no doubt that the structure *sopa* validates most Zumbagua meals. It is the most important and most typical syntagm (dish/meal) of Zumbagua cuisine.

Generally speaking, most main meals eaten in the parish consist of *sopas*. Each person sharing the meal is expected to eat at least two bowls full of soup, and more is always offered. The heavy starch content makes it a very filling meal.

The basis of these meals, like all *sopas*, is boiled water. Even the *secos* eaten in the parish are boiled foods from which the water has been poured off. The word for "to cook," *yanuna*, itself means "to boil." Boiling is absolutely central to Zumbagua cooking practice.

The children, my constant watchers, were disturbed by many of my cooking habits, and their protests frequently brought implicit cooking rules to my attention. One such lesson was that water must be *cooked*: simply to bring it to a boil is not sufficient. It is perhaps for this reason that, instead of simply heating water in which to wash dishes, Zumbagua women actually "cook" dirty dishes in a pot of water on the cooking fire before washing them.

Water for bathing is also cooked, not merely heated, before being poured into a large *batea*, or wooden trough, used only for bathing. I

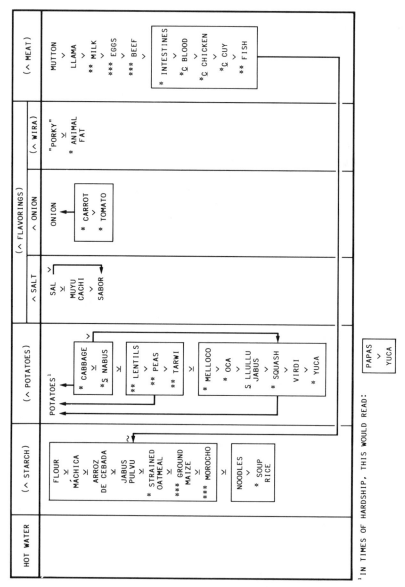

Figure 6. Schematic depiction of the *sopa*.

frequently felt that Zumbagua women were "cooking" their husbands and children when they heated water for them to bathe in, and bathed the little ones. The implements and processes are strikingly similar, involving fire, fuel, water, and the *batea*, which is exactly like the smaller ones used to hold grains and tubers. The bright red little body of a child wrapped in a cloth and set by the fire to stay warm until it is dry brings to mind the pot of potatoes taken off the fire and set to cool. When sick, injured, or exhausted husbands are given baths made with healing herbs in them, the process really does seem like cooking potatoes, the herbs being added to the water to soothe an aching body just as onions and salt season raw potatoes. *Wira*, of course, is used for both purposes.

Beyond this underlying process of boiling in water, it is hard to write a minimal definition of a *sopa*. Starches form a main ingredient in most *sopas*, but they are not the validator.

The two subsets in the second column of Figure 6 divide *sopas* into two basic categories, *colada* and *caldo*. The first are thick, the latter clear soups. (This distinction is not absent from our own cuisine, though it is not clearly distinguished linguistically. Cream soups, bisques, chowders, and bean soups are *coladas;* consommés, broths, noodle and vegetable soups are *caldos*.) Note that potatoes, while important, do not play the role of fundamental thickener in *coladas*. While North American cuisine frequently uses potatoes as the thickening agent for a *colada*-style soup, in Zumbagua potatoes are never allowed to cook long enough to disintegrate in this fashion. Instead, other starches are used as the base of *coladas*. Potatoes are present in both *caldo* and *colada*, but are the validator for neither. A *colada* is validated by its thickening starch food, a *caldo* by its broth.

Whereas a *colada* must have a flour or meal of some sort used to thicken it, *caldos* may be without any starch. It is possible to make a meat broth for the sick that contains no starches at all, or only potatoes. Sick people frequently decide that they have no stomach for one or another starch, aversions that are always heeded; the extremely ill may only be able to eat pure broths. These clear broths in fact represent the quintessential *caldo*. Nonetheless, neither meat broth nor its substitute, "Porky," need to be present to make a *caldo*. Hot water, noodles, and salt make a perfectly acceptable *caldo*, one that cash-poor people consider somewhat desirable.[3]

Overall, *coladas* are more common than *caldos* in everyday cuisine. A good, substantial *sopa*, the kind of meal an average family eats on a regular basis, consists of hot water thickened with *arroz de cebada* or flour, cooked with a spoonful of *wira*, some salt, a packet of *sabor*, and three chopped onions. On most but not all days, a *sopa* also contains some extras: pieces of mutton, perhaps, or cabbage. A *sopa* should always contain enough potatoes so that each bowl served contains several, though in many households it often does not.

Potatoes, though not normally the main ingredient of a *sopa*, are important nonetheless. Note the absolute subordination of all parallel elements in column three to the potato: manioc, *oca,* pulses, lupines, cabbage. What lifts a *sopa* out of the category of simply sustenance and makes it satisfying is the presence of *papas.*

The importance and desirability of the potato is further indicated by its ubiquity in the cuisine. It is an appropriate addition to any meal, no matter how many other starches are already present. And, in fact, two of the classic special-occasion dishes of the parish contain only *papas* as starches: *yawarlocro* and *caldo* made of *cuy.* In both cases, a meat broth flavored with onions and salt, has potatoes cooked in it. *Yawarlocro* is made from blood and internal organs and is the first meal made when butchering is done. Hence it is associated with the beginning of a festive period, whether the occasion is childbirth, a houseraising, or fiesta sponsorship. *Caldo de cuy,* by contrast, is served for the single special meal, as for instance when one's wedding *padrino* visits. In both meals, a tasty protein broth is joined with an abundance of potatoes; nothing else is served.

Either of these dishes is a formal, special-occasion dish that is a *sopa* in form. These dishes are the most traditional forms of acknowledging a special occasion and of honoring someone or paying respect to them. Today, however, their primacy is threatened by another type of special-occasion dish, which takes the form of a *seco.*

The *Seco*

Although white Sierran cuisine and Zumbagua cuisine contain a large number of identical elements and dishes, the contrast between the two cuisines in the manner of composing meals out of these elements and dishes is equally striking. (This difference is probably not accidental, but rather serves to create and maintain sharp—though permeable—boundaries, like those that exist between the two languages.) The contrast between "white" validating *seco* and Zumbagua validating *sopa* has been noted. In addition, in "white" usages the normal *almuerzo* or full-scale meal consists of a matched pair, *sopa* and *seco.* In contrast, Zumbagua meals seldom if ever mix the two. Normally, a meal consists exclusively of *sopa*. If a *seco* is present, the *sopa* is correspondingly absent. Instead of two distinct courses, the meal consists of two (or more) successive servings of the same dish. In the parish, replacement of *sopa* by *seco* characteristically happens under two very different circumstances: seasonally, during the period from Semana Santa to Corpus Christi; and on special occasions at any time of the year. In the first instance the *seco* prepared is markedly informal in contrast to a *sopa,* while the special-occasion *seco* is served at times that a meal more formal than a *sopa* is desired. These two types of *secos,* then, both contrast to the more typical *sopa,* but in opposing ways. One represents an extreme of informality, the other of formality.

The Formal Seco: *Rice and Potatoes*

The *cuy* (guinea pig) is raised specifically to be used in the preparation of special-occasion meals. "To kill a *cuy*" for someone (in other words, to cook a *sopa* of *cuy* for them when they come to your house) is an open declaration that you would like to deepen and formalize the relationship between your household and theirs, perhaps to make them compadre, but have not yet found the opportunity. Or it may be the expression of gratitude for a gift or a favor. (In this context, it is not by any means a repayment, which would close the account between the two parties, but rather a statement that there is now a relationship of mutual giving between the two parties, not simply an unrepaid debt [see Bourdieu's 1977:5–9 discussion of the nature of reciprocity].)

The phrase "to kill a *cuy*" implies a *sopa*. But while *cuyes* are served in this form, they are also served in the form of a *seco*. The starch used in making these *secos* is one of two foods: potatoes or rice. Both are simply boiled, then drained and served without any condiment or seasoning beyond those in which they were cooked. Boiled potatoes may be served, or white rice, or both together. If both are served, the potatoes are placed in the bowl, then rice is mounded on top, totally covering the potatoes. The meat, such as *cuy,* or other toppings (see Figure 7) is then placed on top of the mounded starch. This meal, however, like all Zumbagua meals, may be made solely of starches: potatoes and/or rice are frequently served alone, without any accompaniment.

This type of *seco,* if it does not include *cuy,* is eaten occasionally in many households simply for variety's sake and as something of a treat. It is especially appropriate, however, when guests come to call, and more especially if those guests are wealthy or "white" in comparison to their

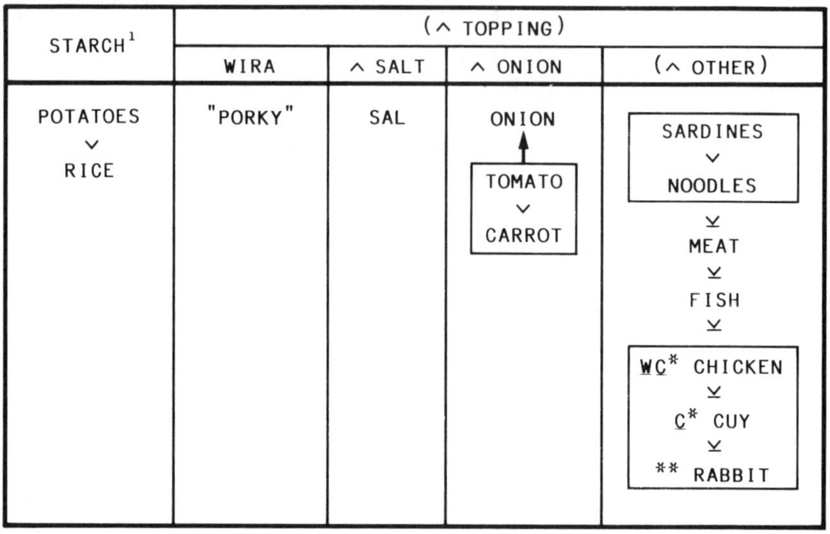

STARCH[1]	($\wedge$ TOPPING)			
	WIRA	$\wedge$ SALT	$\wedge$ ONION	($\wedge$ OTHER)
POTATOES $\vee$ RICE	"PORKY"	SAL	ONION $\uparrow$ TOMATO $\vee$ CARROT	SARDINES $\vee$ NOODLES $\veebar$ MEAT $\veebar$ FISH $\veebar$ WC* CHICKEN $\veebar$ C* CUY $\veebar$ ** RABBIT

[1]ALTHOUGH THIS STARCH IS SERVED <u>SECO</u> (DRY), IT IS FIRST COOKED IN WATER AS THOUGH TO MAKE A <u>SOPA</u>, THEN DRAINED. IN THE <u>SOPA</u> STAGE, THE STARCH IS COOKED AS FOLLOWS:

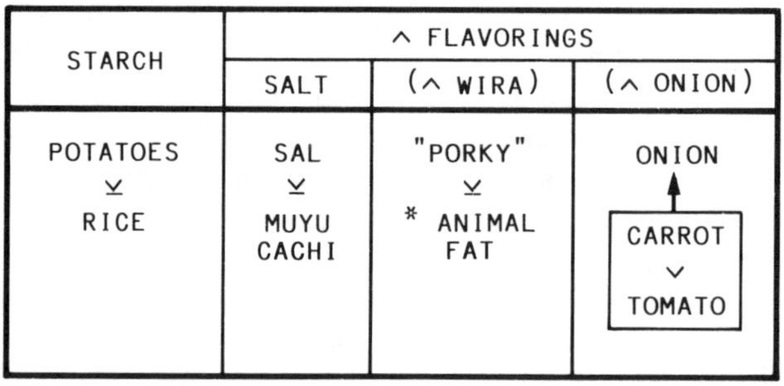

STARCH	$\wedge$ FLAVORINGS		
	SALT	($\wedge$ WIRA)	($\wedge$ ONION)
POTATOES $\veebar$ RICE	SAL $\veebar$ MUYU CACHI	"PORKY" $\veebar$ * ANIMAL FAT	ONION $\uparrow$ CARROT $\vee$ TOMATO

Figure 7. Schematic depiction of the type 1 *seco*.

hosts. If they are very wealthy or very white, however, the issue may not be whether to serve *cuy* as a *seco*, but whether to serve *cuy* at all.

The *cuy*, as I have said, symbolizes certain types of relationships. The meanings it has are most appropriate for the relationship of *compadrazgo;* one raises *cuyes*, in fact, "because one has compadres." But for high-status compadres, *cuy* is not appropriate, or at any rate not sufficient: chicken takes its place. For example, the white bus-driver, Don Lucho, who is *padrino* and compadre to many *indígenas*, does not eat *cuy*. "My wife eats it," he explains, "She's from here. I'm from Valencia [a town on the western slopes]." Lucho is fat, wealthy, many times a father. He is reputed to have shamanic powers. He can afford to drink beer, not *trago,* and he does not eat *cuy.*

There are *secos,* then, of *cuy* or of chicken, of potatoes or of rice. If a *sopa* is made for a special occasion, it may be of potatoes and *cuy,* or of chicken and rice. All of these dishes signify a special occasion and a meal in someone's honor. But not all permutations of these ingredients and techniques are possible. In the special-occasion *sopa,* potatoes, and chicken do not occur simultaneously; neither do rice and *cuy.* The parallelism of rice and potato is only possible in the *seco* form, where the form itself suggests whiteness.

The Informal Seco: Habas

When I helped to plant *habas* (fava beans), the family tried patiently to show me how to handle a hoe. "Like this, Marya, like this." I was a slow learner. Trying to soften a reprimand, Taita Juanchu, the patriarch, added, "So we can eat *jabus* at Easter."

That phrase, *jabus* for Easter, became a refrain for the day. And in the months that followed, as people shared with me soups of *jabus pulvu* (dried *haba* flour) and snacks of toasted *habas,* they would say, "But by Easter there will be *llullu jabus*" (fresh *habas*).

Why, I wondered, did *llullu jabus* matter so much? Anticipation of them seemed to color the months that followed Reyes (the Feast of the Three Kings). When *habas* first appeared in meals, there were just a handful, thrown into a soup. Attentive eyes had picked out those few, ripe before the rest, among thousands of beans not yet ready. Eating the soup, I thought I understood their appeal: in a diet in which most of the ingredients are dried, processed starches, the bright green *habas* seemed unbelievably tasty and appealing. Their freshness, texture, and color contrasted sharply against the grays and browns, the smooth, bland softness of other foods.

As we entered into the fullness of the season, I learned that these qualities are only part of *llullu jabus*'s appeal. In Zumbagua, a great deal of formality is observed when serving and eating everyday meals. The size and composition of each portion, the order of serving, the relative height of seats are arranged to correspond with the relative status of those eating together; respect for the women serving is shown through the uttering of specific words of request and thanks. All of this ceremony changes, once the *llullu jabus* are big enough to be eaten. The etiquette (further described in Chapter 6) that has been scrupulously observed day after day from June to March is suddenly dropped.

S

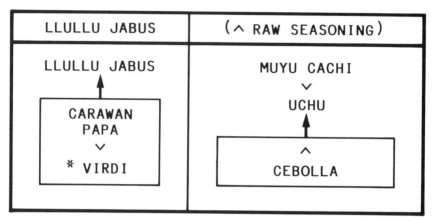

Figure 8. Schematic depiction of the type 2 *seco*.

A fava bean has a thick skin; even boiling does not soften it sufficiently for human consumption. When putting a handful of *habas* in a soup, a woman painstakingly removes the skin from each bean. But most *almuirzus* of the *llullu jabus* season consist primarily of *habas*: to peel them all would be impossible.

For this reason, when a large number of *llullu jabus* are cooked, they are simply cooked in their skins. The water is drained off and the beans are dumped into a wooden trough called a *batea*. In startling contrast to the formality observed during the serving of *sopas*, the entire *batea* is then placed on the floor and everyone eats from it together. This casual sharing, and the relaxed atmosphere it produces, are very much enjoyed. Status hierarchies are for the most part forgotten (although the patriarch or matriarch may be served apart, and the young *kachun* [daughter-in-law] may hesitate to join in). These intimate family meals are especially enjoyed by older children no longer allowed to snatch food from their parent's dish or from the cooking pot, liberties still enjoyed by their younger siblings. Squatting knee-to-knee with his father, a young boy pops beans into his mouth and tosses the skins in perfect contentment.

Llullu jabus seem to make rules irrelevant. Enamelware bowls and spoons lie untouched as the family eats out of a *batea,* a container normally reserved for raw foods or for feeding animals. And when potatoes are cooked with the *llullu jabus,* as they often are, the *papas* are served *carawan:* with their skins on. Like the *llullu jabus,* they are only peeled as they are eaten. Sometimes *virdis* (plantains) are added to the mixture as well. They too are sliced and cooked in the skin, which is discarded as the *virdis* are eaten. All of this peeling and tossing of skins adds to the general air of lively, informal activity as the meal is eaten.

Fanesca

In national Ecuadorian cuisine, Semana Santa (Easter Week) is marked by a traditional *sopa*, *fanesca*. *Fanesca* is made with fish, a Christian symbol, and with a variety of fresh beans, grains, and pulses, symbols of the harvest. *Fanesca* is also eaten in Zumbagua, in forms that vary widely according to the acculturation and economic resources of the household. In the parish, Semana Santa opens the season of eating fresh, green things of all sorts, and the preparation of *fanesca* celebrates this event. Everyone has *llullu jabus;* some buy maize, lentils, squashes, peas. Acculturated households struggle to be able to afford fish, while traditional families butcher a sheep.[4]

The period from Easter to Corpus Christi, the most alive and vital period of the Zumbagua year, is framed by celebrations in the plaza. But, on a daily basis, this period is marked by a change in meals: first, the appearance of *fanesca;* then, the series of *llullu jabus* meals, with their festive atmosphere and brightly colored, fresh-tasting beans, sign of the ripening harvest. The fiesta cycle and the agricultural cycle are closely intertwined, material practice and cosmology reinforcing each other. Between these two extremes lie the small rituals of every day, the cooking of meals, which is both ritual and work, both mundane and signifying.

The Raw and the Cooked: *Uchu* and *Cachi*

When a woman places a *batea* full of hot *llullu jabus* on the floor, she may then take a handful of *muyu cachi*, strong raw salt, and set it on the rim of the *batea* for people to eat with the *habas*. Even better than *cachi* is *ají/uchu*, capsicum pepper.

Uchu is often made into a sauce by pounding the peppers in a special mortar, called an *uchu rumi* (pepper stone), together with raw onion and rock salt. Water is then added to this paste to thin it. Usually the *uchu* stone is simply set in the center of the floor, and people add *uchu* to their food at will, according to individual taste.

The casual manner in which *uchu* sauce is put within reach of people as they eat, instead of being served to them, makes it an appropriate accompaniment to *llullu jabus*. But *uchu* can be eaten with any savory dish, especially potatoes. No matter what the meal context, however, *uchu* is always simply placed within reach of those eating.

Use of *uchu* varies by gender to a much greater degree than any other food. Eating *uchu* is associated with maleness; many women claim it is too "strong" (*chinchi*) or bitter (*jayaj*) for them. Men, in contrast, eat it with great enjoyment. Like other gender prescriptions, there is no rigidity to this division. Many women openly enjoy *uchu*, while some men do not much care for it. Nevertheless, the implicit maleness of *uchu* can be seen in the categories of women likely to eat it: many young, unmarried girls do not eat *uchu*, while postmenstrual women are more likely to eat it than are those of child-bearing age. Women and girls frequently asked me whether I liked *uchu*. I realized that it was a way of finding out about my personality: was I a bold, daring woman, or mild and retiring?

A significant aspect of the maleness of *uchu* is the fact that it is served raw. Few foods, with the exception of fruit, are eaten without being cooked first. Even water is considered dangerous if drunk "raw."

In fact, while *uchu* is never cooked, men eat it in a form that is more "raw" than that in which both sexes eat it. *Uchu* is not always eaten in the form of a sauce. The raw peppers may simply be left lying on a convenient shelf. Men of the family will then grab a pepper at will and hack off a piece to eat along with their meal. Although women eat *uchu* sauces, they will not eat it in its unprepared state, and it is not offered to women visitors when in this form. Thus *uchu* is always uncooked, but women eat it only after it has been somewhat removed from a purely raw state by being subjected to the (feminine) culinary process of making sauce.

The word *jayaj* (bitter), used to describe *uchu* and *muyu cachi*, has connotations of maleness, of rawness, and of strength. The lowland hallucinogen *ayahuasca*, usually translated as *aya huasca*, soul vine, is understood by highland Quichua-speakers to mean *jayaj huasca*, bitter vine. This vine, connected with the male domain of shamanism and cooked by male shamans into a bitter drink is, along with *uchu*, *jayaj*.[5]

It seems that the qualities of *jayaj* foods also belong to *trago*, the strong cane alcohol of the Andes. It, too, is drunk mostly by males (and it, too, is of lowland origins). Its association with maleness is suggested by the practice of blowing mouthfuls of *trago* over the bulls during Corpus Christi to make them more *bravo*."[6]

For men, drinking *trago* is an inescapable part of social life. Women are offered *trago*, but many of them make a show of refusing it because it is too "strong." Again, a woman's willingness to drink *trago* is an expression of her age role—women with children stay away from it more than do the elderly—and of her personality. The same bold women who boast of eating potatoes with *uchu* are those who get boisterously drunk at fiestas. Similarly, cigarettes are harsh, strong products without nutritive qualities, used mostly by men.

It is more difficult to associate *cachi* with maleness. Women use it in cooking, and Cheryl Pomeroy has suggested that, far from being associated with males, salt may in fact have female associations in the Ecuadorian highlands (n.d.). But the applicability of this suggestion to Zumbagua is questionable, for the association is based on salt being produced by women in areas in which salt was obtained from highland springs. Salt is not locally produced in Zumbagua and I know of no indication that it ever was, though it is certainly possible that salt-producing springs were among the resources of the *yunga* zone exploited in earlier times.

Uchu and *cachi* do seem to belong together, and it seems likely that their meanings are similar as well. Frank Salomon suggests that the history and significance of the two seasonings are similar in the Ecuadorian Andes (1980). When eaten with *llullu jabus,* the use of *cachi* parallels that of *uchu,* and *uchu* sauce is actually made of *uchu* and *cachi* together. *Uchu* and *cachi,* when eaten in this form, are unusual items in the cuisine not only for the informality of their consumption but because they are eaten raw. It is these uncooked foods that are *jayaj,* while everything that is cooked, and so made by women, is not *jayaj* but *mishqui.*

Mishqui is a word that is difficult to translate. Sugar is called simply *mishqui,* but so too are the packets of flavorings called *sabor* in Spanish. Either sweet or savory things, if they are well cooked and well seasoned, are *mishqui.* An opposition seems to exist between *jayaj* and *mishqui,* *jayaj* being associated with things that are powerful, strong tasting, or raw, and with maleness, and *mishqui* describing what is tasty, easy to eat, nutritive, cooked, and belonging to the female domain.

Sweet gruels can be made of *arroz de cebada* or of *máchica,* or of other types of flours or meals (see Figure 9), but the ultimate *mishqui* food, the meal that is simply called by the name *mishqui,* is a sweet gruel made of barley and eaten in the morning or at night. *Mishqui* made of *arroz de cebada* is cooked and served like a *sopa,* but when it is made using *máchica,* there are striking parallels to the serving of *uchu. Máchica* is not doled out by the cook like other foods, but is simply placed on the floor where everyone can reach it, in the same way as *uchu.* And, as with *uchu,* hosts may press *máchica* on a guest, but only verbally (while bowls of soup or potatoes are offered and cannot be refused).

There are also parallels in the preparation of the two foods. The Zumbagua kitchen is equipped with two *rumis,* or mortars and pestles, the small *uchu rumi* used for preparing *uchu* sauce and the enormous *kutana*

HOT WATER	∧ STARCH	∧ SWEETENER	(∧ FRUIT)	(∧ ACHIOTE)	(∧ MILK)
HOT WATER W*** COLD WATER[1] →	MÁCHICA ⌄ ARROZ DE CEBADA ⌄ "QUAKER" ⌄ BREAD[2] ⌄ COOKIES[2] ⌄ *** MAIZE	RAPADURA ⌄ SUGAR ←	← S CAPULÍ	C* ACHIOTE	*** MILK

[1] AT TIME OF SERVING, NOT OF COOKING
[2] NOT COOKED

Variant 1: *cafe*

W

HOT WATER	∧ FLAVORING	∧ SWEETENER	∧ BREAD	(∧ HARD-BOILED EGG)
HOT WATER	INSTANT COFFEE ⌄ SWEET HERB →	SUGAR ⌄ RAPADURA ↑	BREAD[1] ⌄ COOKIES	W*** HARD-BOILED EGG

[1] NOT COOKED

Variant 2: *colada morada*

W
C

HOT WATER	∧ STARCH	∧ SWEETENER	W∧ FLAVORINGS	W∧ FRUIT
	MÁCHICA ⌄ ARROZ DE CEBADA ⌄ "QUAKER" ⌄ W* MOROCHO ⌄ W* MAIZE ⌄ W* MAIZ COLORADO	SUGAR ⌄ RAPADURA	W* HOJA DE NARANJA ⌄ W* CANELA ⌄ W* ARRAYAN ⌄ W* ETC.	W** RASPBERRIES ⌄ W** BLUEBERRIES ⌄ W*** PINEAPPLE

Figure 9. Schematic depiction of the sweet *colada*.

rumi, or grinding stone, used for making *máchica* and other flours and meals.

Contrasts between *uchu* and *máchica* are equally striking, however. Whereas *uchu* is a seldom enjoyed luxury, superfluous to the meal, an imported food from lower altitudes, *máchica* is a staple food, entirely produced by the household. Barley is grown from the household's own store of seeds and is ideally threshed, stored, toasted, and ground without ever leaving the family's own property. Even though many households in fact take their grain into town to be ground in the mill, women adamantly insist, as a point of honor, that they themselves grind every grain of *máchica* consumed by their households themselves. Only stone-ground *máchica,* they insist, is *mishqui.*

Meals and Treats: *Wanlla*

As I stated at the beginning of this chapter, foods are several different kinds of things: elements in a diet, signs in a cuisine, symbols in discourse, products of an economy. The semiotic roles given foods are shaped by economic aspects of their use, and both semiotic and economic determinants in turn inform their use as symbols. The category of foods defined as *wanlla* (see Table 1) is a classic example of this interrelationship.

Not every food eaten in Zumbagua is part of a meal. There is *kukawi,* food people carry with them to eat out in the field or pasture, for example, and then there is *wanlla,* food that by definition does not form part of a meal.

In Chapter 3, I defined *wanlla* as treats or snacks. But *wanlla* also has other meanings. The second meaning of *wanlla* is "gift." All of the foods called *wanlla* are primarily purchased in order to be redistributed. The motivation is not so much altruism as the exercise of power: giving *wanlla* is a critically important social and political action in Zumbagua; no one can be a successful social actor without understanding how to give and how to manipulate others into giving. *Wanlla* is double-edged: within the family, or when done on a small scale, the giving of *wanlla* expresses a relationship of superiority/inferiority: men give *wanlla* to women, parents to children, rich benefactors to the humble poor. To give *wanlla* to a social equal, such as a sibling, is both to offer them pleasure and to gain a slight advantage in prestige over them; to offer this type of *wanlla* to those who consider themselves your social superior is to insult them.

Giving *wanlla* is an important part of relations among household members. To return home after a journey without bringing *wanlla* would be unthinkable. The concept of *wanlla* is also involved when several household members go together to the market. Each carries a small hoard of spending money, the exact amount undisclosed to the others. They separate at the market and periodically meet again, making overt and covert purchases of various dry goods and supplies. Each in turn buys a treat: a cooked fish, a plate of *papas,* which is shared out with the others. Each burst of generosity impels the others to follow suit. Generosity and stinginess are never commented on at the time, but each one's behavior will be discussed in detail and with relish later.

In other contexts, *wanlla* expresses respect and the acknowledgment of an ongoing relationship. A woman's siblings bring *wanlla* when she bears a new child. Adult children who have established their own household bring *wanlla* when they go to share festive meals with their parents. *Wanlla* of this sort, while it may be adorned or embellished with fruit, cookies, and the like, is usually in the form of uncooked staples. Noodles, flour, rice, or other purchased foods are the preferred form, but a much larger amount of local produce may be substituted.

Gifts of food may similarly be given to those of superior status prefatory to asking a favor or after receiving one. These gifts, however, are not called *wanlla* but have various names depending on the exact nature of the occasion. (For example, gifts given in thanks are *agradecimiento; ofrenda\sirichi* are foods given to the dead.)

Any food given as a gift can be called *wanlla.* Hence in certain contexts rice, onions, noodles, milk, or any other food could be *wanlla.* Some foods, however, are always *wanlla* in nature. They do not form part of regular meals and their primary purpose, in Zumbagua eyes, is as gifts. Because eating in Zumbagua always takes the form of offering and receiving food, these foods are still *wanlla* even when bought by members of a household and consumed within that household.

Wanlla is by definition food that is unnecessary and insignificant; and yet *wanlla* is not without importance, nutritional, emotional, social, and political. What separates the poor from the rich in the parish is not lack of staples but the keenly felt lack of those special little treats: an orange, a bag of sweet breads, a tasty little something brought home from an excursion. The good husband, the beloved mother, the dutiful daughter, the loving sister are known by the *wanlla* they give, even if it is just half of a cold potato pancake wrapped in a greasy scrap of paper, or a couple of ten-for-a-sucre candies.

Cookies, crackers, and candies are indispensable as *wanlla.* For a man coming home to a house full of kids with only a few sucres to spend on treats, or a girl who wants to buy something at the market that she can share with siblings and playfriends left at home, sweets are the only affordable option. At weddings and fiestas they are necessary to provide part of the general atmosphere of extravagance and fun. Shopkeepers depend on candies as inexpensive *yapas* for favored customers. Sweets are lubricants for social interactions of many kinds, in a society in which the expectation of food gifts conflicts with the inability to provide.

I have said that *wanlla* can mean "snack" or it can mean "gift." The latter translation opens the door to a third interpretation: a *wanlla* is a food that is being used as a symbol: a thing that stands for something else (Turner 1967; Geertz 1973). When something tangible, a food, is used to represent something intangible, that food becomes *wanlla*. The "something intangible" is social in nature: to say "*wanlla*" is to describe a social interaction taking place between two people: mother and child, husband and wife, two sisters, or two comadres. In calling a food *wanlla* the people of the parish are calling attention to a relation between social and material realities that is radically different from that of fetishization (Marx 1977). An object such as a food becomes fetishized when the social relations behind its production are made invisible; it becomes *wanlla* when its material existence is subordinated to its social import. When an object is changed from a possession into a gift, it must become a symbol as well.

Notes

1. A fourth, less significant major cultigen, different from the other three, is the onion. Onions are grown in the higher areas of the parish as a cash crop, primarily by young adults. There is some suggestion that onions are being adopted as a cash crop throughout the higher reaches of the central provinces. Their presence in the Zumbagua landscape is a recent phenomenon, according to maps made by the Instituto Geográfico Militar based on aerial photographs taken in 1963. These maps suggest that twenty years ago there were no significant amounts of onions grown in the parish. Today, an entire upper plaza of the Saturday market is given over to the onion sellers, and buses and trucks going down to the Inter-Andean Valley markets carry loads of onions. It is only in the upper *comunas* that onions are grown in quantity, but their presence in the parish diet is not limited to these higher areas. Almost every family in Zumbagua has access to a steady supply of onions through links of gift-giving and reciprocity, whatever the altitude at which the family itself lives.

2. In using the term "metalanguage," I do not mean to imply that signs lifted out of the semiotic system, in order to serve as metasystemic comments on that system, are then simply constituted into a new system of signs, as Barthes (1965:89–94) would claim. Although these signs exist in patterned relation to

one another, being, for example, organized into contrastive pairs, the operation of elements at this metasystemic level is much closer to Turner's description of the operation of a symbol than to the more limited functions Barthes ascribes to signs.

3. Noodles, like flour, are a purchased food that is fully integrated into indigenous cuisine, without "white" connotations. The proportion of noodles eaten by a household depends on its integration into the cash economy. For more agriculturally based households without a family member working outside the parish, noodles have somewhat of a special value as "bought," hence hard-to-get, food. At the same time, noodle soup is such a common poor-man's meal that landless families and men who work in the cities find no joy in *fideos*.

Nevertheless, one piece of evidence suggests that certain purchased foods such as flour, oatmeal, and noodles (and certain cheap cookies and crackers sold in quantity), though not associated with the white, the wealthy, or special-occasion meals, enjoy a special status distinct from locally produced staples. They are the socially appropriate gift to bring when a raw-ingredient food gift is expected, for instance when one's sibling becomes a parent. Bread, fruit, or special starches such as rice, maize, or potatoes would be incorrect; they are used to ingratiate, to pave the way for a costly demand such as fiesta sponsorship, marriage, or *compadrazgo*. Local products, fava beans or wool, would also be inappropriate. They do not mark an occasion, and rather suggest payment or charity to an impoverished family member or compadre. Bags of noodles, flour, or oatmeal acknowledge an event in the life of an equal.

Although the substitution of flour or strained oatmeal for *máchica* in an everyday *colada* would not occasion any comment, no amount of barley in any form would be appropriate as a gift in the type of circumstances in which these other foods are expected.

4. Dishes such as *fanesca* and *colada morada* (Figure 9, variant 2), which is made for All Souls' Day, are labeled as "traditional indigenous dishes" in national Ecuadorian cuisine. But although these dishes undoubtedly entered national cuisine from an indigenous cuisine, that does not mean that they are native to all indigenous cuisines of the highlands. In Zumbagua, Easter fish and November black maize are equally alien, and both *fanesca* and *colada morada,* having been introduced into the parish by "whites," are considered part of "white" cuisine.

5. In many parts of the world, male cooking of ritual foods contrasts with female secular cooking.

6. This practice is reminiscent of shamans blowing *trago* and/or cigarette smoke over a patient during curing sessions. *Trago* is particularly associated with shamans.

FIVE

Food in Discourse: Everyday Symbols in Ideological Conflict

In this chapter, foods are considered in their role as symbols, material things that evoke a wealth of condensed, ambiguous meanings. The symbolic usages discussed here are those which occur in the context of discourse; the meanings explored are primarily ideological.

In order to illustrate the action of foods as ideologically charged symbols in everyday discourse, I begin by recounting an incident between neighbors taken from my field notes. In interpreting this incident fully, I leave behind the realm of diet and cuisine to look at other aspects of Zumbagua reality: ideology and desire, racism and money, the lives of unmarried girls. After introducing these themes, I return to the topic of food itself: barley, which may be opposed to rice in discourses; and bread, the small, white *panes* that have emerged as the focus of friction in households, illustrating the shift in arenas of discourse over time, new battlefields being staked out as territories are ceded from past defeats.

To begin, a story about neighbors.

In the *comuna* of Yanatoro on the slope they call Rumichaca, a rare warm day coaxes a woman out of her windowless house to enjoy the afternoon sun. As she sits with her children at the edge of the patio, a neighbor couple hails her and, crossing the path that divides her land from theirs, joins her. They are careful to sit on the bank of the path and not on the patio itself, but nevertheless she is a little taken aback. Such casual intimacy is not an everyday occurrence among neighbors who are not family. She is ill at ease at first, and little is said. The women's hands are busy: she picking lice out of her son's hair, her neighbor's wife mending. The man stretches out in the relaxed, reclining position characteristic of men in leisure moments, and makes idle good-humored comments.

Gradually a desultory conversation develops; the woman mentions that she is cooking *nabus*,[1] a leafy green plant that grows as an adventive among cultivated plants. "Oh," exclaims her neighbor, "*Nabus*, those are good. Fried in a little oil, with white rice, that's the way to eat *nabus*." At once the tentative rapport is broken; his wife looks reproachfully at him, and after a few minutes of awkward silence, the neighbors leave. Later the woman will angrily complain to a kinswoman, "Who does he think he is? I say *nabus* and he starts talking about white rice."

Two foods, *nabus* and white rice, function metonymically in this conversation to represent larger differences of economy and status, ethnicity and culture. In announcing with pleasure that she is cooking *nabus*, a poor woman celebrates the availability of a seasonal green, leafy food to supplement an otherwise meager meal of barley. In contrast to vegetables such as carrots, tomatoes, or cabbage, which are available only through purchase from "white" market women from the outside, *nabus* spring up spontaneously in the fields and can be had for the taking. All that is required is the knowledge that they are edible. They are eaten by human and animal alike; in December, when the yellow flowers show their heads in the fields above the tops of the barley and fava beans, people watching the herds stand in the fields picking the long, leggy stalks and throwing them to the sheep, painstakingly gathering these "weeds" from the fields in seed and throwing them into the fallow fields where the sheep graze, so as to ease in any small way they can the overgrazing of fields in fallow. The use of *nabus* is part of the household ecology, the management of farmstead resources in which human and livestock consumption is so closely integrated, and all forms of waste or excess are carefully controlled.

The name of this food also evokes the whole experience of seasonality. Market vegetables are available year-round, but local foods come and go in accordance with the season. Just as fresh fava beans are inseparable from the special period between Semana Santa and Corpus Christi, so the idea of *nabus* must inevitably call to mind the early ripening of crops, the quiescent and impoverished period after the work of planting is done and the debts have been incurred, but when the harvest is still far away.

Nabus are not a very important food, even in Zumbagua. Unlike white rice, they do not frequently turn up as a topic of conversation. Nevertheless, making use of these "weeds" is almost a subversive activity. This food is so far from being a part of the market economy that not only is it not bought and sold, it is not even sown but only gathered. The categories of experience it evokes make the mention of the humble *nabus* counterhegemonic: seasonality, locality, and most of all the casual, spontaneous act of gathering it while doing something else. This experience of productive activity is one that is far removed from the rigid definition of work and play found in a wage-labor system. To a male neighbor with aspirations to a life-style firmly entrenched in the cash economy, this complex of referents must be put in its place, just as the local culture must be known in its "real" status as a backward and old-fashioned enclave in a large and exciting world. "*Nabus?*" he says: "fry them in oil and eat them with white rice."

Rice, grown on the coast where no *indios* live, arrives in Zumbagua as part of the wares of "white" merchants from the Inter-Andean Valley, who sell it along with other expensive processed goods such as white sugar and bottled cooking oil. And with the rice, he suggests serving *fried* greens. Frying is the most expensive cooking method possible in a Zumbagua kitchen. As a method of preparing vegetables, it is also alien to indigenous cooking traditions. So in response to her implicit suggestion, "Isn't it nice for us poor people that we can get something good, *nabus,* for free?" he is trying to establish himself as someone who may eat *nabus,* but not because he is "poor and Indian" and must rely on what he can grow. (His attempt to do so was not a little pathetic, for in fact those who eat white rice and fried foods do not eat *nabus:* his imagined meal is one that belongs to no cuisine.)

Although the man in question certainly could not afford to eat white rice with fried vegetables all the time, his aspiration to do so sets him apart from his neighbor and reflects on her poverty—as her insulted reaction, and his wife's embarrassment, clearly show. In the context of this conversation, *nabus* and white rice represent alternative complexes of practice and experience. In the naked topography of Zumbagua, these two neighboring households live lives transparently visible to one another: husbands' drunken anger, children's misbehavior, slowness in getting the fava beans shelled or the barley threshed are common knowledge between them. Thus discrepancies between the two households, which go beyond relative poverty to life choices about work, language, clothing, money—food—are always known and seen, always enacted against the backdrop of the neighboring family's decisions.

The differences between these neighbors can perhaps most clearly be demonstrated through their daughters. Both have unmarried adolescent daughters, but there the resemblance ends. The poor woman's daughter is absolutely monolingual in Quichua; she lives a circumscribed life, working in the fields surrounding the house, watching the sheep, cooking and tending her younger siblings. She is her mother's workhorse, freeing the older woman to work in the fields of kinsmen. To her neighbors, the daughter is the object of pity and scorn. Their own daughter is exceptional. She is one of a very small group of young women in the parish who have used opportunities provided by the church to gain an education and a paid job as a nurse's aide in the local government clinic. Fluent in Spanish and flush with cash, with a bedroom at the clinic and one at home, and friends in all the nearby towns, she is utterly independent, her parents' pride and their despair.

This young woman is a symbol of success achieved in the nonindigenous world. Twice I have heard the song\monologue of drunks reduced to the simple repetition of her name, though neither time was she or had she been present: the recitation of her name alone was an incantation about winning in the white world. Once it was an older male relative who sang it with pride, but once it was the drunken lament of two girls her age whose own attempts to follow a similar road had met with failure.

Her status in the community is a mixed one. She is beloved of most of the white community as a "model Indian," but her gossiping, arrogance, tight clothes and high heels, and constant flirtations with white boys earn her the censure of much of the indigenous community. The women are especially quick to criticize but also to envy her. Envy of the daughter coexists with pity for her mother, who has lost her daughter's labor in the household economy and gained precious little beyond reflected prestige in return. The parents' continuous efforts to extract cash from her are only intermittently successful. The money she gives them is nowhere near enough to satisfy her father's risen expectations of the life-style such a professional woman's family should by osmosis enjoy.

But the conversation in the sunshine involved foodstuffs, not daughters. Even to mention, however obliquely, the criticisms each had of the way the other's daughter lives, would be to cause an irreparable breach. Such family enmity could last for generations. Talking about cooking is far safer: the sense of insult only lasted a few days.

The mention of *nabus* was fairly incidental; it is neither an important food nor a frequent topic of conversation. White rice, by contrast, is a food with unmistakable symbolic import. I do not mean to say that the appearance of white rice always causes controversy. It may be served and eaten without calling forth a political discourse. Its homology with boiled potatoes in indigenous cooking practice suggest an equation between the two foods. And yet the choice to serve white rice is always a more conscious and deliberate one than a decision, say, to make soup with a base of ground barley rather than fava-bean flour. And, critically, white rice emerges in discourse: people talk about it, and they use their talk about it to discuss other things.

To speak of white rice can call into question the whole complex of foods and cooking techniques that constitute everyday, unreflective indigenous practice. For "Indians," it is a luxury, a special-occasion food, something to serve a guest. Younger families are anxious to assert their identities as knowledgeable and conversant with the ways of the outside world, not the "dumb burros" "everyone" (out there) thinks they are (because they are *runa*). They may make a point of eating a meal that includes white rice once every few weeks even though just the family is present. But they do so quite deliberately, as part of an effort to construct an identity for themselves in contradistinction to what they see as old and ignorant lives.

White families, by contrast, eat white rice every day, with every meal. It is their staple food, the mainstay of their diet. Eating white rice for white families is *doxa:* ordinary unreflective practice. But for "Indians" it is quite different. Not only does the grain itself, with its coastal plantation (non-Sierran) origins, differentiate it from local foods, but the method of preparation and eating, as *seco* rather than *sopa,* distinguishes it from indigenous main dishes. To the indigenous people of Zumbagua, *secos* are expensive dishes, found in social circles from which they are excluded. The *seco de carne (pescado, gallina, chivo,* and so on)—meat served on a bed of rice—is the meal characteristic of restaurants and market stalls, where "Indians" rarely if ever eat. Not only poverty but racism prevents them from entering many eating establishments; even in the lowest of low-class eateries, an "Indian" may be driven away with kicks, slaps, and curses if he dares try to sit at a table.

These experiences have caused white rice to emerge as a topic of discourse in Zumbagua, where it stands for the class of people, "whites," who customarily eat it, and for "Indians" who aspire to be like them. Derogatory comments about those who "pretend to eat rice every day" are heard, such as "who does he think he is, talking about white rice?" quoted before. But rice is often mentioned wistfully, as the emblem of an unattainable life of prosperity. White rice, quite an ordinary sign in the semiotic system of "white" cooking practice, functions metalinguistically in the indigenous food system as a symbol of the alien "white" system.

The symbolic weight accorded to rice differs markedly from that accorded to most foods. White it is true that all foods, insofar as they form part of a semiotic system, must carry meaning, the meanings evoked by most foods remain quiescent, unrecognized. Fava beans, noodles, onions, or flour can be used in actual practice or named in discourse without arousing comment or criticism. They occupy a specific category, a role, a place, in the semiotic system, but it is a silent one. In Pierre Bourdieu's terms they occupy "the field of doxa, that which is taken for granted" (1979:166). They could also be described as falling into the realm of the preconscious. It is not that their symbolic role cannot be known by the conscious mind, but simply that in ordinary usage it need not.

But according to Bourdieu, *doxa,* "the theses implied in a particular way of living," the semiotic system underlying practice, is not always allowed to remain unselfconscious and unexamined. An awareness of the system, even a "practical questioning" of it, "is brought about by 'culture contact' or by the political and economic crises correlative with class division" (1979:168); the mechanism for this questioning lies in the oppositional role accorded to a particular element, in this case rice.

In Zumbagua, white rice poses a question, a challenge, to the doxa of everyday foods. It enters Zumbagua discourse as the consciously recognized symbol of alien cultural practices. Such symbols have ideological valences. They become charged with political meanings. Unlike the complaisant silence of most foods, which fill their roles without calling attention to themselves, the presence of these marked foods is a shout, a call to be noticed. In Zumbagua, white rice occupies a controversial position, a speaking part in the ongoing drama; it confronts the doxa of indigenous foodways and challenges its validity. Its own symbolic burden as "white" food problematizes the status of every other element in the cuisine. Just to bring it up, as in the conversation that opens this chapter, is to cast a shadow on the doxa of everyday indigenous life. In Bourdieu's terms, the role of white rice in Zumbagua creates "a *field of opinion,* the locus of the confrontation of competing discourses—whose political truth may be overtly declared or may remain hidden, even from the eyes of those engaged in it" (ibid.).

It would be possible to say that white rice, once an alien food, is being "integrated" into Zumbagua cuisine, that a form of "assimilation" or "syncretism" between two cuisines is taking place. But to do so would be to gloss over the confrontational nature of its presence in parish life, the political nature of its role there. Within the realm of Zumbagua discourse, white rice is an antagonist, a flag of the hegemonic pressure to subvert the doxa of indigenous practice.

The symbolic power of this "white" food can only be understood through an exploration of whole spheres of meaning in which the insubstantiality and inconsequence of indigenous life are projected. Two such spheres are the ideology of racism and the market of desire. Each sphere contributes something to the power of white rice, which carries an allure, a capacity to beguile, even though it is acknowledged to be a less substantial food than barley, fava beans, or potatoes. It is still the most desirable, and this quality is connected with two facts about it: white people eat it, and it is bought in the market.

Commodity Fetishism and the Marketplace of Desire

The Western European and North American tourists whose jeeps pull into the plaza of Zumbagua on a Saturday, charmed by the mass of brightly colored ponchos and shawls and the "authenticity" of the crowd's windburned faces and work-gnarled hands, think of the market as quintessentially "Indian," a quaint and colorful custom showing that the people of the parish still cling to their traditional ways. As one spends time with the women of the parish, however, the market comes to appear instead as the very instrument of change, for it is the institution that educates women in the desire for purchasable goods. Hegemonic domination is primarily a matter of education, of penetration into a world view and into the structures of desire.

For children, the state provides a formal education that teaches lessons far more profound than the three Rs. Men also internalize new systems of thought. Their education occurs in the brutalizing experience of searching the cities for work, and in the words, gestures, and clothes of the *ingenieros* and work bosses they learn to admire and yearn to imitate. As they rethink the value of work and of money, they come to see the worthlessness of the handmade and the homegrown. But for women, integration into the national economy comes on Saturday mornings, when the dusty wind-whipped plaza is transformed by rows of stalls and piles of shiny, expensive things.

Like their children, Zumbagua women are being educated by the institutions of the larger society. The market is also a school, one in which commodity fetishism is the lesson being learned. At home, the pile of grain in the storeroom transparently represents an accumulation of human labor, the clearly remembered days of hoeing, scything, threshing of the previous year. But the piles of plastic bags filled with rice, noodles, and sugar at the market carry no such message. The moment of exchange in which they fall into one's hands is so effortless, if only one has the money to buy. No wonder the idiom used to describe experiences at the marketplace is that of longing and fulfillment, pleasure and desire.

For the Zumbagua marketplace is truly a marketplace of desire: questions about it always evoke responses not about necessities—it is not an Indian grocery store—but about delights. The question, "What do you buy at the market?" is always answered, "Anything, everything, whatever you want," using the word *gushtana,* which also means to enjoy, as in *fishta gushtana,* to enjoy or celebrate or go to a fiesta. The market is like a fiesta in which the eyes feast on delightful things.

For the men of the parish, home from the big city, the local market holds no such allure. Saturdays provide the pleasures of volleyball and drinking with friends, but the goods of the market itself have no special charm for them. It is only the women for whom the market exerts such a fascination. The goods it offers, food and clothing, are much more important to women than to their husbands. To a much greater degree than the larger markets of the Inter-Andean Valley, the Zumbagua market offers mostly things that appeal to women. Most of the fair is given over to food; the other major offerings are clothing and adornments. The narrow aisle between the clothing stalls is crowded with young couples and family groups fingering the bright plaid shawls and shiny decorated blouses. Big tables hold rows of ribbons, plastic beads, and hair ornaments, placards hung with a hundred pairs of earrings. Mirrors, needles, and acrylic yarn for crocheting underskirts are also piled up there: all are women's possessions.

This weekly playground of desire exerts a strong fascination over the women of the parish. All during the week, while their hands and bodies are given over to the tasks of the subsistence economy, women's conversations linger on prices, mythical bargains a luckier woman landed, the outrageous purchases of a spendthrift, the cruelty of the cholas in making the prices so high. The intensity of interest in the cost of chili peppers and the duration of conversations about it are simply incomprehensible to an outsider. One can only try to understand the fascination of such small purchases in a world in which money has not become the universal unit of exchange, but remains a scarce and precious substance operating in a separate realm of "nonnecessities," which nonetheless form the basis of social success. The cruelty of the steady incursion of expenditures on necessities into this economy of desires and delights is painfully felt and constantly discussed.

I met a very young girl with an unusual story, whose conversation alerted me to the significance of the Zumbagua market to the women and girls who go there. She had been forcibly taken by "whites" to work in Quito. In indigenous communities one frequently hears of this type of kidnapping of indigenous children, but in this case—unlike other rather horrible stories—the girl considered herself lucky. The family who had taken her did some small buying and selling in indigenous communities such as Zumbagua, so they brought her back fairly frequently, always on Saturdays. On these days, carefully dressed, she ostentatiously wandered the plaza meeting old acquaintances and making sundry purchases of hair ribbons and such. I asked her why she did not buy things in Quito, where there is so much to see and buy. She hesitated and finally answered that she knows the market here. It is probably true that she is lost and afraid in Quito, but the return to Zumbagua is not only for the reassurance of the familiar but for the satisfaction of old desires. Celebrating her riches in the eyes of her friends validates her prosperity in a way nothing else could quite match.

What her triumphant return to the market means can be seen by comparison to another young girl whose life is not so exceptional. She was a girl perhaps twelve years old, from a lower *comuna*. She had taken me with her around and around the market, partially to wheedle treats, but also because she simply assumed that anyone would enjoy just walking around the market looking and looking.

Like many young people, she is not allowed to come to the market every Saturday. Similarly, children are not taken every day to Corpus Christi, the seven-day harvest festival. The belief is that so much *gushtana* is bad for them. It would make them foolish instead of industrious and circumspect. Showing up at the market every Saturday, usually with a same-sex friend rather than with the family, is a mark of maturity, of the transition from *huambra* (kid) to *soltero/a,* unmarried young adult. Young people thus demonstrate their independence; also, the market provides a space for them to play out the elaborate games of gossip, teasing, friendships, and enmities among their peers, and to explore from afar, circumspectly, the attractions of the opposite sex.

The girl from the low *comuna* thoroughly enjoyed her day in the plaza, joining her parents to share a fried fish—a real delicacy—then abandoning them to visit her grandmother, a rather destitute old widow who attempts to sell cardboard boxes, spoons, and matches as an adjunct to a good-natured chola who has adopted her (she is a likable old thing, greedy and demanding in the childish way of the very old).

When I accompanied the girl on the road back to her *comuna*, she stopped to point someone out to me, a young woman who, she said, was a widow. The words tumbling out with excitement, she told me of this woman's fabulous life. Unable to support herself when her husband died, she had made the trek to Quito looking for work—a rarity among these women, and one that must have earned her some censure. Now she had a job shelling fava beans in a Quito market. Said the child with shining eyes, she comes back here on the weekends and on Saturday she goes to the market. She has a lot of money, she can buy whatever she wants.

Beauty and Power: Ideologies of Race

To a woman who lives in the subsistence economy and perceives the cash economy as a separate sphere of prestige and special occasions, the enormous magic of "white" people, who live only on food they have bought, becomes apparent. Such people seem scarcely human, eating only white rice day in and day out, a food that is glamorous but insubstantial. *Runa* flesh is made of barley and potatoes, the fruits of their labor, but wealthy white bodies seem to be literally made of money. Children and even grown women with little exposure to strangers would indicate huge containers in my house and ask in all seriousness if they were filled with money. But the shared identity of the commodities at the market with the mysterious Otherness of "white" people was most clearly brought home to me by the girl from the low *comuna*. At first she was bashful when I bought her some sweets, but later she blossomed into an orgy of demands—"Buy it for me!"—that seemed sickening. I regretted that reaction a moment later, when she captured my hand in hers and began stroking it with her own callused fingers, commenting on its softness and whiteness. She looked up and said, half-joking but with great longing, "Buy it for me." Then she laughed at the absurdity of what she had just said and stopped asking for anything.

Phenotypic whiteness is generally considered to be beautiful. It is described by a word, *suca,* which to some extent contrasts with *runa*. The latter is a Quichua word originally meaning "us, people," but it has since taken on, in standard Ecuadorian spoken Spanish and in the vocabulary of Zumbagua Quichua speakers, a purely pejorative meaning. It has also changed from being a noun referring to a person to an adjective that can be applied to anything shoddy or second-rate, not unlike the English "nigger-rigged" or "jerry-rigged." (Note, however, that this usage is definitely not the case for all Ecuadorian Quichua speakers. See Whitten and Whitten 1985:13–16 for the Canelos Quichua of the Oriente; like the word "chicano" in the southwestern United States, it also has become a defiantly proud self-appellation among politicized indigenous people in the Sierra.)

In Zumbagua, *runa* is ugly and *suca* is beautiful. Not all attributes of racial whiteness are prized; facial hair, of which many Zumbagua men have a little, is definitely disliked, and the hirsuteness of white men's bodies, when glimpsed, causes reactions of disgust. But those few indigenous individuals who have light hair or eyes are considered to be blessed.

There is a noticeable admixture of Caucasian blood in the indigenous population of the parish, mostly due to the long years of hacienda living with its institutionalized miscegenation. Many *sucas* are acknowledged to be the illegitimate children of *mayordomos* (hacienda foremen or overseers). Still, while they may try to claim some special prestige due to their real or imagined influence with their absent parent or white half-siblings, they have a separate power, simply by virtue of their physical fairness.

For example, one man who had made a *suca padrino* to his younger son would frequently mention this fact, often coupling reference to the *padrino*'s fairness with a discussion of the glossy, fat healthiness of his toddler. When I gave a gift of photographs to him and his family, he immediately began dreaming of a picture of his son standing next to his *suca* godfather: "What a beautiful photograph it would make, with him so *suca*." Although the physical beauty of this compadre was so frequently brought up, never once did he refer to the man's being the son of an ex-*mayordomo,* now an important political figure in a small town on the other side of the Inter-Andean valley.

Suca is beautiful and *runa* is ugly. Women with flawless skin, long jet-black hair, almond eyes, and high cheekbones assured me that of course they are ugly: they are *runalla,* just *runa* (here used as an adjective describing physical appearance). Some of the most poignant moments of my field experience occurred when these young women reacted to my compliments about their babies with an offer to trade: "Take my *runa* baby and give me a white one."

This kind of self-deprecation, coupled with admiration of whiteness, is intrinsic to hegemonic domination. When the ideology of racism is thus internalized by its victims, the reproduction of the relations of power is assured. According to Henri Lefebvre, racism is among the ideological tools used by the dominant class, which creates and constantly struggles to maintain "an image of itself for other classes which devalues them in their own eyes, drags them down, tries to defeat them, so to speak, without a shot being fired" (1977:263). Eugene Genovese, who like Lefebvre interprets racism as a tool of ideological domination within class relations, describes black culture in the antebellum South as a "shame culture," characterized by "a sense of inadequacy" (1976:121).

It is this generalized sense of inadequacy, of being "just" *runa* that colors Zumbagua self-perceptions. Internalized racism plays on the individual's conception of the division between self and other. The power

of racist ideologies derives from this dichotomy, so central to our understanding of ourselves and of the world. Racial differences form an orectic
pole (Turner 1967:54) that is not truly biological in origin—as Lefebvre
points out, the "real" phenotypic variation upon which racism is based
is extrapolated and transposed to an utterly fantastic degree (1977:269).
Rather, the power of these images is rooted in their articulation with the
psychological processes of creating an identity, processes that James Fernandez describes as the predication of metaphors onto the inchoate self
(1977). Although Fernandez does not address the application of his ideas
to ideologies of domination, it is easy to see how series of pairs such as
runa/suca; ugly/beautiful; worthless/valuable are readily grafted onto the
self/other dichotomy as the growing child seeks to "recast the inchoate
(and ineffable) whole of primary experience into various manageable
perspectives" (1977:126). This process takes place particularly as the
tremendous inequalities of wealth and power become increasingly visible
to him and demand comprehension.

The symbolism of white rice, then, must be seen in the context of this
entire symbolic complex. White rice was said before to function metonymically within discourse, standing for an entire realm of nonindigen-
ousness. Its power as a symbol must be seen in its ability to call up and
make felt this entire complex of metaphors of the distant and superior
Other, the nonindigenous world of wealth and power. And, by the same
token, its entrance into discourse as a metonym for the realm of the
Other throws into question the entire sphere of everyday cooking, all of
the nonprestige foods that might otherwise exist only as *doxa,* unexamined practice.

In 1984 Zumbagua, white rice stands as an antagonist in the arena of
discourse, a symbol for integration into a national way of life. This
arena, however, is not stable over time. What is defined as indigenous
and nonindigenous today is not the same as it was in the past or will be
in the future. Barley itself, which in Zumbagua today is the food of the
poor and Indian, was brought to the New World by its conquerors. It
may have stood for decades where white rice stands today.

Hegemony and Resistance: The Early Morning Meal

Bread and Hegemony

The identification of indigenous practice as "the past" and "white"
culture as "the future" is part of the process by which indigenous culture
is denied validity as a choice for living. In both popular and scholarly

representations, indigenous people are thus denied a history: their culture is "timeless," except insofar as they have slowly over the centuries taken on a few trappings of modernity, borrowed from the outside. They are a "traditional" people.

Although his work is not directed toward the analysis of multicultural societies, Raymond Williams's comments on "tradition" are worth considering in this context: "tradition has been commonly understood as a relatively inert, historicized segment of a social structure: tradition as the surviving past. But . . . [w]hat we have to see is not just a 'tradition' but a *selective tradition:* an intentionally selective version of a shaping past and a pre-shaped present, which is then powerfully operative in the process of social and cultural definition and identification" (1977:115–116).

As I mentioned in Chapter 2, it is questionable whether a pre-Columbian Zumbagua even existed: it is likely that the very existence of its population as a distinct ethnic group is an artifact of the colonial period. And regardless of the origins of settlement there, it is unquestionably true that most of the markers of "indigenous" culture today were introduced into the area by outsiders, often by conquerors. During long centuries of resistance, however, the people of Zumbagua have taken certain elements of alien custom and made them their own, even turned them into symbols of their own, "indigenous" "tradition."

For the purposes of contemporary Zumbagua discourses, indigenous people have "always" eaten barley, spoken Quichua, and raised llamas and sheep. By reclaiming the remnants of previous conquests, Spanish and Incaic, as native to their own tradition, these people continue to define themselves as the possessors of a distinctive culture. In the process, certain practices and meanings are safely understood as *doxa,* to be taken for granted as "ours," while others are contested.

Even preparation of the simplest of meals, early morning *café,* is not a wholly unreflective practice. For most "white" Ecuadorians, *café* consists of a cup of hot water, served with a saucer and a spoon, into which the individual consumer mixes coffee and sugar. It is served with two bread rolls. This meal is also the *café* served in the early morning at restaurants and market stalls in the "white" towns Zumbagua people frequent.

In older households within Zumbagua, the early morning meal takes quite a different form. Though still called *café,* it does not contain any coffee at all. The main component is *máchica,* finely ground toasted barley meal. This *café,* like the "white" one, involves the serving of hot water, but there are no cups or saucers in evidence. Like most other meals, this one is served in deep enamel bowls.

Water is heated to boiling, and a big hunk of *panela* is dissolved into the water. Each person is handed a bowl of this sugar water along with a spoon. At the same time, a container filled with *máchica* is placed on the ground within reach, and everyone is invited to have some: *chapuvay, chapuilla,* "go ahead and mix yourself some." There is some range in personal tastes, but most people put about an equal amount of *máchica* to sugar water in their bowl. It is frequently done gradually, with leisurely actions interspersed with morning conversations. At first, spoonfuls of hot, sweet water are sipped, then bit by bit spoonfuls of *máchica* are added, until at the end the bowl contains mostly dry *máchica.*

Although most households consider *máchica* an absolute necessity, a substance one simply cannot live without, the alternative construction of *café,* familiar to everyone, consists of bread and water flavored with instant coffee and white sugar. Despite being a quite different form of a starch food than *máchica,* in the actual consumption bread becomes somewhat similar: as people drink spoonfuls of coffee, they break the breads up into pieces and mash them into the cup, producing a sweet, soupy mass not unlike a gruel.

There are various combinations possible between the two extremes depicted above: one may be served *máchica* with white-sugar-and-coffee-water, *máchica* with white-sugar-water, bread with *panela*-water, or—least palatable to me—bread with white-sugar-water. The distinction between white sugar and *panela* is the reverse of what one might expect. *Panela* is more expensive than white sugar and considered to be far tastier. Whereas insisting on having *panela* all the time is a "traditional" attitude seen more among older couples, it is a choice that demands something of a cash outlay. Instant coffee is a real luxury good, something that most families either do not have or hoard for occasions when they really want to impress someone: if the nurse or schoolteacher should for some reason come to the house, for example. Usually sweetened water is considered perfectly adequate. In the evening various *aguitas* or herbal teas may be made, with or without medicinal purposes.

There is conflict, however, over the question of bread. Here the generational cleavage is between very young children and their parents. Even fairly "modern" young parents, conversant with "white" foodways to some degree, find themselves forced into conflict with their children on this issue: they simply cannot afford to provide bread at every morning meal. Preschool children, especially, demand bread as their right, and refuse to accept *mishqui,* sweet gruels, or *máchica* in its place. Refusal is difficult for parents, because young children, especially the youngest child, are commonly indulged a great deal. Quichua-speaking mothers mimic their children's Spanish cries for bread: "*Sulu tandata munan, 'pan, pan, pan,' nin. Sulu wakan*" ("They only want bread [*tanda* in

Quichua]. 'Bread, bread, bread [*pan* in Spanish]' they say. They just cry").

In current practice, bread is definitely a member of the *wanlla* set of foods, along with bananas, oranges, and other fruits, hard candies, and cookies. As such, bread is a necessity in certain social situations: it is included among the offerings to the dead on Finados, the gifts exchanged during marriage negotiations or when asking someone to be a godparent, or as part of the redistributive flow surrounding fiesta sponsorship. Unless they are very poor, most families also buy some bread on Saturday as a treat for the children and for gift giving in the web of *wanlla* presentations that defines much of social life. Some of this bread is stored in the kitchen for any special occasions that might arise during the week. Many battles of will take place as mothers struggle to dole out the breads bought on Saturday as special treats, while the children demand them as daily fare. Fathers who witness these scenes seem to feel shame at their own inadequacy, their inability to fill their children's hands with bread. They may react with anger toward the child for his unreasonable demands, or toward the mother for denying the request: "Let him have it! I can buy more," as though resenting the implication that he in fact cannot.

What seems to be taking place is a struggle on the children's part to redefine what had been a treat (*wanlla*), a luxury food that most families can afford to buy but not for everyday consumption, into a staple, a necessary part of the morning meal. Sidney Mintz describes this process as intrinsic to the needs of capitalism: demand must be created, new foods must be "transformed into the ritual of daily necessity and even into images of daily decency" (1979:65). The children desire bread as the validation of a meal, that which seals it and marks it as satisfactory. They are pushing to redefine the role of bread in the domestic economy, not as a mainstay in the diet but as something without which a meal would be incomplete, a role similar to that "minimum of comfort" (Salomon 1980:145) perhaps once the definition of *uchu*. In the pre-Conquest era, *cachi* and *uchu*, products from the western slopes, came up to the highlands through networks of exchange that operated on a smaller scale than that of elite luxury goods, the movement of which was politically significant. Similarly, *panela* today is produced by household-level manufacturing on the western slopes and then reaches the markets of the Sierra through a multitude of intermediaries operating on a very small scale. White sugar, by contrast, is produced in large capital-intensive coastal plantations and mills and circulates through large-scale centralized marketing.

For sweetness, then, there is a contrast between, on the one hand, small-scale networks between two adjacent ecological zones, which despite their cash basis echo similar exchange patterns of several centuries ago, and on the other, capital-intensive, national-level production and marketing. The starches offer a different contrast, between ethnically indigenous *máchica* and ethnically "white" bread. The contrast between gruels and breads has had ethnic and imperial connotations in various times and places. It played a part in the changes in taste that accompanied the spread of the Roman Empire. "Bread . . . was established as being more desirable than grain-pastes and porridges" (Tannahill 1973:57). According to Jack Goody, "In Europe . . . the northern extension of bread from the Mediterranean was associated with its use by the conquering Romans and by the missionizing Christians, who sacralized this high-status food through its use in the Mass" (1982:180). (In Zumbagua, the intonation by European priests during the Mass of the phrase "Give us this day our daily bread" has similar connotations of white validation of a high-prestige food to indigenous listeners.)

Oats and barley, and the porridges and unleavened breads that are made from them, symbolized the provincialism of the Scots to the eighteenth-century writer Samuel Johnson. According to Raymond Sokolov, Johnson's jibes on the subject of Scots culinary tradition, with its emphasis on such gruel-based dishes as haggis and flummery, are revealing of the dependent relationship between London and the hinterlands of the British Isles. "[Johnson's] complete insensitivity to the real situation that condemned the Celtic fringe (and the north of England) to oat and barley breads is an unappealing, but, once again, typical expression of the imperial status of London" (1984:110).

In this century, the opposition between porridges and breads is one facet of the colonized/colonizer dichotomy in Ghana, where rising black elites, who previously made much of their familiarity with European culinary habits, have only recently begun to eat porridge publicly as an affirmation of their ethnicity (Goody 1982:177 and passim). Goody's comments on the production aspects of this opposition are relevant to the Andean case. He points out that the early success of bread among European foods introduced into the area can perhaps be attributed to the possibility of producing it on a small, localized scale (1982:180). In Ecuador, bread baking and sales figure importantly among the entrepreneurial possibilities open to the lower-class "white" and cholo populations whose livelihood is based on products that appeal to and are affordable for people from the small towns and rural hinterlands of the Sierra.

As Goody points out, the contrast between leavened breads and gruels or toasted grain products is one of technology; baking bread implies use of an oven, a technology that contrasts with that of the rural household, in which cooking techniques are limited to boiling and toasting (1982:180–181). Because of the high energy input required for their use, ovens in turn require some type of commercial or communal organization of production in low energy-consuming economies such as that of Zumbagua.

In rural Ecuador, then, bread has for some time now been a high-status food that contrasts with local products, whether Zumbagua ground barley or lowland manioc. Its European origins and present-day class connotations parallel the Incaic use of maize as a high-prestige food associated with imperial power (Murra 1975). It remains to be seen whether the children's cries for bread and the continued erosion of the household's ability to sustain itself through subsistence agriculture succeed in incorporating its use into everyday local practice.

Máchica and Resistance

The presence of "white" foods and foods bought with money earned through wage labor challenges the doxa of indigenous cuisine; but it remains to be seen whether this challenge ultimately weakens the parish's self-identity as indigenous, or strengthens it. Bourdieu states that it is only with the emergence of such conflicts that doxa, previously mute and invisible, is created as an actual discourse: "The truth of doxa is only ever fully revealed when negatively constituted by . . . the confrontation of competing discourses. . . . It is by reference to the universe of opinion that the complementary class is defined, the class of that which is taken for granted, doxa, the sum total of the theses tacitly posited on the hither side of all inquiry" (1979:168).

For the people of the Andes, at no time in the centuries since the Conquest (if ever) has it been possible to live a life in which the doxa of one's way of living could remain utterly implicit, completely taken for granted, "on the hither side of all inquiry." The polarities and contradictions of race and class have irrevocably polarized the languages of food, drink, clothing, and speech. In Zumbagua, a distinctively "indigenous" way of life has been marked out and contrasted to "white" ways, and despite the radical changes in economy and society that historical process has created, changes that have altered the content of "Indian" and "white" practice beyond recognition, the boundary between them has constantly been reproduced.

In Zumbagua today, the aggressive presence of "white" foods is met

by the stubborn, uncelebrated existence of barley at the core of indigenous doxa. If children's longing for bread and the fetishization of white
rice as the sign of superiority represent pressure to assimilate, barley
products stand for cultural resistance. Barley is the focus of agricultural
production; as I described in Chapter 2, the landscapes of the parish are
filled with it, and the sacks of it in every household's storeroom represent
an unfaltering assurance that, whatever the vicissitudes of the barley and
habas harvests or the wage-labor market, the family will not go hungry.
Its centrality in the subsistence economy is marked in the ritual cycle by
the tremendous importance of Corpus Christi, the festival that falls at
the barley harvest, overshadowing every other calendrical rite.

In the realm of discourse, barley seems to play a silent, unmarked role
in the *doxa* of everyday practice; it does not call attention to itself, as
rice does. But certain curiosities of Zumbagua speech suggest that it does
pose a challenge. I suffered much confusion, for example, until I learned
that if one says "rice" in the parish, it is assumed that barley is meant.
In common Zumbagua parlance, the word *arruz*, from Spanish *arroz*,
rice, is taken to mean not white rice but *arroz de cebada*, "riced" barley,
the coarsely ground barley used in soups and sweet gruels. To say "white
rice" the phrase *di castilla* must be added, "*Castilian* [Spanish]" rice.

This linguistic usage subtly likens the contrast between barley and rice
to that between Quichua and Spanish: in highland Ecuador, the Spanish
language is commonly referred to as *castellano*. Like white rice, within
the parish the Spanish language must be referred to by name, while the
unmodified *shimi*, language, always refers to Quichua.

Verbally, rice and barley, the two *arrozes*, appear to stand as an opposed pair, like Spanish and Quichua, the two *shimis*. In actual practice,
however, *máchica*, finely ground toasted barley, is parallel in position,
and opposed in value, to bread in the structure of the early morning
meal. Hence barley functions in opposition to either white rice or bread,
depending on context. (Potatoes can also be seen as paradigmatically
matched with white rice in meal structures and hence as a possible can-
didate for opposing white rice in ideologically charged discourse.)

Barley, especially *máchica*, could be seen as a core cultural symbol for
Zumbagua. It is referred to as "good, substantial food," as being "as
filling as meat," as "food that warms you up." *Máchica* is central to the
whole cozy familial atmosphere of early morning inside the house, giving
it an aura of "Mom and apple pie." It is the food that is given to kittens
and young puppies, and the first solid food given to human babies.
Mothers give little bags full of *máchica* with *panela* chopped up in it to
their children when they send them off herding, and they worry all day
if a careless youngster leaves his behind.

Because it is the essential symbol of the home, *máchica* is the quintessential symbol of hospitality. Some is always kept on hand to offer to visitors. It is not offered to formal guests and certainly not to the white nurse, schoolteacher, or priest, for whom, after much frantic searching, the crusty year-old jar of instant coffee is unearthed while a kid is sent racing downhill to buy bread. *Máchica* is for the familiar guest, for your comadre who always comes to help harvest or for the neighbor who has come to castrate your pig. A woman loves to bring out the *máchica* when her family visits from her natal *comuna,* or when sisters visit from the *comunas* into which they have married. It is as though with this single act she can recreate the disbanded family home.

Conversations about *máchica* marked the steps of my integration into the parish. When I first lived in the *centro* and was trying to establish contacts in the outlying *comunas,* townspeople's skepticism about my ability to do so changed when they learned that I was being served *máchica.* In fact, this news was worthy of being repeated: "Did you hear? In Chami they offered her *máchica.*"

Months later, the family with whom I lived in the *comuna* of Yanatoro would introduce me to visitors with two boasts. One was that I spoke Quichua, and the other was that I ate *máchica.* And after weeks of my struggling, in my awkward Quichua, to explain participant observation, I heard the family patriarch explain it to a visiting in-law in one simple phrase: "In the early morning she mixes *máchica* in her coffee with us." (By "coffee" he meant hot, sweet water.)

That same old man, who loves to sit in the morning feeding warm, moistened *máchica* to the kitten off the tip of his finger, gifted me with another usage of the term *máchica* in discourse. I had been trying for weeks to elicit some term that people of the area use to identify themselves as an ethnic group or distinct population, but aside from the Spanish *naturales,* used even when speaking Quichua, and the derogatory *longo* and *runa,* I had found none. One afternoon the old man initiated once again a conversation about airplanes, a topic of which I was heartily sick. "What was it like to be in one? What could you see?" He looked at me as if guessing my impatience and said, "What would we know about airplanes, we who eat *máchica?*"

I was struck by the aptness of the phrase, and even more so when I realized later that the ethnic boundaries that mark off the Zumbagua-Tigua-Apagua people as a distinct group correspond roughly to the upper limits of maize cultivation: below that line, maize farmers; above it, barley eaters.

The statement in which this self-apellation, "we who eat *máchica,*" is found is a negative one, expressing ignorance. Thus the name *"máchica* eaters" would seem to have predicated onto it a traditional national ideological judgment about indigenous people of the Sierra. Ignorance is part of a whole series of metaphorical statements that present highland "Indians" as being mute or dumb, an image that gains support from their not speaking Spanish and from the stubborn silence and incomprehension with which white men's demands are often met. Other powerful metaphors are those comparing indigenous people to domesticated animals, especially burros and sheep.

This range of metaphors is frequently used by white officialdom in their efforts to stir the local populace to change, to leave behind old superstitions and embrace modernity. "You are no longer burros, now you must be men"; "you must no longer expect to live like sheep, like little children, with a *patrón* to care for you, but like men"; and the repeated exhortation to be *racionales.* (*Gente racional* is a commonly heard phrase that means literally "rational or reasonable people" but implies "people who are culturally if not racially white.") The implicit demand is that these people embrace a market economy, the Protestant work ethic, and the Spanish language. They should abandon poncho and hat, shawl and sash, kin-based economic relations, the conspicuous consumption involved in fiestas, and the Quichua language. This rhetoric also emerges when indigenous groups threaten hostility against whites. The threat to do violence to the priests was met with exactly this rhetoric on the part of government officials, coupled with religious exhortations that Jesus preached that to be poor and humble is better than to be rich.

The rhetorical framework in which all of these oppositions can be found, together with the racist ideology that produces the *suca/runa;* beautiful/ugly; valuable/worthless pairs, certainly form an overarching metaphorical structure the "truth" of which few in Zumbagua would dispute. Every indigenous individual in Zumbagua, no matter how isolated from the white world, has internalized all of these meanings into his or her understanding of self and other, of usness and themness: they constitute a specific discourse within Zumbagua reality. A particular set of statements forms a field of discursivity—what Bourdieu would call an arena of discourse—when a "site of the possibility of proof and disproof" is established (1979:168). The existence of a discourse implies "the constraint of truth" (MacCabe 1979:279–280). Thus, the discourse about being *runa,* once established, concerns itself with the truth or untruth of statements within the confines of that discourse: are Zumbaguans "burros" or are they "*gente racional*"? Is *runa* ugly, or can it be beautiful?

This kind of Zumbagua discourse is clearly a variant of other Ecuadorian discourses on ethnicity (see Stutzman 1981:71; Whitten 1981:

788–790; Whitten 1985:224, 233). What Norman E. Whitten, Jr., refers to as "national oppositions" permeate Ecuador from "the Quiteño pinnacle of Ecuadorian power structure and the ideology emanating from it there to a Puyo saloon and the paradigmatic imagery generated there" (1981:791). Within the framework of the Zumbagua discourses on "whiteness" and indigenousness, the possibilities for real resistance to these hegemonic images seems limited.

Nevertheless, it is my contention that the nature of discourses, and the complexities of self-knowledge, suggest that the constitution of reality in Zumbagua also contains other truths. Colin MacCabe criticizes the idea that the boundaries of specific discourses are hermetically sealed. He points to the possibility of rejecting one discourse by recourse to another (1979:294) or of a single statement acting to "homogenize" two intersecting discourses (1979:293). For example, the metaphor of the burro, intended to evoke images of passivity, docility, and stupidity on the part of the Indian, is often reinterpreted in indigenous discourse so as to become social criticism: "We live like burros," meaning that labor is incessant, rewards barely enough to sustain life, and gratuitous punishments frequent. In other areas of Ecuador, where indigenous resistance has taken overt political form, multiple, contradictory discourses about human worth, race, and cultural identity have in fact become part of the political arena. Whitten's work on the Canelos Quichua of the Oriente (1976, 1985) depicts what he calls the "pulsating system of indigenous insolence/acquiescence in Ecuador's growing system of confluent antinomies" (1985:224). Whitten maintains that understanding of these symbolic systems "does not lie in raising the question as to the exact relationship between ideology and 'reality'. Rather, it lies in the critical appraisal of the ebb and flow of dialectical and transactional processes wherein cultural transformation and social reproduction of opposites can be understood within a unified frame of reference" (1981:792–793).

As Bourdieu's image of competing discourses suggests, and as Whitten's ethnographies show for lowland Ecuador, however, a single, all-encompassing framework of meaning does not necessarily exist in social life. In fact, competing discourses may not even be directly placed in conflict with one another, as in Bourdieu's analysis. Just as the human psyche is capable of simultaneously holding contradictory thoughts and impulses (Bowie 1979:123), so a human society maintains and plays with a multiplicity of discourses with incompatible truth constraints. It is not so much that there exist in Zumbagua discourses in which white superiority is challenged, but that there are whole spheres of living and speaking in which the question cannot even come up; it is irrelevant. The possibility exists, though only as a latent force, that these discourses could be used to challenge the dominant one.

It is this human capacity to embrace competing discourses simultaneously that makes resistance to domination possible. According to MacCabe, in contrast to the Althusserian theory of ideology, which leaves

> no theoretical perspective for ideological struggle in the face of dominant ideologies, for there is nothing which escapes or is left over. . . . [A Marxist reading of Lacan would] theorize the individual's assumption of the place produced by him or her by the complex of discursive formations and would insist that these places would be constantly threatened and undermined by their constitutive instability in the field of language and desire. (1979:302)

It is this kind of theory of discourse, in which the contradictions of material life are matched by the complexity of competing discourses, that offers a theoretical basis from which to understand ideologies of resistance.

As I stated earlier, Fernandez's image of the inchoate "I" seeking metaphorical predication in order to create an identity for itself lends itself to an understanding of the workings of dominant ideologies, as depicted by Louis Althusser (1971). But the Lacanian theory to which MacCabe refers subverts the Freudian notion of the self that underlies Fernandez's work. While acknowledging the existence of the process of searching for a stable, comprehensible identity, Lacan insists that this fixed sense of self represents only a part of one's entire identity, most of which remains always unfixed, inchoate, energized, and processual. The individual does "seek and foster the imaginary wholeness of an 'ideal ego' . . . [but t]he unity invented at these moments, and the ego which is the product of successive inventions, are both spurious" (Bowie 1979:122). Beneath this superficial unity of the ego lies the enormous, active energy of the unconscious, "a set of instinctual impulses which are able to coexist without mutual influence or contradiction; it knows no negation, no doubt, no degree of certainty; it is the realm of the primary process, in which psychical energy is freely transmissible between ideas by means of displacement and condensation" (Bowie 1979:123–124).

This kind of theory, acknowledging as it does the capacity of the human mind to incorporate a multiplicity of contradictory images into a dynamic identity, full of ambiguities and contradictions, is necessary for one to begin to understand the realities of Andean life today. As I lived in Zumbagua, I constantly struggled to understand the contradictory statements about race, class, ethnicity, and identity made by the people who lived there. No single "truth" can encompass their attitudes to the contradictory position they hold within Ecuador today; and far more volatile, emotion-laden, and deeply conflictual than their discourses about outside realities are the images of themselves exposed through the statements they make about whiteness, jobs, language mastery, foods.

To say that the people of Zumbagua hold contradictory images of themselves, images that reflect the existence of multiple ideological statements, does not imply that they are totally free to make of their situation what they will. The symbolic realm does not exist divorced from reality. The ability of a human being to displace, condense, subvert, remake ideological statements is ultimately constrained by the need for discourse to express material reality. The "symbols" used in discourse are not freely taken from life, but must refer back to actual praxis. Instead of acting through a two-stage mental operation in which certain material objects symbolize ethnicity and repression, which are then understood as abstract concepts, burros, muteness, white rice, and barley flour actively create and constitute these understandings, through the social and productive processes in which men know them.

In the body of theory to which I have been referring, this constraint is expressed through the statement that the unconscious is not unlimited "psychical energy," but rather energy structured by language; and language, in turn, is socially constructed. From the point of view of the individual, it is a preexisting symbolic order. As the human being acquires speech, the libido must submit to the systematic pressures of this socially constructed order (Bowie 1979:126). Although Lacan's psychoanalytical theory represents an advance over Althusser's monolithic image of ideology, it is not usable in critical social analysis until the individual's construction of himself through the use of language is reinstated into the actual sites of language use—the family, the school, the workplace (MacCabe 1979:302), thus partially recapturing Althusser's notion of these sites as ideological apparatuses (1971). The constitution of ideologies in language must be understood as a process inseparable from material practice. The ideology of cultural and racial inferiority prevalent in rural Ecuador today may be, in the classic Marxist image, a *camera obscura* in which the truth is only seen upside down; but the projected images have their basis in material life. Poverty in Zumbagua is a reality, not a rhetorical construct, and no rhetoric will emerge from that reality that does not speak to this basic fact.

Nevertheless, neither racist explanations of social inequality nor the national insistence that cultural assimilation will improve economic conditions in the parish clearly dominates Zumbagua interpretations of their existence. Both of these ideas exist, and both are active in thought and discourse in the parish. But the potential for resistance is present in the multivocalic power of symbols, as can be seen in the indigenous affirmation, "Yes, we are burros," which consumes the white stereotype and reproduces it as social criticism. At the same time, the nature of discourses and that of the impermanence of the images the self predicates onto its inchoate existence point to the possibility that multiple and competing paradigms for understanding the world exist. The "truth" of white superiority may be absolute and yet coexist with an equally true realization that white people are largely irrelevant to an indigenous woman's life.

I spoke earlier of the power of the white world to make indigenous life seem insubstantial, of white rice to throw doubt on the value of barley. But in current Zumbagua understandings, each world has the power thus to make the other feel illusory. Passing buses may fill a boy's heart with longing for adventure and make home seem shabby and unimportant; but these same boys, when they are a little older and working in Quito, are capable of spending almost all of their days and nights in the city while never faltering in their assertion that they *live* in Zumbagua: Quito is just where they work. The knowledge that the crops are ripening, the sheep are giving birth, and the women are still cooking soup is enough to render life in Quito unpleasant but inconsequential.

Those women making soup may occasionally express shame at not serving white rice instead, or the sight of their baby in the arms of a stray North American anthropologist might move them to wish that its hair was a different texture and its skin a different color, but these experiences, though telling, are evanescent. It does not seem at this point as though women see the glamor of the white world as seriously challenging the integrity of everyday indigenous doxa. White rice is the object of desire, but *máchica* is the locus of satisfaction. To the women, white rice or breads my be longed for as treats, but not as substitutes for the entire *doxa* of known and familiar, satisfying foods: barley and potatoes, warm soup and toasted grain.

The children's demands, by contrast, do show the possibility that these boundaries are being redefined. This redefinition is not the result of purely superstructural phenomena. Foods may function as symbols, but they do not cease to have a material reality. Concrete economic change, as it occurs, inexorably restructures kitchen practice, and thus the *langue* of cuisine. Still, change does not necessarily imply the loss of cultural identity. Just as barley, an Old World cultigen, is defined as the essence of indigenousness today, bread, white rice and instant coffee may slip into indigenous doxa. If so, new arenas of discourse must emerge. The ongoing process of discussing and defining what it means to belong to the parish of Zumbagua will continue to inhabit the interstices of every-day conversations about mundane affairs, even as the fields of discursiv-ity are shifting to new terrains. Some aspects of what is eaten, and when, and how, will continue to excite commentary, gossip, envy, and desire as long as there is food to eat and women to cook it.

Note

1. Wild mustard (*Brassica campestris L.*), not turnips, Spanish *nabos* (*Brassica napus D.C.*). See Gade 1975:159, who notes the plant's use as food and fodder in the Vilcanota Valley of Peru, and comments, "Undoubtedly this potherb pro-vides significant vitamins to country people who might not otherwise get them."

S I X

Practice: Kitchen Life

The previous chapter outlines the use of symbols derived from cooking in discourses about ideologies. But the issues of ethnicity and modernity, of the role of the parish as a whole within the nation of Ecuador, are not the only messages that images of cooking can carry. Much of the social significance of cooking has to do with matters internal to the household. People joking, gossiping, arguing about cooking are frequently not at all concerned with "the people of Zumbagua" in general, but with the relations between individuals: mother and daughter, husband and wife, host and guest.

These relationships are symbolized not so much by single foods, *nabus* or rice, as they are by practices. The disaffected wife signals her displeasure not just with soup but with cold, leftover soup; the obedient daughter-in-law is known not by the bowl of potatoes but by the bowl of potatoes quickly and competently peeled. It is to this aspect of food and cooking practices, and to their relations to the social and economic structure of the household, that we now turn.

There are three kinds of relationships under consideration here: women among themselves in the organization of kitchen work; women and men, in the etiquette that governs eating; and the household itself with the outside world, in networks of exchange as well as in larger systems. These matters of production, consumption, and exchange illuminate two contradictory aspects of the household: its image as a self-sufficient, internalized sphere, and the actuality of the producing, consuming, and redistributing activities that connect it to the other households within Zumbagua, to the ecological zones above and below it, and to the economic systems of the nation and the world.

Inside the Kitchen: Household Politics

Women, Power, and Work

In Zumbagua, the hearth defines the home. It supplants the marriage bed as the symbol of conjugal living and the bond of blood as the emblem of parenthood: the Zumbagua family consists of those who eat together. The hearth's importance can be seen in the great significance attached to the founding of a new kitchen. A man and woman are ready to marry after a year's courtship, but it may be ten years before they begin to cook apart from their parents and siblings.

Physically, a household in Zumbagua consists of a series of one-room buildings around a patio. These rooms always include a kitchen and a storage room, but additional dormitories may be added at need. The word "kitchen" in itself implies much more than a room in which food is prepared. It is there that meals are made and eaten, male and female heads of the household sleep and live, baths are taken, decisions made, wakes held, babies born, and the sick nursed back to health. Other buildings are storage rooms and sleeping places; only the kitchen is a home.

Zumbagua households have a long life cycle, undergoing several distinct phases. At first, there is a married couple and their children. They all sleep in the kitchen together. Later, as the children mature, they may begin to sleep in the storage room or to build small separate dormitories. Finally, as they marry, if they do not join their spouse's family they will build a new, more substantial dormitory within their parents' household, still bordering the same patio as the kitchen in which they were born, where they still eat their meals and where their own first children are born.

The married children cook, eat, work, and play with their parents for a number of years. The kitchen begins to feed three generations. Not until the young couple has several children over the age of five will they consider building their own, separate kitchen and so establishing their own household. Ideally, the youngest child never leaves home; the natal household finally enters a last phase in which the youngest couple and their children sleep in the central kitchen building while an elderly parent inhabits a small dormitory nearby.

The nuclear family is the conceptual basis for the Zumbagua household, but in fact the biological relationships among its members tend to be complex. Girls of the family may marry a man who is not their first partner and leave the offspring of their first match to be raised by their grandparents; grandparents also simply choose to "keep" some of their grandchildren, whose parents now live elsewhere. In addition, various forms of adoption are common. The ethos surrounding these decisions attaches neither shame nor disadvantage to adoption: in a society in which more kin means more wealth, to add adopted kin to blood kin never seems like a bad idea. Adolescents cheerfully take off to visit their "real" families from time to time, and adults sometimes go to "honor" blood relatives whom they scarcely know.

An outsider might guess that a young girl's decision to leave a first child born out of wedlock with her parents is motivated by shame or unwillingness to accept responsibility; but residents of Zumbagua would not so readily make this assumption. Premarital sex is not stigmatized but is considered normal adolescent behavior. Shame comes from leaving elderly parents without young people to help around the house and to bring joy to it. Young women may be under considerable pressure to leave a child at home even if it was born to her after marriage, or if her husband is the father. For example, I know a young woman who chose to live at home, nominally a *soltera* (single girl), until her child was a year old, although she had every intention of marrying the man who had fathered her child and who is today her husband. She and the child live with her husband and his family now; every time they visit home, the entire extended family falls on the toddler with cries of delight, demanding that she be allowed to stay, feeding her, spoiling her, and asking her if she does not want to come back to live with them again. In a few years, when she is old enough to fetch water and help with other chores, she may in fact be "borrowed" to live with her grandparents if she is not needed at home.

Young children are loved and enjoyed as one of the greatest reasons that life is worth living; no one wants to live in a house without children in it. But they are also considered to be pragmatically necessary to the running of a household. There are so many small tasks to be done: drawing water, fetching piles of *ujsha* from patio to hearth, feeding the dogs and the pig, watching infants, delivering little pots of food to the homes of nearby kin. Although adults do perform any and all of these tasks, taking care of all of them would make it impossible to attend to the larger jobs of the farmstead. In contrast, these little activities are ideally suited to the short attention span of a child, who would be incapable of performing a single task for hours on end. It is because of all these little jobs that young couples usually wait to establish their own kitchen until they have two children of the age of five or six, and why, once they have several children of their own, they may send one back to their aging parents' house to live.

There is a general feeling in the parish that no home should be without children. Physiological incapacity to reproduce for whatever reason is overcome by social mechanisms. Redistribution of children among extended and fictive kin also ensures that the demands on each household match its ability to provide; as a result, older, more established households tend to have more young children than do new ones, and poor families often give children away. Over the years, every family comes to have a generational and sibling structure constructed out of everyday usage that is frequently substantially different from actual consanguineal kinship.

Figure 10 depicts the difference between "everyday" kin relationships and underlying blood relations in one family. The household is shown during two developmental phases. About 1955, this family was raising three children, whose "birth order" was oldest female (1), second female (2), and son (3). The first child was in fact the mother's child from a different father, adopted by the husband; the boy child was adopted. By the 1980s, the picture had become more complex: the second daughter's oldest child was being raised by her grandparents, while the husband's daughter by another woman had also given one of her sons to the family to raise, at their request. Yet these two young people were sometimes listed in "birth" order as the couple's fourth and fifth children. Figure 11 shows the spatial distribution of this family into three households.

This picture of the family is in fact enormously simplified; there were various other "children" who had spent part of their childhood in the household, and the next generation was already beginning to realign blood lines to fit their own household arrangements. This family was by no means unusual in its kin relations, except inasmuch as, having some means, it tended to acquire rather than to lose children.

On a day-to-day basis, then, the use of parent–child terminologies refers to the people who share a hearth: the older generation that feeds and the younger one that is fed. All of the children that a couple raise in their household (*viñachishka*) are referred to by them as their sons and daughters. Food, not blood, is the tie that binds.

There is, however, one category of people who eat under the same roof, yet are not really kin: those who have entered the household through marriage. A man or woman refers to his/her mother-in-law or father-in-law as "mother" and "father," but the reciprocal terms *kachun* (daughter-in-law) and *mashi* (son-in-law) clearly identify them as in-laws and not kin.

I went to take family photographs for a household that lived high up in a high *comuna*, just below the *páramo*. There was a flurry of activity on my arrival: children's hair was combed, everyone bathed, trunks and storehouses were raided for "best" clothes. Young men went into agonies of indecision over whether to be photographed in hand-spun Zumbagua

1. "SURFACE" RECKONING: KINSHIP BY HEARTH

1950's

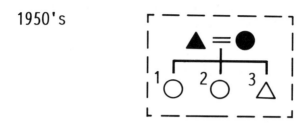

1980's

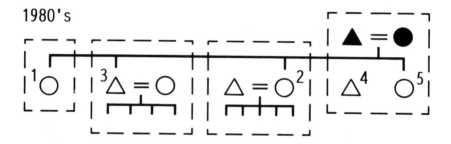

2. "DEEP" RECKONING: KINSHIP BY BLOOD

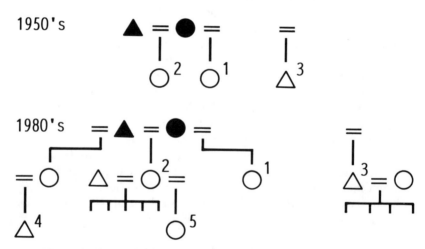

Figure 10. Everyday kin reckoning versus consanguineal kinship
in one extended family.

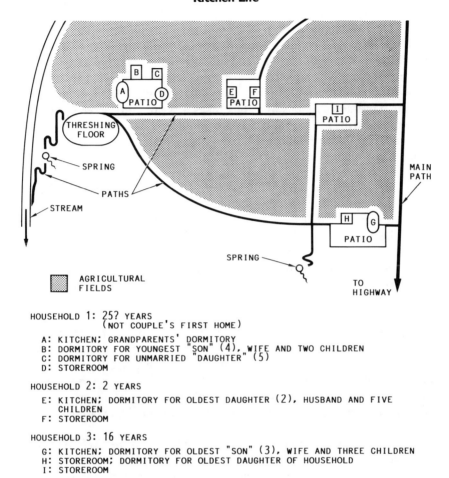

HOUSEHOLD 1: 25? YEARS
                (NOT COUPLE'S FIRST HOME)

A: KITCHEN; GRANDPARENTS' DORMITORY
B: DORMITORY FOR YOUNGEST "SON" (4), WIFE AND TWO CHILDREN
C: DORMITORY FOR UNMARRIED "DAUGHTER" (5)
D: STOREROOM

HOUSEHOLD 2: 2 YEARS

E: KITCHEN; DORMITORY FOR OLDEST DAUGHTER (2), HUSBAND AND FIVE
   CHILDREN
F: STOREROOM

HOUSEHOLD 3: 16 YEARS

G: KITCHEN; DORMITORY FOR OLDEST "SON" (3), WIFE AND THREE CHILDREN
H: STOREROOM; DORMITORY FOR OLDEST DAUGHTER OF HOUSEHOLD
I: STOREROOM

Figure 11. Plan of households in one extended family.

poncho or modern *chompa* (short jacket); their sisters had similar diffi-
culties over whether to wear their best hat, kept carefully wrapped in
plastic, or go bareheaded like a "white" woman.

Not everyone participated in the bustle. One young woman stayed in
her old clothes, cleaning ashes from the hearth and drawing water while
the others bathed, a modern-day Cinderella. She would not be included
in the picture because she was not part of the family: she was *kachun,* a
daughter-in-law. In a traditional family with a strong, dominant mother,
as this one had, the role of the young in-law is unenviable. The very
words *kachun* and *mashi* evoke images of unquestioning, lifelong servitude.

The ideal residence pattern in Zumbagua is virilocal, though perhaps one-third of young couples opt for uxorical residence instead. Married couples who live with the husband's family typically spend several days a month at the wife's parents' farmstead and are expected to make a substantial contribution of labor there, for she will inherit some of her parents' land and animals and thus takes a proprietary interest. A wife enjoys these trips home, but her family often puts heavy demands on her husband, the *mashi;* failure to comply willingly on his part can be grounds for separation.

A young wife typically spends much more time playing *kachun,* because she actually resides with her affines. The homesickness of new brides reflects not only the absence of loved ones but also the unpleasant transition from *ushi* (daughter) to *mushuj kachun* (new daughter-in-law). The inseparable relation of *kachuns* and work is revealed in various uses of this expression, *mushuj kachun.* Whenever an older woman let me tag along after her during her long, active days, neighbors who saw me following behind, weighted down with buckets of water or chasing an unruly ewe, would laugh at the incongruity of the sight and call out, "Mushuj kachungá?" ("Is that your new daughter-in-law?")

Kachuns are also assumed to be inept: my clumsy attempts to help at simple household tasks were frequently met with a good-humored "Mushuj kachunshna": just like a new daughter-in-law. In fact, however, my labors differed from those of a *mushuj kachun* in important ways. My attempts to help were voluntary and frequently of short duration, while a *kachun*'s ability to work tends to be maximally exploited by her affines.

Semiproletarianization has affected the situation of the *kachun* in contradictory ways. If the husband is fairly steadily employed, a young couple may be able to buy cement blocks and tin roofing to build their own house years before they would be able to establish the network of mutual obligation necessary to put on a traditional house-building, in which the materials are free but the labor involved requires having many compadres. Some young women thus gain a degree of independence from their mother-in-law earlier in their marriage than would have been possible without their husband's wages.

Nevertheless, having her own house frequently does little to alleviate her work responsibilities, for she still works, cooks, and eats with her affines during her husband's long, frequent absences. It is in fact these very absences that exacerbate her situation, as her own labor becomes proportionally more necessary to the family as they lose his. Claude Meillassoux in a personal communication suggests that the parents also attempt to use their control over their daughter-in-law to "capture" their son, because older households need the cash provided by wage labor, so they fear the growing independence of their male children.

The labor of the *kachun* is important to the older household. Spending the night in the high-*comuna* household mentioned before, rolled up in old ponchos on the floor by the ashes of the fire, I would be awakened in the wee hours of the morning by the *kachun*'s voice calling out "Alabay" softly as she crossed the threshold, the traditional asking of permission uttered on stepping through a doorway. She and her husband slept in their own, separate room, some distance away, and each morning in the darkness and numbing cold of 4:00 A.M. she crept to her in-laws' to start cooking.

As a guest, I was urged to stay cozy in my blankets till the fire was lit and the morning meal cooking. Soon all the other women were up, the young ones, *kachun* and daughter, grinding barley and the old woman presiding over the fire, toasting barley on a flat griddle, keeping a sharp eye on the younger ones' progress and punctuating her emphatic, humorous comments with a wave of the stirring stick. The men stayed in bed, making sleepy jokes and waiting to be served hot water and *máchica*. *Kachun*'s husband came in after a bit, wrapped in a blanket with sleep still in his eyes, and lay down next to his father's bed. His mother remarked tartly that he must have gotten cold in his own bed with his wife gone, and his father snorted at the double entendre: young couples come in for a great deal of this type of mildly ribald teasing.

This household was well into the most expanded phase in its life cycle, with in-laws and grandchildren in residence. This fact was represented by the presence of two *kutana rumis*, big grinding stones, on the kitchen floor. The early morning meal was prepared here the "right" way, the "old-fashioned" way: the toasting, grinding, and sifting of the barley was done just before the *máchica* was eaten, as the water was boiled and the *panela* dissolved in it. The smell of toasting barley filled the room, and men and children happily poked fingers into the bowl of still warm, powdery fine meal.

It is easy to make *máchica* like this, freshly prepared from scratch, in a big household, with one woman to do the first grinding and another to do the second, fine grinding and the sifting, leaving the senior woman to toast and boil and fill the bowls, handing them to a young granddaughter to carry to the men. A woman who runs a kitchen by herself, with only young children to help her, must grind barley the day before. Many newly established kitchens do not even have a *kutana rumi;* the woman still goes back to her mother's or mother-in-law's in midafternoon to

make *máchica* for her morning meals. Or the gift of labor may be reversed: after so many years, as a young bride, of grinding barley at the
older couple's home, now she may be awakened herself by a child bearing a bowl of warm *máchica* from the "big" house, ground by a grand-
child or new daughter-in-law. For years after a new kitchen is established,
neither household cooks anything without sending a small pot to the
other, visible sign that affective ties still bind.

The movement of cooked food between households is also the mark
of ongoing exchanges of labor: the families who share food are those
who also share agricultural tasks. In Figure 11, household 3, in which
the couple has been married for twenty years, has established its independence from household 1, but still engages in reciprocal labor exchanges with both household 1 and household 2. It is only on these
occasions and a few formal celebrations that meals are shared. Household 2, a "new" marriage only seven years old, still sends and receives
pots of food at every meal. Households 1 and 3 have their own *kutana
rumis,* while the woman in household 2 does not.

When a couple finally establishes its own kitchen, the mother or
mother-in-law may lose direct control over some of the younger woman's
kitchen activities, but she still can expect that, in the management of the
farmstead as a whole, she can coordinate tasks with the fledgling households scattered around her. One or two people to herd sheep; one or two
to go up to the *páramo* to cut *ujsha;* one to feed the pig and the dogs,
clean house, and cook *almuerzo,* doing a little weeding in the field near
the house in the meantime: it works so much better to organize the tasks
among several households. One woman simply cannot herd sheep, weed
habas, and nurse a sick relative at the same time.

The absence of adult men and schoolchildren has put tremendous pressure on the household labor supply. Because male and female agricultural
tasks are not sharply differentiated, the absence of men is a generalized
problem that makes a woman's day longer and her efforts more inadequate, without her ever being able to point to a specific task and say,
"that's not really my job." The absence of schoolchildren creates a more
specific need: adult women in Zumbagua have had to take over the task
of pasturing sheep, work theoretically done by older children.

Men come back at the periods of peak agricultural activity and when
their wives are soon to give birth. At the latter time they take over all
household tasks. (The sight of a man washing clothes by himself automatically signals a new father.) But on a day-to-day basis, women must
manage the farm and care for old and young on their own.

Alain Janvry characterizes the strain put on the wives of semiproletarianized men as pushing women beyond the brink of endurance:

In the peasant sector of the peripheral economy, . . . women's subordination . . . originates in their role as production agents of use values and petty commodities to cheapen semiproletarian male labor. . . . Exploitation of women in the periphery often manifests itself in brutal forms, for women assume an enormous number of physically demanding tasks to be carried out under highly primitive conditions—caring for the animals, preparing food, rearing and feeding children, tending the dwelling, going to the market, and in many cases also cultivating the subsistence plot. As CIDA observes, "Intense work wears her out to the point of exhaustion. At an early age, she appears old and weary." (1981:88)

This description shows one of the hidden effects of semiproletarianization and its concomitant effects on ideology: it appears to be the nature of the domestic economy itself that is exploitative, so that many First World feminists see the exhaustion of peasant women as evidence of the oppressive nature of precapitalist systems. They fail to perceive that the burden a peasant woman bears is the absence of the men who should be sharing her work, men whose labor is being absorbed by the capitalist sector.

The need for women's labor on the farm binds young women to the parish. It is not unusual to meet older women who worked as maids in Quito in their youth, or ventured out of the parish to live with distant kin in other places. Young women, in contrast, have for the most part never been allowed to leave home. Here too, female "backwardness" and isolation is partially a product of the community's involvement in the capitalist sector.

Women, Men, and Table Manners

The organization of work in the kitchen is largely a female concern: here, more than in any other realm, the relations among women are unmediated by men. Once the food is ready to be served, however, the kitchen becomes the locus for a centrally important interaction between the sexes.

According to accepted practice in Zumbagua, food is served in a regular sequence of four meals arranged symmetrically throughout the day: *café-almuirzu-almuirzu-café*. There are two very light meals, often sweet, eaten in predawn and nighttime darkness, and two larger meals, predominantly salty, eaten during the day, in late morning and late afternoon. This meal structure is suited to a woman's productive activities, as it allows for a long uninterrupted period of daylight, midmorning to mid-afternoon, in which to pasture the flocks.

Schools and city jobs, however, have a temporal structure incompatible with this arrangement. Through the conflict between mothers who must herd sheep and children who come home hungry at midday, it has been borne in upon local people that the national pattern is three meals a day, the major meal falling in the early afternoon.

Many young people feel strongly that one "ought to" eat meals according to the latter pattern. I had seen some friction over this question, but was amazed on one occasion to witness what amounted to a sit-down strike on the part of a group of young adults because of it. Three siblings and their spouses had come to harvest their father's barley. Normally this patriarch's word was obeyed without question, but when he threw down his sickle at eleven o'clock and announced that it was time for *almuirzu,* he was met with firm opposition from his wristwatch-wearing children. It was too early; it was not right to go down to eat before at least twelve. The young people eventually backed down, somewhat shamefacedly. An unacknowledged compromise was reached through the delay caused by the whole incident, by which with a little dawdling they managed to not sit down to eat until twelve—though all agreed that one o'clock "would have been more appropriate."

In objecting to the announcement that an *almuirzu* was being served, these young people were making a social breach in several senses. Not only were they defying the most senior male of the extended family, they were also breaking one of the most sacrosanct rules of proper behavior, that proffered food must always be accepted in the manner in which it is given. The fact that this incident occurred during harvesting made their behavior even more surprising. On this occasion, the usual structure of family relationships, in which age and gender demand respect but may be informally questioned, was superseded by the more formal relations of host and guest. The adult children had given the gift of their labor in working their father's fields, and the meal was offered to acknowledge that gift. Because of this fact, the *almuirzu* under discussion was a somewhat more formal and elaborate meal than usual.

The fact that, with the exception of the oldest son and his wife, these people all eat together on a fairly regular basis, does not affect the formal nature of the harvest or planting-time *almuirzu.* The request to work in the fields on these days is always made formally, and the repayment includes at least one formal meal as well as gleaning rights and, at the discretion of the field owner, a small portion of the harvest as well. Even when, as was true in this case, the family was basically harvesting all of their fields as a unit, working one day on one member's fields and the next day on another's, the *almuirzu* retained its formal air. In fact, there was a degree of added anxiety for the women preparing the meals, for these meals were immediately comparable to the ones prepared by sisters or *kachuns* the day before and the day after.

In more asymmetrical labor situations, as when a wealthy family asks poor comadres to come and help harvest, it is assumed that they will enjoy their meal. Often, the chance to eat a two-course *almuirzu* of meaty, potato-filled *sopa* and sweetened *mishqui* dessert is indeed enjoyed by poor women living largely on unseasoned barley gruel. Compassionate compadres often send a big pot of soup home to the hungry children too.

No matter what the relations between workers and field owner, a harvest *almuirzu* is always something of a formal affair. Zumbagua houses lack tables, so everyone eats scattered around the room on benches or on the floor, eating soup out of tin bowls and tossing bones to the dogs. Despite the apparent haphazardness, a strict hierarchy is observed in the seating arrangements. Tiny chairs or low seats are offered to the most honored diners, usually the senior male(s). Then, according to a flexible series of social criteria that puts old before young, male before female, and guest before host, others are seated on still lower seats or on cloths or straw spread on the floor. As a general rule, men sit above the ground while women sit on it. Even if a more senior female is offered a chair and a young man not, he will not actually sit on the ground, but rather crouch so that only his feet actually come in contact with it.

The order in which people are served is another indication of social status. Decisions regarding this order belong to the woman doing the serving, normally the senior woman of the house. She herself merely ladles the food into bowls, remaining seated by the fire, while a child or younger woman does the actual serving. But it is the woman at the hearth, as she hands over the bowl, who indicates to whom it will be served: it is specifically understood to be her prestation to the person receiving the food. The recipient directs his/her thanks to the woman at the hearth, not to the one delivering the bowl.

If those being served are important people, *padrinos,* for example, the husband himself may do the serving; but he does so under his wife's direction. On occasions fraught with social anxiety, the man of the house sometimes hovers nervously about the cooking pot, urging his wife in whispers to serve in a certain sequence, but such undignified behavior is hardly becoming. The man should be calmly seated, awaiting his portion, sublimely unaware of kitchen politics.

The woman at the cooking pot controls not only the order of serving, but a veritable arsenal of tools for expressing her opinion of those she serves. First among them is the wide discrepancy in size, shape, design, and materials among the bowls and spoons. Far from simply reflecting a sporadic sequence of acquisition, as I at first assumed, the dissimilarities in cutlery and dishes are necessary in order to emphasize the social inequality of those who eat together.

The biggest, newest, and most ornate should go to the person first served, and so on down the ladder, thus reinforcing the status distinctions already expressed in the serving order. To some extent, this pattern is pragmatic: children get the smallest and least damageable bowls, while the men, who do the heaviest work, get the biggest portions. In practice, the dishes offer yet another scale on which social worth can be measured. The server may subtly express an opinion by incongruities between serving size and serving order, or by saving an especially pretty bowl for a favorite relative. Many women consider one sister to be their best friend, one child to be the most loving, and the deployment of bowls and spoons provides an opportunity to express these feelings.

A third indicator is found in the soup itself. To North American minds, a soup is by definition a homogeneous and amorphous kind of dish: one might quibble over the larger of two pork chops or the selection of a piece of chicken, but soup is all the same. This conception of soups is plainly not held by Zumbaguans. Each bowl of soup is carefully constructed, meats, vegetables, and broth being apportioned with a specific consumer in mind. To aid in this process, meat tidbits are often removed from the pot in advance and kept in a dish to the side; sometimes potatoes are separated as well, or even cooked separately; they are then simply placed in the bowl, meat is put on top, and soup is then poured in to the brim.

This act of composing each bowl of soup is an acknowledged stage in making a meal. There is nothing furtive about a woman's fishing about in the soup pot, looking for more pieces of cabbage to add to a serving, or putting some back if she gave someone too much. Selecting potatoes, or poking through the meat dish to find just the right piece, is done with a flourish: a woman thus displays her skill in assembling a filling, aesthetically pleasing, and socially appropriate serving.

When the members of a Zumbagua household include others in their *almuirzu,* the meal is not so much a sharing of food as it is the giving of food by hosts to guests. Even when the meal includes only household members, it is still conceived as a gift: parents to children and woman to man. All of the ritual of the meal is still present in even the most intimate, casual family meal. Somewhat less attention is paid to the symbolic associations of seating arrangements in the latter case, men sometimes joining their wives on the straw by the fire, or women sitting on chairs. But the entire etiquette of serving is still enforced. Each diner verbally thanks the server, both on receiving the full bowl and on returning it empty; and if the woman replies with a formal "Please eat more," rather than a casual query about whether more is wanted, the food cannot be refused without grave offense.

The latter aspect of table manners takes on interesting dimensions when spouses are at odds. The woman's obligation always to have ready hot, fresh food when her husband comes home is of course the source of much conflict, along with serving as a symbol for conflicts initiated elsewhere. When an angry spouse, surrounded by a phalanx of supportive same-sex kin, decides to indulge in a full-fledged, public airing of grievances, the accusations that *she* has no food ready when he is hungry, or that the meal waits while *he* never comes home, are heard more often than any other claim. The centrality of the woman at the hearth as the very image of the home is revealed in these interchanges.

If the wife is supposed to serve food to her husband, he in turn is supposed to eat it. This job may seem agreeable enough, but like most aspects of married life it can be turned into a torment by a vindictive spouse.

I first became aware of its use as a weapon during a fiesta. A recently married couple went down to the plaza together early in the day, but discovered that fiestas were not as enjoyable as they once had been. Accustomed as a *soltera* to leaving the children at home with her mother, the young wife now found herself nursing one infant and additionally burdened with a toddler. As a result, she did not want to drink and tired early. He, finding the children a nuisance and his wife unaccountably bad-tempered, disappeared "for a few minutes" with his friends and never reemerged from the crowd.

After a difficult trip home carrying both sleeping babies up steep slopes in the dark, the wife was very angry indeed. When her husband arrived home many hours later, drunk and sleepy and ready for bed, she informed him that he must be very hungry; as an obedient wife, she had prepared a nice dinner for him. Almost unconscious, he forced himself to sit upright long enough to eat two enormous bowls of soup under her reproachful eyes. The meal over, he crept off to bed, but his ordeal had only begun. The next day found him in an extremely delicate physical state, such that the three very elaborate meals she prepared for him, which he dutifully consumed, resulted in several hasty exits from the kitchen to the bushes outside. She appeared to enjoy cooking for him very much that day, smugly playing the virtuous wife in front of her in-laws, who watched with some amusement and did not interfere.

After this incident, I became aware that this form of revenge on drunken husbands is not uncommon. Wives find their husband's drinking to be one of the most difficult aspects of married life: newlyweds resent being left behind with the babies, while more experienced wives learn to dread the unpredictable and often violent behavior of drunken husbands. As long as a man restricts his drinking to fiestas and market days, however, it falls well within the scope of acceptable male behavior, and a wife cannot by rights object to it.

When husbands have drunk too much, the etiquette of the meal provides the perfect means for retaliation, for it entails culturally impeccable behavior, which nonetheless makes one's partner's life miserable. And if a husband should be so rash as to refuse the proffered food, he will at last have strayed into the realm of culturally inappropriate behavior, thus giving his wife a perfectly legitimate opportunity for protest. She can then vent all of her anger in a single, vitriolic stream unlikely to soothe her husband's already aching head.

Arguments and physical violence are endemic to many young marriages in Zumbagua, a problem that worries older residents. In addition to the heavy drinking that plagues the indigenous Andes as it does the underclass of much of the world, another cause is the widening cultural gap between young men and women in their teens and twenties: older couples share a similar life experience and world view, but the knowledge and attitudes of young husbands and wives are very different.

This difference starts to develop when they are still children, as boys and girls begin mapping out their dreams. Girls think about running the farmstead, owning animals, having children, seeing the harvests ripen. Boys want to buy electronic goods—wristwatches and radios—and long for speed—bicycles, motorcycles—things far beyond their reach. They dream of travel, movement, the buses and trucks that carry those with money for the fare to the towns and cities where they can try their fortunes, to Quito and Guayaquil, which are *lindo,* beautiful, because of their big buildings and many cars; to the coast, which is *lindo* because it is warm. These desires leave the young girls quite unmoved. "Here I will die," said one *soltera* to me spontaneously—and in fact the fear of dying away from Zumbagua haunts many men. When a man from the parish was hit by a car in Quito, it was said that he grew two heads as he lay in his coffin, and two powerful *yumbos* (shamans) had to be called in.

But the boys still dream of going, knowing they will have the girls here to come home to, still speaking Quichua, cutting *ujsha,* living out their lives. The stability of indigenous life represented by the female role is of tremendous psychological importance to young men as they try to survive in the city, a battle that often involves hiding one's indigenous heritage. The women and children left behind think of the journey to Quito as an adventure, but the thrill soon fades for those who do it on a regular basis. Most men come back on the weekends because the *comuna,* not Quito, is where they think of themselves as living, even though they spend less time there than in the city. The five- or twelve-day sojourn in Quito is an exile, lived out in cramped quarters.

The men spend as little as possible there, eating lunches of Coke and bread and suppers of noodles and salt. Despite their efforts to economize, constant inflation erodes their scant earnings as the week goes by. Bus fares to and from Zumbagua alone may eat up one to two days' wages. As his family grows, a man's return home is met with increasing demands for shoes, clothes, groceries, medicine, and school supplies. It is not altogether impossible to understand why fathers sometimes respond by lashing out, especially after drinking.

Others respond by partially or totally abandoning their wives. It is not uncommon to see young wives who live in abject poverty for weeks on end, barefoot and in rags, living on unseasoned barley gruel alone. When their children sicken on this inadequate diet, they lack the money to buy medicine. Their husbands come back to the *comuna* occasionally but may not even visit their wives and children; these men belong to a totally different economic class, show up in the *centro* sporting new clothes, shoes, and a wristwatch, carrying a radio/cassette player and buying everyone drinks.

The extreme version of this kind of abandonment is only possible under one of two uncommon circumstances: if the husband earns enough in the city to be relatively independent, or if his family conspires in the abandonment of the wife by providing him with a place to eat and sleep when he comes home. Normally, if a husband's mistreatment of his wife exceeds certain limits, the two extended families, *padrinos,* and compadres all descend to correct the situation.

The community does tolerate the differential economic status of husband and wife to a degree, however, partially because it is reinforced by traditional values. Within the agricultural economy, men and women do not join their properties at marriage, but maintain separate ownership. A land-poor man's standard of living improves on marrying into a landholding family, but his actual worth does not. It is his children who will gain, through inheritance from their mother.

Similarly, a man is not automatically expected to share his cash income with his wife. He may buy her or his children presents, and will do so if he is a good husband, but at his discretion. Women often live a feast-or-famine life, subsisting on barley and water during the week, awaiting the return of a husband who takes the whole family to the market on Saturday morning and treats everyone to sodas, potato pancakes, pieces of pork, mutton and fish, oranges and bananas and bread, only to disappear again on Sunday afternoon.

Under these circumstances the category of *wanlla*, snack or treat, is coming to have a meaning reciprocal to the *almuirzu*, the home-cooked meal. As mentioned before, one of the many rules of household etiquette requires that, on venturing into the outside world, one must return bearing gifts: *wanlla*. When husbands come and go on a weekly basis, *wanlla* prestations become an important fixture of married life.

Wives anxiously prepare the best meal they can on Friday nights, knowing that their husbands have missed country food during the week. The return home should find the wife at the hearth and the cooking pot full of all the best products of the parish. Men relax visibly at the sights and smells that greet them as they enter the doorway, the "Alabay" on their lips marking their reentry into indigenous ways.

The man answers the woman's *sopa* with *wanlla*: food purchased in the Inter-Andean Valley on the journey home. It may include bread and noodles, *capulies* in season, whatever he can afford. When times are bad, penny candies for the children take the place of groceries.

The symbolic role of *wanlla* remains that of snacks and treats: frivolous little elaborations to a diet that depends on the basic sustenance of barley, potatoes, and *habas* provided by the family farm. In actuality, the ability of subsistence farming to support the family is eroding, and the groceries bought with wages are of ever-increasing importance. But Zumbagua ideologies, those of the boys who work in the city and those of their elders alike, continue to emphasize the primacy of the agricultural and domestic world and its ability to maintain the family. Not only the economic primacy of farming, but the social hierarchy within the family demanded by the relations of production in the agrarian sector, are sustained by the people of Zumbagua today as centrally important to their cultural identity.

The Kitchen and Outside: Household Economies

It is age that gives authority in these agricultural and domestic realms. The oldest man and woman wield a great deal of power over their heirs: they are owners of most of the property and livestock and generally assume their unquestioned right to continue managing those assets which they have ceded to their children and grandchildren.

Wise parents gradually give control of some portion of their property to their children, teaching them responsibility. The first major transfer of property usually occurs at marriage, but gifts of livestock begin when a child is young. Among the sheep a family herds, the guinea pigs underfoot in the house, the dogs in the patio, one or two are allocated to children, who learn the joys and anxieties of ownership as their charges prosper or die and bear the brunt of another's anger if at fault when a sibling's sheep strays while in their care. Young children are encouraged to feel pride in their contributions to the family's wealth; as they mature, they begin to sell an occasional sheep to purchase their own clothing, or volunteer to contribute *cuyes* when the family participates in food gift exchanges with another household, thus beginning to invest in social networks of their own.

The grandfather where I lived was a good teacher: in one of his fields, he gave (*mingana*) one row to each of the young grandchildren, some still toddlers. He encouraged them to care for their plants, asking them each morning if they had gone out to the field to look at them. There was more than one lesson to be learned: in thus teaching them to pay individual attention to a few dozen plants, he was teaching them the kind of meticulous, personalized investment of time and attention that characterizes Zumbaguan agricultural practice. He himself rose early each morning and spent the sunrise hour walking the fields, bending to check the undersides of leaves for blight, mounding earth around a bean plant uprooted by a careless passerby. Children and adults alike feared incurring his displeasure by accidentally harming a plant; no damage, however slight, escaped his vigilant eye.

This kind of minuscule, "waste not, want not" attention extends from Zumbagua agriculture into food processing and cooking. A woman threshing *habas* with a stick will spend her rest periods sifting through the refuse, pulling out unpopped pods; children sitting on a pile of threshed barley stalks stacked for use as fuel unthinkingly ply their fingers as they talk, stripping the grains off the few stalks that had escaped the threshing stick, stuffing them into their shirts to add to the bags in the storeroom later.

In preparing meals, the same attitude of investing labor, even when the return seems so small as to be not worth the effort, is one of the most striking characteristics of household management in the parish. For example, women from the high *comunas* milk their sheep. The small amount of milk thus produced is added to soups in the manner of eggs, half a cup of liquid in several gallons of soup broth. It provides a small, almost unnoticeable protein supplement and, the women believe, adds a little "something" to the taste of their soups.

The desire to make use of absolutely everything, no matter how insignificant, implies a second characteristic of household management: the tight integration of all aspects of production, processing, consumption, and waste management. Tully Cornick and Roger Kirby have pointed out the interrelation of crop and animal management in agricultural practices in the Ecuadorian Sierra, animal-dung fertilizer for maize plants being produced by cows fed on maize husks and stalks, only the ears being diverted to human consumption (1981). This kind of closely interrelated cycle extends into kitchen practice. Waste products such as potato peels, onion skins, dirty dishwater, and other vegetable wastes produced in the kitchen are valuable products, used to feed the precious family pig. (There was stiff competition among my neighbors for my garbage, as I kept no animals.) Not only nutrients but recycled water are provided through the pig slops, meaning that the laborious task of fetching water does not have to be performed for animals, but only for humans.

Cuyes eat weeds that grow in the fields, daily gathered by women while "resting" from harder agricultural tasks. The few vegetable remains disdained by the pigs, such as *haba* pods, are saved and fed to the sheep. Nothing is wasted: even onion rootlets are saved and used as pot scrubbers.

Dogs eat what people do: the soup pot always contains more than the humans of the household can eat, and the rest is fed to the dogs and cat. This practice has ideological value, for even poor households eating unseasoned gruel have the all-important sense of being able to provide amply for themselves: the soup pot is full, one can eat as much as one wants. Also, because the underfed dogs always eat every drop of what is left, the Zumbagua kitchen knows no leftovers: every meal is cooked fresh.

Because fuel is scarce, nothing is ever overcooked: foods are consumed boiled until just tender, or lightly toasted. Impure water kills babies, and lack of protein makes small bodies, but the diet in the parish, low in fat, high in fiber, is healthy to an extreme.

Nutritionists are critical of many Sierran kitchen practices seen in Zumbagua, such as the peeling of potatoes and the rinsing of vegetables, as being wasteful of needed nutrients. As Cornick and Kirby observed about agronomists' suggestions for improving Sierran agricultural practices, however, some approaches ignore the basic strategy of household management, which is not solely producing as much food as possible for humans, but rather deploying resources so as to maintain the entire household, extracting surpluses and returning nourishment to best advantage (1981:15). Fields, dogs, cats, sheep, guinea pigs, and real pigs must be maintained as well as people, and each performs a necessary function within the household economy. Even the cat earns its keep by preventing the field mice from damaging stored grain.

Outside experts unaware of this orientation of peasant kitchen practice see waste and ignorance where there is none. Zumbagua cooks are well aware that potato peels and rinse water contain valuable nutrients; it is precisely for that reason that they put them in the pig bucket in the first place.

The careful recycling of everything the household produces, including "waste," adds to the conception of the household as a closed circle, a unit of production and consumption (and a social unit) complete in itself and self-sufficient. This notion, important in much of Zumbagua ideology, is illusory. The boundaries of the household in fact are permeable, and its entire energy flow is dependent on this fact. Like the isolation of the valley of Zumbagua from the outside world, the self-sufficiency of the farmstead is a necessary fiction, a self-image contradicted by practice. Zumbaguan households receive products from other ecologies, and their members invest labor in other economies. In addition, some of the products that enter the household leave it again, to enter the web of food prestations that link households within the parish to one another.

Things That Go out from Inside

Reciprocity and redistribution have long been recognized as the mainstays of Andean social organization (Alberti and Mayer 1974). In Zumbagua, no household can survive without ties of kin and *compadrazco* to give it a support network. These ties, which exist primarily to provide access to labor and mutual aid, are created and maintained largely through the ritualized exchange of food and drink.

There is a rich vocabulary of food gifts to acknowledge events and relationships. Despite the impression sometimes given in the anthropological literature that such gifts have an invariable, rigidly defined form, in Zumbagua the rules governing food prestations are fluid enough to admit the expression of emotions about the relationship, not simply to acknowledge its existence. There is also always the possibility of making a presentation well or doing it badly, of delighting or insulting the recipient, whether deliberately or through simple incompetence. Thus the gift that accompanies a request to be a *padrino* must involve eggs, but they could be cooked or raw, accompanied by bottles of wine and beer for a friend, or the more expensive and impersonal raw chickens for an influential stranger. Similarly, a godmother should remember her godchildren on Finados (All Souls' Day), but whether she chooses to do so simply with *colada* for the parents, with bread and candies for the child, or—if the child is very special to her—to conform to the cultural ideal and buy a *tanda wawa* (a bread baby) is at her discretion.

When labor or services are activated between two parties, food again passes between households: if compadres let you use their storeroom to keep your onions overnight, some onions must stay behind when you leave, or next week your friend may accidentally forget to be home when you bring the next load; those who help to plant *jabus* early in the year will act pleasantly surprised at the basket of *llullu jabus* that arrives on their doorstep months later, but if none are given, the gossip that eventually reaches your ears will prove that they neither forgave nor forgot.

One may mark a *compadrazgo* tie with a wealthy "white" one hardly knows just through the minimal formalities. If relations between siblings cool, only the annual pot of *colada* at Finados acknowledges the tie between them. But most kin and compadre relations are both affective and instrumental, and are frequently reinforced through casual prestations of food and drink.

Men only offer food to their families; their relationships with other men are affirmed through the sharing of drinks. Through *trago*, friendships and agreements are sealed and kinship is acknowledged. *Compadrazgo* and affinal ties are also renewed through the offering of the glass. For men, market days are characterized by *trago*. Ringing the marketplace are the *trago* shops, where moonshine cane liquor is siphoned out of barrels into smaller containers (the similarity between containers used for gasoline and kerosene and those used for *trago* is unmistakable, as is the smell characteristic of both), or directly into glasses for immediate consumption. For most men, market day begins early, down by the potato wholesalers or at the livestock market. But Saturdays end in the afternoon with rounds of drinking, done in the formal Andean style with its endless permutations of politeness and offense in the sequence of offering, refusal, and offering again. As when a meal is shared, a drink in Zumbagua is always a prestation in which one gives and the other receives; honor is always involved, along with the attempt to place another in one's debt.

For women, market day is marked by gifts of *wanlla* (*golosinas*, as they say in Spanish): little food treats shared among sisters or friends, but especially in cases of a blood bond. It is at the marketplace, among other women and girls, that the giving of *wanlla* becomes a woman's affair. A woman gives her comadre a two-sucre sweet bread; it is divided in half to be shared with the comadre's sister, who breaks it again to split between her two children. Some *wanlla* can be tucked away to be redistributed later; not the least of the pleasures it gives its recipient is the possibility of using the treat as a gift for someone else. A woman's pleasure and power derive from choosing when and how to distribute food, in the market as in the kitchen.

The market thus serves as a big weekly playing field for the games of giving and receiving by which the rural economy and society are linked. At the same time, it is where the outbreaks of verbal dueling, men's fist-fights, and the occasional hair-pulling and face-slapping of a women's fight occur that mark the schisms and conflicts generic to the same system. But this fabric of interactions is a thin overlay that decorates the main economic moment of the market, adorning without concealing the real movement of significance. While a network of kin and neighbor is being sustained through interaction among locals at the market, the economically significant relation is that in which sucres are changing hands between local people and mestizos. Mestizos from the coast and the Inter-Andean Valley come up to the *páramo* to make money by selling goods. They charge a high price to cover their long trip and the cold and discomfort they must endure there; if they did not make a profit, they would not come at all.

Despite the ideology of reciprocal gift-giving still strong in the parish, the articulations that support the indigenous household as a unit of production and consumption are less and less those of the community and more and more purely economic ties with the anonymous capitalist system. In this altered reproduction of the peasant household, an isolated unit of consumption and production replaces the family sunk in a web of personalized, unabstractable, thick relations.

Ironically, the demands of the gift-giving relation among households is itself one source of Zumbagua families' need for cash. Increasingly, food produced in the parish is not used in prestations between households. Barley, *habas,* onions make very poor *wanlla;* the only really acceptable *wanlla* foods are those sold in the market. The event of the market day is also the occasion of *wanlla* giving, either in the marketplace itself or on returning home. Thus even the social and affective ties that bind household and parish together have been permeated by the demand for cash.

Things That Come in from Outside

The modern Zumbagua household survives through strategies that involve it in a variety of ecological zones and economic arenas. The division of labor through which this survival is accomplished places women in spheres that are within parish boundaries, while men move between the parish and the world outside.

Women's association with cooking has given them one means of earning money: cooking food for the Saturday market. Many women complain that they actually lose money in these enterprises, because they are expected to feed the entire extended family gratis. Their food stall, by providing household members with market treats without demanding precious cash, subsidizes the whole family, despite the fact that expenditures and profits from market cooking are considered to be the cook's own, separate from household finances. A woman who does not know how to control these demands on her products quickly goes into the red. Experienced women usually only serve chicken soup to an elite few within their network: perhaps a woman's parents, her favored youngest child, an especially prestigious compadre. Others receive small plates of rice with fried topping. Even this dish represents a special-occasion food.

Selling at the market, a woman participates in the cash economy but never leaves the cultivated, inhabited zone of the parish. But women's work also takes them into the wilderness called *ujsha sacha*, the grasslands above their fields and houses.

The *páramo* is *sacha* (wilderness), but it is a *sacha* that lies within Zumbagua's territory, not beyond it. For all its wildness, the *páramo* belongs to the picture of life within the parish, unlike the other *sacha*, the *yunga* that lies to the west. Religious symbolism connected with the *páramo* involves masculine fertility, but on an everyday basis the *páramo* seems to have strong feminine connotations. It is primarily women and girls who go up to the *páramo* to herd sheep and to cut *ujsha* for fuel. This *ujsha*, once brought into the homestead area, is intimately associated with women and their activities.

Ujsha is the fuel used in cooking. A woman at the hearth sits on a pile of *ujsha*, and it is piled up everywhere around her; even when she sits elsewhere in the house, *ujsha* will be spread out underneath her. *Ujsha* is used in many other feminine tasks as well. It is used in sweeping: women first scatter *ujsha* on the dirt floor to absorb moisture and pick up vegetable matter, then sweep up straw and debris together. It serves as packing material and as the medium for storing potatoes, because of its capacity to absorb moisture. Beds are made of *ujsha* covered with blankets. It is furniture, tool, cleanser, fuel: women use it in all aspects of kitchen work.

There is also an unmistakable visual association as well, of the rounded *páramo* hills, covered with *ujsha*, with the round shape of the *ujsha*-thatched houses that are women's domain, and with the rounded shape of women themselves, covered with layers of skirts and shawls.

Hills, houses, and women all have layers of coverings and hollow interiors that can hold lives within them. (According to popular mythology, the wild hills, sentient beings, sometimes trap children inside them.)

Symbolic associations and economic significance both link the *páramo* to women's lives. Pasture for sheep and fuel for cooking, both associated today with feminine tasks, are its two major contributions to the household. Also, work done in the *páramo* is unpaid labor utilizing a communally owned resource; it thus belongs strictly to the domestic economy that is itself an increasingly feminized domain.

The *yunga*, in contrast, is masculine in both symbolic associations and economic exploitation. Although husband-wife pairs sometimes travel down to the *yunga* to get wood, the image of a journey to the *yunga* is strongly evocative of maleness. Men go together to the *yunga* and speak of the trips as experiences that create male bonding and a kind of emotional high. Very young children travel to the *páramo* with their mothers, but young children are not taken to the *yunga*. Boys nearing adolescence may be taken there by their fathers: the trip to the *yunga* separates the young male from his childhood, when he was symbolically female, part of his mother's domain.

The association of shamanism with the *yunga* zone adds to the aura of glamorous masculinity that surrounds the western slopes. Although both men and women cure, the complex of shamanism is heavily masculine in its symbolic overtones, and truly powerful and dangerous shamans are male. The most famous and wealthy *yumbo* (shaman) of the parish resides in Cocha Uma, a high and remote *comuna* on the western edge of the parish, on the borders of the *yunga*. In addition, Zumbagua has been visited by shamans from the west who are Tsátchelas (Colorados). They are an indigenous people famous throughout Ecuador for their shamanic powers; they are also the only major indigenous population of the littoral still extant. The word for shaman in Zumbagua is *yumbo*, a term that in colonial times referred to inhabitants of the western slopes (Salomon 1981:193; Carrera Colin 1981:145). This fact in itself is suggestive, the more so because young consultants sometimes confused the terms *yumbo* and *yunga*, suggesting an unrecognized relation between the two words. Zumbagua Christmas festivities feature dancers called *yumbos*, who are supposed to be "wild men" from the *yunga*, half-animal, who bear western-slopes products.[1]

Among the *yumbo* dancers in 1983 was my neighbor, a man who worked *machitiwan*, "with a machete." This phrase denotes someone who performs wage labor in the littoral, on small *fincas* toward the upper limits of the sugar-cane production zone. This form of labor is common in the parish, though more men commute to Quito than travel to the western slopes. *Machiti* work represents an earlier form of wage labor; whereas Zumbagua men have only found construction work and other jobs in the capital for a decade at most, many of the men who go to the *monte* are older men who have worked there for twenty years or more.

The labor relations on the *finca* also follow an older style than do those of the city. In Quito, workers find their own housing, buy their own meals, and are paid strictly in cash. *Finca* relations resemble those of the hacienda in that payment is partly in kind: workers receive housing and meals and are often given *yunga* products to take back home to the *páramo*. Many older men are more comfortable with these kinds of relations than with the more impersonal structure of the construction site: they expect to be taken care of by their employers and find in the meals cooked for them an indication of an affective bond as well as a work relationship.

The *yunga* provides another opportunity for making money, one that is also primarily—though not exclusively—exploited by men: the transport and sale of contraband *trago*, cane liquor. *Trago* is big business in Zumbagua, because of the parish's location between the western lowlands, where sugar cane is grown and illegal stills maintained, and the enormous market for *trago* in the Inter-Andean Valley. *Trago* moves from the *monte* into Zumbagua by mule, llama, and horse trains, then down into the Inter-Andean Valley, money frequently changing hands several times in the process. These trains avoid the highway, using *yunga-páramo* trails that may be of some antiquity. Some *trago* also travels by truck and bus, hidden under more innocuous *yunga* products such as oranges or *panela*. The full-time *trago* runners are something of an outlaw group, typifying the wildness associated with the *yunga*, but many Zumbaguan households have one or more members who are involved in the *trago* business to some degree.

"Machete work," *trago*, and shamanism all support the association between men and the *yunga*. It is perhaps not surprising, then, that lowland products have something of a male aura in Zumbagua cuisine. *Trago, uchu,* bananas, and oranges are all eaten raw; the first two are primary examples of *jayaj* foods, the bitter, strong substances contrasted with women's *mishqui* cooked foods in Chapter 4, while the latter two foods are quintessential examples of *wanlla,* the foods that men give to wives and children. *Trago,* oranges, and bananas all figure heavily in the flow of consumables that surround the largely male domain of the fiesta.

It is perhaps because of this association of maleness, rawness, and *yunga* foods that the people of Zumbagua find eating soups made of *yuca* so distasteful. The substitution of *yuca* for *papas* as part of a meal is experienced as unsatisfying to a degree that seems inexplicable in terms of the qualities of the two foods themselves; the problem may lie in the violation of cultural categories when a *yunga* product, something men bring in from outside, is substituted for the food that women produce inside. A soup made with a product of the *yunga* could never taste *mishqui*.

The foods that men bring home from Quito are, of course, also from outside; they are even more foreign than *yunga* products. The urban Inter-Andean Valley is treated as a kind of production zone in the organization of the Zumbagua market. One area of the market features onions, mutton, and llama meat, all local products. Another offers *yunga* products: *muyu cachi, rapadura,* oranges, bananas, *yuca,* and plantains. A third is given over to manufactured foods, all sold by Inter-Andean Valley women: processed salt and sugar in plastic bags, rice, flour, candles, sardines, cookies. These kinds of foods are what men bring home from Quito as *wanlla.*

Conclusion

The fact that foods are grouped in the market according to their origins—where they were produced, how, and by whom—reveals that some of the categories by which foods are known and understood derive from the productive process. As earlier discussions of *sopas* and *secos, wanlla* and meals, rice and barley made clear, the semiotic ordering of foods in cuisine refers to their role in consumption as well. Cooking, a process that involves not only processing and combining but also categorizing and naming (one food becoming a snack, another a main course, one a *seco,* one a *sopa*), is truly a "gateway" between production and consumption, as it has been called (Niñez 1984:9), transforming the results of labor into the means for the satisfaction of desire.

This process, as I have suggested, is not only one of transformation but also one of homogenization, by which the peasant household, so greatly diversified in its economic strategies, reasserts a unified cultural and individual identity in its consumption style. The foods eaten in the Zumbagua household originate in the parish itself, the *yunga,* or the Inter-Andean Valley; they are grown or raised on the farmstead, or they are acquired through barter, or with money obtained from wage labor, from *trago* running, or from selling cooked food in the market. Once they enter the household, the structures of cuisine are used to transform these products of diverse ecologies and economies into something that is uniquely of Zumbagua, a culturally domesticated creation ready for consumption.

It is because of this function of cooking and eating as a means of asserting cultural identity that cuisine features among the important markers of ethnicity. The act of cooking food, and thus transforming it, is a means of expressing what a people think of themselves, who they are, where they live, and what their place is in the natural and social world and in the political and economic systems of the nation. It follows that when the cultural identity of a people is in question, as in the parish of Zumbagua today, symbols taken from the realm of cuisine, eating fried vegetables or eating foraged vegetables, buying bread or buying *panela,* become active in the arenas of ongoing discourse in which questions of cultural identity are confronted. The multiclass, multicultural social universe in which a people find themselves is mirrored in a multiplicity of cuisines; and certain foods, such as white rice and *máchica,* become metonyms for these cuisines and the kinds of people associated with them.

This process, though occurring in the realm of discourse, has both economic and cultural referents; the metonymic associations of food symbols refer not only to people and to styles of living, but to productive processes as well: *máchica* calls to mind not just the indigenous woman but her grinding stone, sifting screen, threshing stick, and hoe; white rice represents not just the marketplace but the shedding of the poncho, the bus ride to Quito, the awkward feel of Spanish syllables in a Quichua-speaker's mouth. By the same token, changes in production must inevitably alter symbolic associations, for changes in the content of the life experience that people bring to bear on their understanding of symbols and discourses must in turn alter the content of the latter. This process of interaction between symbolic and economic structures is not unmediated: not only is life experience directly shaped by the act of working, but the experience of work and pleasure is also molded by political and social forces. Whether the task is bitter or sweet, the meal desired or detested has to do with their class and cultural associations and with the dominant ideologies current in society and the hegemonic processes by which these ideologies make their presence felt.

In view of the fact that economic, sociopolitical, and ideological forces inform cuisine, it is not surprising that the etiquette of meals contains a politics all its own. The shared meal represents the unity of the family that gathers to eat it, but the manner in which it is served and eaten also speaks to the divisions between household members. Sex, age, and kinship are used to place household members in separate social categories, each with their own productive role and their own right to claim household resources for their own purposes; each social category also defines a particular role in the family's power structure. The etiquette of the meal reveals both the social structure of the household and the resultant social rifts; not only is the structure reflected by the meal, but it may be either reinforced or broken through the political processes contained within its etiquette.

If the etiquette of the meal thus reproduces household relations, the flow of exchanges and reciprocities in food between households creates the larger social structure of the parish as a whole. As I have suggested in this work, the modern Zumbagua household increasingly finds that these movements of labor and products among families are eroding, while anonymous market exchanges increase; symbol and ideology struggle to encompass these changes.

The structures of cuisine, discourses about food, and practices of cooking and serving together form a complex central to the culture and society of Zumbagua. Zumbagua today finds itself at a historical juncture in which a contradictory economic situation demands resolution, but the choices to be made are difficult and possible outcomes unclear. These choices are by no means nakedly economic, but lie embedded in complexes of cultural, social, and political practices. The practice of cooking, the structures that underlie it, and the discourses about it not only reflect these conflicts but are an active part of the processes by which they emerge and through which they will be resolved.

Note

1. See Salomon 1981 for a complete description of the *yumbo* dancer complex in the northern Quito area. While they differ from the Zumbagua *yumbo* dance in many aspects, the essential symbolic attributes of the *yumbo* are the same. According to Salomon, the *yumbo* dancer stands for, "a wild green universe, a shamanistic world" (171). A further discussion of the *yumbo* dancer is found in Fine 1983.

APPENDIX:
ETHNOGEOGRAPHY

Ucu: **The Center**

Throughout this work I refer repeatedly to "Zumbagua," and "the people of Zumbagua," as though Zumbagua were a place the existence of which is universally recognized. Certainly the name appears on maps, and it occupies a place in the history of Ecuador. Many early documents contain references to a hacienda of that name, and there have since been a succession of ecclesiastical and civil parishes called Zumbagua. The boundaries of these have fluctuated, but all of these "Zumbaguas" clearly contained the area in which I lived and the predecessors of the people among whom I did my fieldwork. Historians and map makers, politicians and clergymen would all agree that the place I am writing about is called "Zumbagua."

Ironically, the only people who would be mystified by this label are many of "the people of Zumbagua" themselves. In the minds of indigenous residents of the modern-day parish, no such place as "Zumbagua" exists. It is not a word people ever use, except for those who have had dealings with government employees, and have learned, as part of the esoteric lore necessary on such occasions, that the place where they live bears that name to the outside world.

When I first moved to Zumbagua and lived in a house near the plaza, I conceived of the parish as a large rural hinterland to a small central settlement, both parish and town being called Zumbagua. Walking far from town, I would tell people that I had come from Zumbagua or was returning to Zumbagua. Blank faces met this statement. I learned after several confusing conversations that the cluster of houses, stores, church, and clinic that I knew as Zumbagua was in fact called *hazinda* (hacienda) or *ucu*. *Hazinda*, used primarily by older people, is a term dating back to the days of the hacienda, when the main hacienda buildings were located there.

Ucu is more complex. In this context, it is usually translated as *el centro*, the center. This translation is deceptive, however: it makes the cognitive map of the people of Zumbagua seem like our own, with settlements as discrete units, boundaries clearly defined, and central place theory assigning relative importance to each unitary location.

Ucu, however, like the famous Incaic/Andean concept *llajta*, is a geopolitical concept that can apply, Chinese-box fashion, to a nested series of units. Thus *ucu* can also refer to the entire valley in which most of the people of Zumbagua live. In this case, *ucu* is translated as *adentro*, inside, and is contrasted to *jawa* (Spanish *afuera*), outside. *Jawa* refers primarily to the towns of the Inter-Andean Valley.

The meaning of *jawa,* and by extension of *ucu,* can be seen from an example: Women looking for buses to ride home from Saturday market shout "Maymun?" ("Where is this one going?") The bus drivers, answering in the monosyllabic Quichua they have learned in order to work these despised Indian routes, answer "Jawa": away from here, to the white world, so forget it. If you do not speak Spanish you are not going there.

Ucu in this sense, within as opposed to without, widens the concept of where these people see themselves as living, but still does not seem to challenge a model of their cognitive map as being like our own. It simply adds another layer to their vision: the closed corporate community operates here, along with central place theory.

But there is a third usage: the contrast *ucu/jawa* can also be used to differentiate west from east. In this case, both terms refer to what is beyond the central valley of the parish: *jawa,* as before, is the Inter-Andean Valley to the east, but *ucu* now refers to the moist, green cloud forest that begins at the edge of Apagua. Asked to translate the term when used in this way, people may offer "*monte*" or another Quichua term, "*yunga*", or they may say, again, "*adentro*". The *monte* is, somehow, even more "inside" than Zumbagua itself in contrast to the "outside" of the Inter-Andean Valley. (Reconcile this with central place theory if you will.)

According to a description of Zumbagua provided to me by one girl, there is a north-south dimension as well, called *janaj/ura* (up/down)[1]. She herself lived towards the very uppermost edge of the *comuna* of Yanaturu, close to the *páramo*. From her house, a dazzling view of the entire valley in which Zumbagua "*centro*" lies is spread out just below one's feet. According to her own conception of geography, this position at the northern and upper edge of the valley, sitting almost in the highest *páramo*, at approximately 3900 m, was *janaj*; the valley below and to the south, a flat expanse at 3400 masl bisected by a deeply cut channel, was *ura*, below or down.

She rejected the terminology *jawa/ucu* for east and west, insisting that *jawa* lies beyond the parish, in no specified direction. East and west in the visible landscape, which form the two sides of the valley, both lower than the northern rim and roughly equal in elevation to one another, are both called *chimba*. Moving her hand from one to the other, tilting it to match each slope, she emphasized their equality in her mind, saying of them *chimba–chimba*. How, she asked, could they have different names when they were the same?

One cannot, then, simply translate EW–NS into *ucu/jawa, janaj/uru*. The directionality of *ucu* is not universally conceded by the people of Zumbagua and what is more, we have not yet exhausted the meanings of *ucu*.

The interiors of caves and houses are *ucu*, as is the inside of any container. The human body is conceived of as a bony shell that protects a hollow, "*kwirpu ucu*" ("inside the body"), where the organs rest. The butchering of animals, in which the body is slit and the organs dumped out, is *pascay*, opening, and killing cuyes is "cuyta pascana", "opening *cuyes*."

Ucu has metaphysical meanings as well. Malevolent hills may trap unwary children *ucupi*, inside their secret cavities, and must be offered food before they will relinquish their captives, who are rendered mute by the experience. Small children are afraid of, and fascinated by, any opening in the earth, even the small cavities in the banks of the highway: magical beings are believed to dwell in them, and they are considered to be doorways into the interior of the world.

The most sacred places all have visible *ucus*, caves or crevices in which offerings and candles may be left. The crater lake Quilotoa, a huge caldron that is shaped like a container, is salty because a black man, a dog, and two sacks of salt are buried within it (*ucupi*), and children tantalize each other for hours with speculations as to what else its waters might hide. Somehow from Quilotoa one may gain entrance to Ucu Pacha, the interior world where creatures from other epochs—giants and dwarfs—live, and where we will live when the apocalypse comes and the earth swallows us up *ucu*, inside itself.[2]

One cannot comprehend what *ucu* means by forcing all of these referents into a single conceptual frame, and then somehow making it equivalent to the word "Zumbagua." The nature of places referred to as *ucu* and *jawa* can only be comprehended if these words are understood to be relative in meaning. *Ucu* is not a word like "Zumbagua," which refers to an unchangingly defined entity, but a relational term, like "here" or "there," which changes according to the speaker's point of reference.

Ucu, I believe, is best understood as "inside," when "inside" is not "here" but "there": the *centro* is the inside of the valley to those who live on its slopes, and the *monte* is *ucu* when one imagines traveling there from the *centro*.

I first became aware of the importance of relational concepts in Zumbagua ethnogeography while listening to a mother and daughter discuss visiting each other. (The daughter lived in her husband's *comuna*.) In attempting to follow their conversation, I became increasingly bewildered until I finally realized that the geographical terms they were using were all relational in nature; none referred to a fixed point. Like a community in which everyone calls one another by kinship terms, eschewing proper names, this conversation contained no place-names.[3]

What makes these terms so difficult for the observer to grasp is the fact that they are not always used relative to the actual position of the speaker, but rather relative to the location of the speaker's household. In the conversation between mother and daughter, for instance, they were standing side by side, yet referred to each other's houses as they stand in relation to their own. Although the mother stood in the plaza, her daughter's house above and to the north of her, she referred to it not as *janaj* but as *washa*, behind, or on the opposing slope. It was in this way that she conceived of the location of her daughter's house in relation to her own. Her daughter, likewise, referred to her mother's house as *washa*, in mirror image to the other.

In conceiving of their houses as *washa* to one another, the two women were not referring to relative spatial location as it is experienced in traveling from one to the other. The two *comunas* are rather distant from each other and not in any way contiguous. On her frequent trips home, the daughter descended to the highway from her own home, then followed the road past town, along a long, uninhabited stretch of road that bordered a steep gorge, past two other *comunas*, and entered her natal *comuna* from below. She then climbed up to the mother's house, a steep ascent that left me breathless whenever I accompanied her. Nothing about this route suggested that the two houses should be seen as in any sense back to back, as the word *washa* would suggest, a relationship that would seem to require some sort of contiguity. One might expect that the two houses would be considered as above and below each other, because the mother's house was located at a much higher altitude than the daughter's, or perhaps as east and west of one another, because the route of the highway is basically east-west, though it is continually winding due to the topography; the houses in fact stand on a northwest–southeast axis.

To be seen as *washa* to each other, each *comuna* must be conceptualized primarily in reference to its relation to the *páramo*. Both *comunas* are long slopes of farmland, the upper reaches of which extend into the huge communal grassland that stretches from the northern reaches of Zumbagua all the way to Angamarca. Along the flanks of this huge expanse, farmland descends into valleys bisected by waterways. Both mother's and daughter's houses lie on valleys oriented to the northeast; but because they rise to the same expanse of *páramo,* they are *washa* to each other. The *páramo* joins them together, and both *comunas* are on its "sides." If they faced each other across a single valley, or if one of them were associated with another *páramo,* such as the one that joins Zumbagua and Tigua, or the one that joins SaraUjsha to Apagua, then they would be *chimba* to each other.

The relational nature of these terms, then, is qualified. These geographical constructs do not suggest a world in which there are no fixed points, but one in which one's own home provides a point of reference that cannot be superseded by any other place, however large, however central in the minds of others. And at the same time, this point of reference provides conceptions of space that are derived not from one's own travels to and from home, but from a conceptualization of the location of the homestead in reference to the total geography of the entire area, and especially in reference to the high places. It has been stated for the central Andes that "These two points are essential to Quechua conceptions of space: every place has (1) a unique spatial orientation, as well as (2) an ever-expanding regional orientation, defined by ever higher mountain peaks" (Allen 1978:48).

Sacha: The Wild Places

The *Páramo*

Both *páramo* and *monte* can be called *sacha,* wilderness. Because they are unlike the areas in which people live and work and are less subject to direct human control, the *sachas* are characterized in indigenous thought as places of great natural beauty, but also of inexplicable and sometimes threatening supernatural forces. Paintings made in the nearby parish of Tigua show three distinct spatial zones, sometimes as clearly defined as in the art of ancient Egypt. In the forefront is human activity; the middle ground is given over to fields, paths, and houses; the upper third of the painting is given over to *páramo,* mountain peaks and sky.

This third area is inhabited by wild creatures, such as condors, deer, and felines, all of which show up in local mythology as creatures that cross the boundaries between human and animal, natural and supernatural, life and death.

The *páramo* is the source of dangerous winds and the home of malevolent hills. Illnesses such as *huaira japishka* and *urcu japishka* ("caught by the wind," "caught by the hill") originate in the *páramo*. I have seen strong young men stricken while in the *páramo* with an illness that I attributed to the debilitating effects of high altitude, but which their families knew to be the act of an *urcu*.

From the *páramo*, too, came the *locos* and *ladrones* (crazies and thieves). I did not at first realize that these terms refer to supernatural inhabitants of the *páramo*. There are a few mentally disturbed and/or retarded individuals in the parish, familiar to everyone and treated with a mixture of compassion and contempt, and people do get robbed both by marauding whites from outside the parish and (they claim) by antagonistic neighbors. But the *loco* brought down from the *páramo* by a rainy wind, who kept everyone awake by wailing and crying around the house; or the *ladrón* on a black and silver motorcycle with dark sunglasses and a special mirror, found in the bottom of a *páramo* pond, which reflected people's secret hiding places, are a very different kind of phenomenon. Aside from the stories that "took place long ago," like the one about the condor that ravished the shepherd girl, everyday anecdotes blend natural and supernatural elements in a way that indirectly reinforces images of *ucu* and *sacha* as mythologically powerful. A rabid horse, remembered from one's childhood as a terrifying beast with its blood-flecked, foaming mouth, is described as having entered the waters of the stream and gone *ucupi* (inside). Not only is Quilotoa the gateway to Ucu Pacha, the interior/other/past-and-future world, but older boys who have been to Quito assure the younger ones that the city contains stairways leading into Ucu Pacha as well.

The *páramo*, the winds and mists that roll down from it, and the watercourses that originate high in the hills and disappear into the earth below, are mythic elements that recur in all kinds of contexts as the origins of the inexplicable. There are ghost stories for children, boogeyman tales that no one quite believes even as they tell them. But other things found in the *páramo* are taken quite seriously by everyone.

There are two stone shrines, Tayta Rumi Cruz (Father Stone Cross) and Rumi Cruz Chico (Little Stone Cross), that represent sacred places. I first heard about Tayta Rumi Cruz when I attended a Sunday Mass at the large, modern church in Zumbagua *centro*, soon after arriving in the parish. Sunday Masses are normally attended mostly by the "white" community, but on this occasion a small, somber contingent of indigenous men and one or two women waited quietly through the Mass so that afterward they could have the privilege of "carrying Tayta Rumi Cruz." This Rumi Cruz was a boulder-sized rock, roughly rectangular, incised with a cross and painted blue and white. It was tied onto the back of one of the men, who carried it around the plaza.

I was staying at the time at the house of a middle-aged white woman who was sacristan of the church. I asked her about Rumi Cruz, and she told me that it was a sacred stone that had been found in the *páramo* long ago and was associated with various miracles. The bishop, she said, always told the *longuitos*[4] when he came to the parish that they ought not worship it as they did, calling it "Tayta" (Father), because there is only one Tayta and that is Tayta Dios, our Father in Heaven. But nonetheless, because they are ignorant and do not understand, they continue in their ways. Always Tayta Rumi Cruz is covered with money and lit candles that devotees have brought, while our poor Virgencita next to him in the church has only a few.

The sacristan's explanation notwithstanding, it is not only *longuitos* who worship Rumi Cruz. A white man from Valencia, a lowland orange-growing town, came knocking on the door one day soon after, begging to be let into the church. His son was dying, he said, and he had come to lay money before Rumi Cruz that he might be saved.[5]

The mythology that surrounds Rumi Cruz concerns men from lower-altitude towns of the Inter-Andean Valley who, because of disasters and afflictions in their community, begged to take Tayta Rumi Cruz away with them to help them change their luck. When they tried to remove it, however, it became heavier and heavier until it could not be moved at all, whereas once they turned around to bring it home it became as light as air. These tales seem European in their story line, but very Andean in their concern with place and altitude.[6]

The stone in the church is only a representative of an actual Tayta Rumi Cruz located in the *páramo* at the highest, southern part of the parish. At first, as I struggled to learn the names of the rocky crags that crown the *páramo,* I assumed that this most sacred place would also be the highest point in the parish.

It was not until I had lived in the *comuna* of Yanatoro for more than a year that I finally was taken to see Tayta Rumi Cruz and its companion shrine, Rumi Cruz Chico. To my surprise, I found that they were not peaks at all, but stone shrines built on high saddles between peaks. Looking at topographic maps when I returned, I realized that these shrines mark the watershed between the parish of Zumbagua and that of Angamarca to the south.

The importance of the *páramo* as the origin of water, and of watersheds as boundaries, is a recurrent theme in the parish. *Comuna* boundaries are based either on watersheds at the tops of hills, or on streambeds at the bottom of them. Places that are separated by a stream are *chimba* to each other: those separated by a watershed are *washa*.

The people of Zumbagua do not use the word *huaca* to refer to these shrines, as do Andean peoples from the Inca heartlands; but the location of these sacred places at the watersheds, and the mythological importance given to Quilotoa, are reminiscent of the concept of *huacas*. Jeanette Evelyn Sherbondy has written of the relation between hydrological and mythological systems in Andean thought. *Huacas,* according to Sherbondy, are "shrines that are usually landscape features, such as rocks, hills, and springs. . . . [O]ne-third of the 329 *huacas* [in the Cuzco area] are sources of water" (1982:74). In this connection, it is noteworthy that, according to Teodoro Wolf's classic study of Ecuadorian geography, the Zumbagua–Angamarca watershed is of regional significance, being "an important point for the division of the waters; on it rise the rivers of Toachi, Pilalo, Quindigua, Angamarca, and Pujili" (1892:85).

The image of the *páramo* as the origin of water is strongly reinforced by the experience of living in the parish. Rain, mists, and clouds, when they arrive, always seem to roll down into the valley from the *páramo*. It is an unforgettable experience, standing on a sun-drenched slope, to see mist enveloping the upper fields across the valley, and then realize that the first gray fingers are already reaching the place where you are standing.

The image of water as lying under the whole earth, a notion that pervades all of indigenous South American thought, is also reinforced in the *páramo,* where the curious half-dead, half-alive vegetation creates thick, spongy cushions that completely hide the surface of the ground. Alfredo de Costales and Piedad de Costales call the *páramo* vegetation of Zumbagua a "living sponge" (1976). Walking across it, one's ear sometimes picks up the sound of invisible running water, hidden from sight far beneath one's feet.

In addition to the two Rumi Cruzes, the *páramo* is the origin of another class of sacred icon, the *niños*. *Niño* is a spanish word meaning "child" or "infant," but in all of Ecuador it has been replaced by the Quichua *wawa*. In Zumbagua, human infants are *wawas;* the word *niño* is reserved for images of the Christ child. Several people own these images, inherited from parents; they have a certain fame in the parish, and white women even travel to other parishes to visit well-known *niños*. I had at first thought of the cult of the *niños* as something of a white phenomenon, extrinsic to indigenous parish life. This hasty conclusion had to be reevaluated when I learned that, while the recent history of the *niños* might be one of inheritance, their ultimate origin was the *páramo*. These images of chubby, pink-skinned, blue-eyed white infants had been found miraculously by solitary walkers in the high hills.

Rumi Cruz and the *niños* are distant presences in many Zumbagua lives. But the third class of *páramo* beings that descend to the parish arouse a high excitement in everyone. They are the *toros* (bulls). In Niñu Fishtu (Christmas), the first fiesta of the year, the *niños* are brought out to the plaza. In the last fiesta of the year, *wagra fishtu* or *toro fishtu* (Corpus Christi), the plaza is completely taken over by the bulls, who, like the *niños*, are in origin of the *páramo*.

The *páramo* is inhabited by cattle that are almost feral; their owners go up periodically to make sure they have not strayed beyond parish limits, and to bring down gravid or ailing individuals for special care; but otherwise they exercise no control over them. For Corpus Christi, the fiesta sponsor and his male support group ride up into the *páramo* and round up bulls, driving them down through their own *comunas* and into the *centro*, where they are penned in anticipation of the bullfighting that is the high point of the fiesta.

These *páramo* bulls, small, thin, and timid, are supplemented in the ring by bulls raised for bullfighting. But regardless of their actual provenance, conceptually all of the bulls are wild beasts that come down from the *páramo*. They are called to come down by the blowing of musical instruments called *bocinos*, wooden tubes some three meters long that are described as being made of bull's horn. The *bocinos* are first blown on the last day of the Easter week.

Seasons and Fiestas

The *llullu jabus* season, which begins at Easter and lasts until Corpus Christi, seems to be a special time in the Zumbagua calendar. The landscape, as the people of the parish were continually pointing out to me, is at its most alive and beautiful then. The fields are green, lush, and full in April, then gradually turn to gold. Every breeze moves the barley in waves and ruffles the leaves of the *habas*. The rains have stopped, and the harsh August winds have not yet begun. The weeding is done, but the back-breaking part of the harvest is still ahead. People dare to make purchases on credit, for the means of repayment are daily visible in the ripening fields; it is too late for frost, blight, or drought to do much damage.

Best of all, the young men begin to come home. After missing a few days' work for the Easter fiesta, some, looking ahead to harvest and Corpus Christi, simply do not bother to go back to the city. Others will return to the parish as the season progresses.

In the houses of the Corpus sponsors, preparations intensify. The fiesta season opened with Niñu Fishtu, the late December celebration for the Christ child, performed not so much for Christ himself as for the *niños*.

Niñu Fishtu and Riyis Fishtu (December 25 and January 6) are small fiestas at the time of planting. The agricultural year and the fiesta cycle are both in their infancy (on Año Viejo, New Year's, the old year's widow mourns and the newborn year mocks her; young men and boys dance together, reviling and abusing the effigy of the Old Year, which is finally burned).

With Semana Santa, the new year is reaching its full potency and vigor. The Christ figure from the church rises from the dead and is paraded around the plaza, once for the *indígenas,* separately for the whites. During the indigenous celebration, the priest tries in vain to control the drunken, rowdy sponsors. Unlike other, solemn occasions, on Semana Santa the sponsors insist on a ludic comportment even inside the church, while outside in the secular fiesta fake policemen burlesque the power order of the nation.

The last, secular day of the indigenous fiesta does not belong to Easter at all, but to the fiesta of the *toros*—Corpus Christi. Guns are fired in the air. Men on horseback descend on the plaza in wild swoops. For the first time, the sound of the *bocinos* is heard. "We are calling the bulls down from the *páramo,*" the fiesta sponsors say. It is as though mythical wild beasts are being urged to begin a long, slow journey that will be going on during the entire season in which the *llullu jabus* are eaten. The bulls move toward the plaza, the barley harvest comes closer and closer. When the grain is ripe, it will be *wagra fishtu,* Corpus Christi, the biggest fiesta of the year. The *bocinos* will sound continuously for days. Everyone will dress in their finest clothes, and the plaza will be transformed into a bullring. The *hombre gordo* and his transvestite *mujer* will dance, fight, and have intercourse; the splendid *danzantes,* their costumes stiff with ornaments, coins, and mirrors, will dance their slow, spinning dance. And most exciting of all, the brave, beautiful young men of the parish will court death in the ring with the bulls in wild bullfights reminiscent of Pamplona. It is a festival of abundance, of fertility, and of masculinity, the high point of the year.

After Corpus there are no more *llullu jabus;* the year dies. It is the quiet time, without fiestas, marked only by All Souls' Day in November, when the dead are fed and, in return, bring the rains. The post-Hispanic Andean year is divided into a living and a dead half (see, for example,

Bastien 1978:78), separated by the important feast of Finados (All Souls'; Hartmann 1973, 1974, 1978; Nash 1979:149; Michaud 1970; Allen 1978; Villavicencio 1973; Parsons 1945; Karsten 1930). This November observance apparently has pre-Hispanic roots (Arriaga 1621: 56, 78; Karsten 1930:14; Poma de Ayala 1936:256; Valcarcel 1963: 472–473). This division of the year into dead and live halves takes on a vivid reality when one lives through a year in Zumbagua and sees the dry, windy, barren months and then watches the fields once more fill with green. Magical children and mythical bulls, big parties and quiet times come and go in accordance with the practice of agriculture by which the whole system is able to reproduce itself. The arrival of each fiesta marks a change in the seasons and in the agricultural activities of the year.

The *Yunga*

If the *páramo* is the source of both dangerous illnesses and powerful icons, the hot, green *yunga* is the source of death and of powerful curers. The connections are more elusive than are the *páramo* themes, probably because the *páramo* is more commonly frequented and better known than the *yunga*.

The association between shamanism and the *yunga* is discussed in Chapter 6. Stories that relate the *yunga* to death occur in the context of talking about the hacienda. Older people express their experience of the hacienda period in a mixture of mundane details and mythologized and apocryphal tales. Among the latter are endless variations on the theme of deaths that took place in the *yunga*. The theme of the body never being found figures heavily in these tales; frequently it has been borne away by tempestuous waters.

While in the field, my tendency was to interpret these tales simply as reflecting hatred of the hacienda, a pan-Ecuadorian distrust of other climates than one's own, and the deep-seated fear that the people of Zumbagua have of dying outside the parish. But R. T. Zuidema and Frank Salomon have both commented to me in personal communications that these tales reflect long-established Andean themes of the *yunga* as a place of death, which Zuidema further relates to the symbolism of the color green.

As discussed in Chapter 6, the *yunga* is associated with the male sex, but only in the sexually mature state. Whereas very young children travel to the *páramo* with their mothers, and later on their own, the first trip to the *yunga* separates the young male from his childhood, when he was symbolically female, part of his mother's domain. It is a trip typically taken by a boy nearing adolescence, taken there by his father or uncles.

The *yunga* suggests not only masculinity but untrammeled sexuality. When I mentioned that I was going to Apagua, a *comuna* associated with the *yunga,* it evoked howls of laughter and ribald jokes. I had better be careful, or wild Apagua men would drag me down into the *yunga* and never let me go; perhaps I would come back with a wild *yunga* husband, or even an *oso* husband. (The *oso,* spectacled bear, is an inhabitant of the *yunga* zone that figures heavily in highland mythology. Like the condor, he is always male.)

The *páramo* too has its sexual connotations. Young couples frequently escape to the *páramo* to make love; courtship may begin there, as well as being consummated there. During Carnaval, when throwing of water and flour and other practical jokes are commonplace, pitched battles with heavy sexual connotations take place among adolescents in the *páramo.*

Both *sachas,* then, are wild and magical places, both fecund and dangerous. The *páramo,* source of water, and the lush, green *yunga* with its explosive vegetation border the controlled productive zone of the parish itself, just as the adolescent sexuality celebrated in these *sacha* zones precedes the controlled reproduction of marriage. Bears, *yumbos,* and *trago;* condors, deer, and *tigres* (felines) symbolize the wild and sexual nature of these areas; tales of death in the *yunga* and health-sapping winds from the *páramo* warn of an implicit threat to society.

In Zumbagua culture, these lessons are transmitted by unspoken association; they are not formally taught. My neighbor who danced the *yumbo* had a son who was growing fast, moving from a thoughtless childhood into a rather somber adolescence, preoccupied with his family's rocky finances and unenviable social position. His father, on one of his rare visits home, said nothing about the boy's moodiness but announced that they would go together to the *yunga.* Some months after this trip, he and the boy's godfather accompanied the youth to the church and sponsored him to carry Rumi Cruz. These two events had immediate benefits in his relations with his peers. Still poor, he had tales of the *yunga* with which to tantalize his wealthier playmates. He had also undertaken a man's religious duty, while they remained children.

Both of these pilgrimages helped him to move into adulthood. Whatever connections he also made between Rumi Cruz, masculine sign of the uppermost watershed of the parish, and the wet, hot *yunga* lands below, laden with images of masculine sexuality, he made them without the help of an explicit verbalized cosmology in which to place his experiences.

Similarly, although my compadres seemed to think it important to take me to Rumi Cruz and other named places in the *páramo*, they felt little need to say anything to me about them. When we reached Rumi Cruz, one of the family members placed a lit candle inside. "What happens," I wanted to know, "When you light a candle and place it inside there?" He looked at me, "It burns," he replied.

Notes

1. These are dialect variations of the terms *hanan/urin* used in the central Andes to refer to upper and lower, familiar in the anthropological literature as the names of the moieties of Incaic communities (see, for example, Rowe 1963:262). Although some areas of Ecuador have similar divisions, for example pre-Hispanic Quito (Salomon 1975:292–293) and modern Cañar (Fock 1981: 406–408), it should be noted that both of these areas experienced Inca influence. In Zumbagua, the *comunas* do not seem to be formally divided into upper and lower *comunas*, though I repeatedly witnessed the pairing of *comunas*, during fiestas, such that a group of performers from a *comuna* located below the plaza appeared on the same day as one from above it. Nevertheless, I was never able to elicit any usage of *janaj/ura* that was not purely relative; no parishwide or areawide assignation of *comunas* as high or low seems to exist.

Evidence for marriage patterns is similarly inconclusive. Although consultants repeatedly refused to acknowledge it as a rule or preference, *comuna* exogamy is clearly the norm. Based on marriages for which I knew both partner's origins, I was unable to find any regularities that would suggest a further upper-lower division. (Parish marriage and birth records do not record *comuna* origins, and the similarities of names makes it impossible securely to identify individuals mentioned.) My intuitive feeling is that marriage strategies involve choosing a partner from a *comuna* lower or higher than one's own, but this practice would not result in a binary pattern on a parishwide level. For instance, two brothers in a *comuna* higher than the *centro* married cousins from an even higher *comuna*, thus giving themselves access to high grazing lands. Other marriages may provide access to different types of altitudinal zones even though the two *comunas* involved are of similar maximum and minimum elevations, as for example when the husband's family lives at the bottom of his *comuna*, while the wife's household is located at the upper reaches of hers.

2. These beliefs have obvious similarities with Andean cosmologies described elsewhere. See, for example, Núñez del Prado 1969; Casaverde Rojas 1970; Sharon 1978:80; Isbell 1978:207–215.

3. Thousands of place-names do exist in the parish for geographical points of every size, names for large landmarks overlapping with those of smaller features.

4. *Longo*, a derogatory word referring to indigenous persons, plus the diminutive (and affectionate) *-ito*.

5. The fact that a resident of a zone below the *yunga* would come up into the

Sierra to pay homage to a probably pre-Christian icon of the *páramo* opens up tantalizing but insupportable suggestions of a unified pre-Hispanic vertical system. This supposition is lent credence by the popularity of Zumbagua shamans among "whites" from towns such as Valencia. Nonetheless, in addition to the perils of treating modern practices as "survivals," the fact that Ecuadorians of all races and classes are prone to a happy eclecticism where religious, mystical, and health practices are concerned militates against taking such reconstructions too seriously. A more valuable aspect of this incident is that it contributes to a scant but growing body of published information on the pan-Ecuadorian network of religious practice, including pilgrimages, folk Catholicism, shamanism, cursing and curing, and mystical vision questing, that binds together Ecuadorians throughout the nation in a web of communication and power that coexists with the infrastructure of the nation-state, yet remains invisible to and unacknowledged by it.

6. See Moya 1981 for other Ecuadorian examples of tales that reiterate the theme of an unbreakable bond linking sacred shrines, geographical areas, and the people who are born to them.

BIBLIOGRAPHY

Acosta-Solís, Misael
1968 *Divisiones fitogeográficas y formaciones geobotánicas del Ecuador.* Quito: Casa de la Cultura Ecuatoriana.

Alberti, Giorgio and Enrique Mayer, eds.
1974 *Reciprocidad e intercambio en los Andes peruanos.* Lima: Instituto de Estudios Peruanos.

Allen, Catherine (also cited as Catherine Allen Wagner)
1978 "Coca, Chicha, and Trago: Private and Communal Rituals in a Quechua Community." Ph.D. dissertation, University of Illinois.

Althusser, Louis
1971 "Ideology and Ideological State Apparatuses." In his *Lenin and Philosophy*, pp. 127–188. Ben Brewster, trans. New York: Monthly Review Press.
1977 *For Marx.* London: Verso. Ben Brewster, trans. (originally published as *Pour Marx*, Francois Maspero, 1965).

Amin, Samir
1976 *Unequal Development.* Brian Pearce, trans. New York: Monthly Review Press.

Anderson, E. N.
1982 "Food and Ethnicity in East Asia and in the World." Paper presented at the American Ethnological Society.

Appadurai, Arjun
1981 "Gastro-Politics in Hindu South Asia." *American Ethnologist* 8(3): 494–511.

Arnott, Margaret L., ed.
1975 *Gastronomy: The Anthropology of Food and Food Habits.* The Hague: Mouton.

Arriaga, Pablo José de
1621 *Extirpación de la idolatria del Piru.* Lima: Geronymo de Contreras. Edited and translated by L. Clark Keating as *The Extirpation of Idolatries in Peru*. Lexington: University of Kentucky Press, 1968.

Atuñez de Mayolo R., Santiago E.
1981 *La Nutrición en el antiguo Peru.* Lima: Banco Central de Reserva del Peru.

Babb, Lawrence A.
1970 "The Food of the Gods in Chhattisgarh: Some Structural Features of Hindu Ritual." *Southwest Journal of Anthropology* 26(3):287–304.

Bibliography

Bakhtin, Mikhail M.
  1968   *Rabelais and His World.* Cambridge, Mass.: M.I.T. Press.
  1981   *The Dialogic Imagination.* Austin: University of Texas Press.
Barsky, Osvaldo
  1980   "Los Terratenientes serranos y el debate político previo al dictado de la ley de reforma agraria de 1964 en el Ecuador." *In Ecuador: Cambios en el agro serrano,* Osvaldo Barsky et al., eds., pp. 133–206. Quito: FLACSO-CEPLAES.
Barthes, Roland
  1957   *Mythologies.* Paris: Éditions du Seuil. Translated by Annette Lavers. London: Granada Publishing, 1972.
  1961   "Pour une Psycho-sociologie de l'alimentation contemporaine." *Annales: Économies, Sociétés, Civilisations* 16(5):977–986. Translated by Elborg Forster as "Toward a Psychosociology of Contemporary Food Consumption" in Forster and Ranum 1979, pp. 166–173.
  1965   *Eléments de sémiologie.* Paris: Gonthier. Translated by Annette Lavers and Colin Smith as *Elements of Semiology.* New York: Hill and Wang, 1967.
  1970   *L'Empire des signes.* Geneva: Skira. Translated by Richard Howard as *Empire of Signs.* New York: Hill and Wang, 1982.
Basile, David Giovanni
  1974   *Tillers of the Andes: Farmers and Farming in the Quito Basin.* Studies in Geography 8. Chapel Hill: University of North Carolina Department of Geography.
Bastien, Joseph W.
  1978   *Mountain of the Condor: Metaphor and Ritual in an Andean Ayllu.* New York: West Publishing.
Beck, B.
  1969   "Colour and Heat in South Indian Ritual." *Man* 4:553–572.
Belote, James Dalby
  1984   "Changing Adaptive Strategies Among the Saraguros of Southern Ecuador." Ph.D. dissertation, University of Illinois, Urbana-Champaign.
Belote, Linda
  1978   "Prejudice and Pride: Indian-White Relations in Saraguro, Ecuador." Ph.D. dissertation, University of Illinois, Urbana-Champaign.
Bonnet, Jean-Claude
  1976   "Le Réseau culinaire dans l'encyclopédie." *Annales: Économies, Sociétés, Civilisations* 31(5):891–914. Translated by Elborg Forster as "The Culinary System in the *Encyclopédie,*" in Forster and Ranum 1979, pp. 139–165.
Bornstein-Johanssen, Annika
  1975   "Sorghum and Millet in Yemen." In Arnott 1975, pp. 287–295.

Bibliography

Bourdieu, Pierre
1977 "The Economics of Linguistic Exchanges." *Social Science Information* 16:645–668.
1979 *Outline of a Theory of Practice.* Richard Nice, trans. Cambridge: Cambridge University Press.

Bowie, Malcolm
1979 "Jacques Lacan." In *Structuralism and Since: From Lévi-Strauss to Derrida,* John Sturrock, ed., pp. 116–153. Oxford: Oxford University Press.

Brillat-Savarin, Jean A.
1926 *The Physiology of Taste.* New York: Liveright.

Bruneton, Ariane
1975 "Bread in the Region of the Moroccan High Atlas: A Chain of Daily Technical Operations in Order to Provide Daily Nourishment." In Arnott 1975, pp. 275–285.

Brush, Stephen B.
1977 *Mountain, Field, and Family: The Economy and Human Ecology of an Andean Valley.* Philadelphia: University of Pennsylvania Press.
1980 "Potato Taxonomies in Andean Agriculture." In *Indigenous Knowledge Systems and Development,* David W. Brokensha, D. M. Warren, and Oswald Werner, eds., pp. 37–47. Washington, D.C.: University Press of America.

Burgos, Hugo
1970 *Relaciones Interétnicas en Riobamba.* Mexico: Instituto Indigenista Interamericano.

Carrera Colin, Juan
1981 "Apuntes para una investigación ethnohistórica de los cacicazgos del corregimiento de Latacunga S.S. XVI y VXII." *Cultura* (Quito) 4(11):129–179.

Carvalho Neto, Paulo de
1964 *Diccionario del folklore ecuatoriano.* Quito: Editorial Casa de la Cultura Ecuatoriana.

Casaverde Rojas, Juvenal
1970 "El Mundo sobrenatural de una comunidad." *Allpanchis* 2:121–244.

Chang, K. C., ed.
1977 *Food in Chinese Culture: Anthropological and Historical Perspectives.* New Haven: Yale University Press.

Chiriboga, Manuel
1985 *El Sistema alimentario Ecuatoriano: Situación y perspectivas. Ecuador Debate* 9:35–84.

Cisneros Cisneros, César
1948 *Demografía y estadística sobre el indio ecuatoriano.* Quito: Tall. Gráf. Nacionales.

Bibliography

Clark, Gracia
  1985 "Domestic Work and Trading: Pressures on Asante Wives and Mothers." Paper presented at the 1985 meetings of the Society for Economic Anthropology, Urbana, Ill.
Clark, Priscilla
  1975a "Thoughts for Food I: French Cuisine and French Culture." *French Review* 49(1):32–41.
  1975b "Thoughts for Food II: Culinary Culture in Contemporary France." *French Review* 49(2):198–205.
Cordero, Luis
  1950 *Enumeración botánica de las principales plantas, así útiles como nocivas, indígenas o aclimitadas, que se dan en las provincias del Azuay y del Cañar en la República del Ecuador.* 2d edition. Madrid: Afrodisio Aguado.
Cornick, Tully R. and Roger A. Kirby
  1981 *Interactions of Crops and Livestock Production in the Generation of Technology in Sloped Areas.* Publication of New York State College of Agriculture and Life Science. Ithaca, N.Y.: Cornell University.
Costales, Alfredo and Piedad de Costales
  1976 *Zumbagua-Guangaje: Estudio socioeconómico.* Quito: Instituto Ecuatoriano de Antropología y Geografía.
Coward, Rosalind
  1985 *Female Desires.* New York: Grove Press.
Coward, Rosalind and John Ellis
  1977 *Language and Materialism: Developments in Semiology and the Theory of the Subject.* Boston: Routledge and Kegan Paul.
Crawley, Alfred Ernest
  1902 *The Mystic Rose.* London: Macmillan. Second edition. London: Methuen, 1927.
Crespi, Muriel Kaminsky
  1968 "The Patrons and Peons of Pesillo: A Traditional Hacienda System in Highland Ecuador." Ph.D. dissertation, University of Illinois at Urbana-Champaign.
Deere, Carmen Diana
  1976 "Rural Women's Subsistence Production in the Capitalist Periphery." *Review of Radical Political Economics* 8(1):9–17.
Detienne, Marcel
  1977 *The Gardens of Adonis: Spices in Greek Mythology.* Hassock, Brighton: Harvester Press.
Diaz, Sonia Eagle
  1963 "Salasaca: A Closed Corporate Community." Unpublished student paper, Department of Anthropology, University of Illinois at Urbana-Champaign.
Dobyns, H. F.
  1965 "Drinking Patterns in Latin America: A Review." Paper presented at

Bibliography

the meeting of the American Association for the Advancement of Science.

"Doña Juanita"
n.d. *Comida tradicional del Ecuador.* Quito: Gangotena y Ruiz.

Donham, Donald
1981 "Beyond the Domestic Mode of Production." *Man* 16(4):515–541.

Dorfman, Ariel
1984 "Bread and Burnt Rice." *Grassroots Development* 8(2):3–25.

Doughty, Paul L.
1971 "The Social Uses of Alcoholic Beverages in a Peruvian Community." *Human Organization* 30:187–197.

Douglas, Mary
1971 "Deciphering a Meal." In *Myth, Symbol, and Culture,* Clifford Geertz, ed., pp. 61–82. New York: W. W. Norton.
1983 "Culture and Food." In *The Pleasures of Anthropology,* Morris Freilich, ed., pp. 74–101. New York: New American Library.
1984 "Fundamental Issues in Food Problems." *Current Anthropology* 25(4):498–499.

Douglas, Mary and Baron Isherwood
1979 *The World of Goods: Towards an Anthropology of Consumption.* London: W. W. Norton.

Evans-Pritchard, E. E.
1940 *The Nuer.* Oxford: Oxford University Press. Reprinted 1976.

Ferdon, Edwin N., Jr., with Malcolm H. Bissell and William C. Steere
1950 *Studies in Ecuadorian Geography.* Monographs of the School of American Research 15. Santa Fe, N.M.: School of American Research.

Fernandez, James
1977 "The Performance of Ritual Metaphors." In *The Social Use of Metaphor,* David J. Sapir and J. C. Crockett, eds., pp. 100–131. Philadelphia: University of Pennsylvania Press.

Fine, Kathleen
1983 "The Molecaña and the Yumbo: Masked Dance Performance and Protest in Urban Ecuador." Paper prepared for the meeting of the American Ethnological Society.

Firth, Rosemary
1966 *Housekeeping Among Malay Peasants.* London School of Economics Monographs on Social Anthropology 7. New York: Humanities Press.

Fock, Niels
1981 "Ethnicity and Alternative Identification: An Example from Cañar." In *Cultural Transformations and Ethnicity in Modern Ecuador.* Norman E. Whitten, Jr., ed., pp. 402–419. Urbana: University of Illinois Press.

Fonseca Martel, Cesar
1966 "La Comunidad de Cauri y la Quebrada de Chaupiwaranga." Cuadernos de Investigacion 1: *Antropología,* pp. 22–33. Huánuco: Universidad Nacional Hermillo Valdizán.

1972   *Sistemas económicas en las comunidades campesinas del Peru*. Lima: Universidad Nacional Mayor de San Marcos.

Forbes, R. J.
1954   "Chemical, Culinary, and Cosmetic Arts." In *A History of Technology,* vol. 1: *From Early Times to Fall of Ancient Empires,* Charles Singer et al., eds., pp. 238–298. Oxford: Oxford University Press.

Forman, Sylvia Helen
1978   "The Future Value of the 'Verticality' Concept: Implications and Possible Applications in the Andes." In *Papers of the 42nd International Congress of Americanists,* vol. 4, pp. 233–256.

Forster, Robert and Orest Ranum, eds.
1979   *Food and Drink in History: Selections from the Annales: Économies, Sociétés, Civilisations.* Baltimore: Johns Hopkins Press.

Fortes, M. and S. L. Fortes
1936   "Food in the Domestic Economy of the Tallensi." *Africa* 9:237–276.

Foster, George M.
1967   "The Role of Food and Drink" in "The Dyadic Contract," chapter 11 of *Tzintzuntzan: Mexican Peasants in a Changing World.* Boston: Little, Brown & Co. pp. 221–223. Reprinted New York: Elsevier, 1979.

Foucault, Michel
1969   *L'Archéologie du savoir.* Paris: Gallimard. Translated by A. M. Sheridan Smith as *The Archaeology of Knowledge and the Discourse on Language.* New York: Pantheon Books, 1972.

Frank, André Gunder
1969   *Capitalism and Underdevelopment in Latin America.* Revised edition. New York: Monthly Review Press.

Fredman, Ruth Gruber
1981   *The Passover Seder: Afikoman in Exile.* Philadelphia: University of Pennsylvania Press.

Frisch, Jack
1968   "Maricopa Foods: A Native Taxonomic System." *International Journal of American Linguistics* 34(1):16–20.

Gade, Daniel W.
1975   *Plants, Man and the Land in the Vilcanota Valley of Peru.* The Hague: W. Junk.

Geertz, Clifford
1973   *The Interpretation of Cultures.* New York: Basic Books.

Genovese, Eugene D.
1974   *Roll, Jordan, Roll: The World the Slaves Made.* New York: Pantheon Books.

Giddens, Anthony
1979   *Central Problems in Social Theory: Action, Structure, and Contradiction in Social Analysis.* Berkeley: UCLA Press.
1982   *Profiles and Critiques in Social Theory.* Berkeley: UCLA Press.

Bibliography

Gillin, John
  1947 *Moche: A Peruvian Coastal Community.* Smithsonian Institution, Institute of Social Anthropology, Publication 3. Washington, D.C.: U.S. Government Printing Office.

Gómez Huaman, N.
  1966 "Importancia social de la chicha como bebida popular en Huamanga." *Wamani* 1(1):33–57.

González Holguín, Diego
  1608 *Vocabulario dela Lengua General de todo el Peru llamada Lengua Qquichua o del inca.* Los Reyes: Francisco del Canto. Modern edition Lima: Imprenta Santa María, 1952.

Goody, Jack
  1982 *Cooking, Cuisine and Class: A Study in Comparative Sociology.* Cambridge: Cambridge University Press.

Greene, Lawrence Stephen
  1976 "Nutrition and Behavior in Highland Ecuador." Ph.D. dissertation, University of Pennsylvania.

Guevara, Dario
  1960a "Expresión ritual de comidas y bebidas ecuatorianas." *Humanitas* 2(1):37–84.
  1960b "Comidas y bebidas ecuatorianas." *Folklore americano* (Lima) 8–9:217–284.
  1972 *El Castellano y el Quichua en el Ecuador.* Quito: Editorial Casa de la Cultura Ecuatoriana.

Hammel, Eugene A.
  1967 "The Jewish Mother in Serbia or Les Structures alimentaires de la Parenté." In *Essays in Balkan Ethnology,* William G. Lockwood, ed., pp. 55–62. Kroeber Anthropological Society Special Publication 1. Berkeley: University of California Press.

Hartmann, Roswith
  1973 "Conmemoración de muertos en la Sierra ecuatoriana." *Indiana* 1:179–189.
  1974 "Creencias acerca de las almas de los difuntos en la región de Otavlo/Ecuador." In *Ethnologie Zeitschrift Zuerich,* volume 1: *Festschrift Otto Zerries,* pp. 207–228. Berlin: Verlag Herbert Lang.
  1978 "Juegos de velorio en la Sierra ecuatoriana." *Indiana* 6:225–274.

Heath, Dwight B.
  1958 "Drinking Patterns Among the Bolivian Camba." *Quarterly Journal of Studies on Alcohol* 19(3):491–508.
  1971 "Peasants, Revolution and Drinking: Interethnic Drinking Patterns in Two Bolivian Communities." *Human Organization* 30:179–186.

Hémardinquer, Jean-Jacques
  1970 "Faut-il 'démythifier' le porc familial d'Ancien Régime?" *Annales:*

Économies, Sociétés, Civilisations 25(6):1745–1766. Translated by Patricia M. Ranum as "The Family Pig of the Ancien Régime: Myth or Fact?" in Forster and Ranum 1979, pp. 50–72.

Hill, Jane W.
1985 "The Refiguration of the Anthropology of Language." *Cultural Anthropology* 1(1):89–102.

Hilliard, Sam Bowers
1972 *Hogmeat and Hoecake: Food Supply in the Old South, 1840–1860.* Carbondale: Southern Illinois University Press.

Hugh-Jones, Christine
1978 "Patterns of Production and Consumption in Pirá-Paraná Society." In *Sex and Age as Principles of Social Differentiation,* S. J. LaFontaine, ed., (pp. 41–66) Association of Social Anthropology Monographs 17. New York: Academic Press.
1979 *From the Milk River: Spatial and Temporal Processes in Northwest Amazonia.* Cambridge: Cambridge University Press.

Hurtado, Oswaldo
1973 *Dos Mundos superpuestos: Ensayo de diagnóstico de la realidad Ecuatoriana.* Quito: Instituto Ecuatoriano de Planificación para el Desarrollo Social.

Icaza, Jorge
1953 *Huasipungo.* Buenos Aires: Editorial Losada.

Isbell, Billie Jean
1978 *To Defend Ourselves: Ecology and Ritual in an Andean Village.* Austin: University of Texas Press.

Janvry, Alain de
1981 *The Agrarian Question and Reformism in Latin America.* Baltimore: Johns Hopkins Press.

Karsten, Rafael
1930 *Ceremonial Games of the South American Indians.* Societas Sciendiarum Fennica, Commentationes Humanarum Litterarum 3.2. Helsingfors: Akademische Buchhandlung.

Katona-Apte, Judit
1975 "Dietary Aspects of Acculturation: Meals, Feasts and Fasts in a Minority Community in South Asia." In Arnott 1975, pp. 315–326.

Khare, R. S.
1976a *The Hindu Hearth and Home.* Durham, N.C.: Carolina Academic Press.
1976b *Culture and Reality: Essays on the Hindu System of Managing Food.* Simla, India: Indian Institute of Advanced Study.

Kuper, Jessica
1977 *The Anthropologist's Cookbook.* Boston: Routledge and Kegan Paul.

Laderman, Carol
1981 "Symbolic and Empirical Reality: A New Approach to the Analysis of Food Avoidances." *American Ethnologist* 8(3):468–483.

Bibliography

Lefebvre, Henri
  1977 "Ideology and Sociology of Knowledge." In *Symbolic Anthropology: A Reader in the Study of Symbols and Meanings,* Janet L. Dolgin, David S. Kemnitzer, and David M. Schneider, eds., pp. 254–269. New York: Columbia University Press. Previously published as pp. 59–68 in his *The Sociology of Marx,* New York: Random House, 1969. (French ed. Paris: Presses Universitaires de France)

Lehrer, A.
  1969 "Semantic Cuisine." *Journal of Linguistics* 5:39–56.
  1972 "Cooking Vocabularies and the Culinary Triangle of Lévi-Strauss." *Anthropological Linguistics* 14:155–171.

Lerche, Grith
  1975 "Notes on Different Types of 'Bread' in Northern Scotland: Bannocks, Oatcakes, Scones and Pancakes." In Arnott 1975, pp. 327–336.

Lévi-Strauss, Claude
  1958 Postscript to chapters 3 and 4; chapter 5 of *Anthropologie structurelle.* Paris: Plon. Translated by Claire Jacobson and Brooke Grundfest Schoepf as *Structural Anthropology,* volume 1, pp. 81–97. New York: Basic Books, 1963.
  1964 *Mythologies,* volume 1: *Le Cru et le cuit.* Paris: Plon. Translated by John Weightman and Doreen Weightman as *Introduction to a Science of Mythology,* volume 1: *The Raw and the Cooked.* New York: Harper & Row, 1975.
  1966a "The Culinary Triangle." Peter Brooks, trans. *Partisan Review* 33(4):586–595.
  1966b *Mythologies,* volume 2: *Du Miel aux cendres.* Paris: Plon. Translated by John Weightman and Doreen Weightman as *Introduction to a Science of Mythology,* volume 2: *From Honey to Ashes.* New York: Harper & Row, 1973.

Lira, Jorge A.
  1948 "Elaboración de la chicha amarilla." *Revista del Instituto Nacional de la Tradición* (Buenos Aires) 1(1):115–117.

MacCabe, Colin
  1979 "On Discourse." *Economy and Society* 8(3):279–307.

Malinowski, Bronislaw
  1950 *Argonauts of the Western Pacific.* London: Routledge and Kegan Paul.

Mangin, William
  1951 "Drinking Among Andean Indians." *Quarterly of Studies on Alcohol* 18(1):55–65.

Marriott, McKim
  1968 "Caste-Ranking and Food Transactions: A Matrix Analysis." In *Structure and Change in Indian Society,* Milton Singer and Bernard S. Cohn, eds., pp. 133–171. Chicago: Aldine.

Marx, Karl
  1859 *Grundrisse der Kritik der politischen Ökonomie.* Berlin: Franz

Duncker. Translated by Martin Nicolaus as *Grundrisse: Foundations of the Critique of Political Economy.* New York: Vintage Books, 1973.
1977   "The Fetishism of Commodities and the Secret Thereof." In *Symbolic Anthropology: A Reader in the Study of Symbols and Meanings,* Janet L. Dolgin, David S. Kemnitzer, and David M. Schneider, eds., pp. 245–253. New York: Columbia University Press (original date not given).

Mauss, Marcel
1954   *Essai sur le don.* Translated by Ian Cunnison as *The Gift: Forms and Functions of Exchange in Archaic Societies.* London: Cohen.

Maycr, Enrique José
1974   "Reciprocity, Self-Sufficiency and Market Relations in a Contemporary Community in the Central Andes of Peru." Ph.D. dissertation, Cornell University.
1985   "Production Zones." In *Andean Ecology and Civilization,* Shozo Masuda, Ixumi Shimada, and Craig Morris, eds., pp. 45–84. Tokyo: University of Tokyo Press.

Mazess, R. and P. Baker
1964   "Diet of Quechua Indians Living at High Altitude: Nunoa, Peru." *American Journal of Clinical Nutrition* 15:341–351.

Meigs, Anna S.
1984   *Food, Sex, and Pollution: A New Guinea Religion.* New Brunswick, N.J.: Rutgers University Press.

Meillassoux, Claude
1972   "From Reproduction to Production: A Marxist Approach to Economic Anthropology," *Economy and Society* 1(1):93–105.
1978a "The Social Organisation of the Peasantry: The Economic Basis of Kinship." In *Relations of Production: Marxist Approaches to Economic Anthropology,* David Seddon, ed., Helen Lacker, trans. pp. 159–170. London: Frank Cass.
1978b "Kinship Relations and Relations of Production." In *Relations of Production: Marxist Approaches to Economic Anthropology,* David Seddon, ed., pp. 289–330. London: Frank Cass.
1981   *Maidens, Meal and Money: Capitalism and the Domestic Community.* Cambridge: Cambridge University Press.

Mejía Xesppe, Toribio
1978   "*Kausay:* Alimentación de los indios." In *Tecnología andina,* Rogger Ravines, ed., pp. 205–225. Lima: Instituto de Estudios Peruanos.

Michaud, Andrée
1970   "La Religiosidad en Qollana." *Allpanchis* 2:7–18.

Mintz, Sidney
1979   "Time, Sugar and Sweetness." *Marxist Perspectives* 2:56–73.
1982   "Choice and Occasion: Sweet Moments." In *The Psychobiology of Human Food Selection,* Lewis M. Barker ed., pp. 157–169. Westport, Conn: AVI Publishing Co.

1985   *Sweetness and Power: The Place of Sugar in Modern History.* New York: Viking Press.

Moya, Ruth
1981   *Simbolismo y ritual en el Ecuador andino.* Otavalo: Instituto Otavaleño de Antropología.

Murra, John V.
1963   "The Historic Tribes of Ecuador." In *The Handbook of South American Indians,* Julian H. Steward, ed., volume 2: *The Andean Civilizations,* pp. 785–822. New York: Cooper Square.
1975   *Formaciones económicas y políticas del mundo andino.* Lima: Instituto de Estudios Peruanos.

Naranjo, Marcelo
1978   "Etnicidad, estructura social y poder en Manta, Occidente Ecuatoriano." Ph.D. dissertation, University of Illinois at Urbana-Champaign.

Naranjo, Plutarco
1985   *Desnutrición: Problemas y soluciones.* Quito: Olmedo.

Nash, June
1979   *We Eat the Mines and the Mines Eat Us: Dependency and Exploitation in the Bolivian Tin Mines.* New York: Columbia University Press.

Niñez, Vera K.
1984   *Household Gardens: Theoretical Considerations on an Old Survival Strategy.* Potatoes in Food Systems Research Report 1. Lima: International Potato Center.

Núñez del Prado B., Juan Victor
1969   "El Mundo supernatural de los Quechuas del sur del Peru a través de la comunidad de Qotobamba." *Revista del Museo Nacional* (Lima) 36:143–163.

Orlove, Benjamin
1982   "Tomar la bandera: Politics and Punch in Southern Peru." *Ethnos* 3–4: 249–261.
1983   "Stability and Change in Highland Andean Dietary Patterns: Causes and Consequences." Paper prepared for the Wenner-Gren International Symposium, Cedar Key, Florida.

Ortner, Sherry
1978   "Hospitality: Problems of Exchange, Status, and Authority." In *Sherpas Through Their Rituals,* pp. 61–90. Cambridge: Cambridge University Press.

Paredes de Martínez, Irene
1963   *Tulpa, Nifu, Ekinda.* Quito: Editorial Artes Gráficas.

Parsons, Elsie Clews
1945   *Peguche: Canton of Otavalo, Province of Imbabura, Ecuador, a Study of Andean Indians.* Chicago: University of Chicago Press.

Patino, Victor Manuel
1964   *Plantas cultivadas y animales domésticos en America equinoccial.* Volume 2: *Plantas alimenticias.* Cali: Imprenta Departmental.

Bibliography

Peloso, Vincent C.
1985   "Succulence and Sustenance: Region, Class, and Diet in Nineteenth-Century Peru." In *Food, Politics, and Society in Latin America,* John C. Super and Thomas C. Wright, eds., pp. 46–64. Lincoln: University of Nebraska Press.

Pigott, Jeralyn
1981   "Infant Feeding Practices and Beliefs in the Rural Sierra of Ecuador." M.A. thesis, Michigan State University.

Plath, Oreste
1962   "Aportaciones popular sobre el vino y la chicha." *Anales del Instituto de Lingüística* (Mendoza, Chile) 8:361–413.

Pollock, Nancy
1986   "Food Classification in Three Pacific Societies: Fiji, Hawaii, and Tahiti." *Ethnology* 25(2):107–117.

Poma de Ayala, Felipe Guamán
1936   *Nueva corónica y buen gobierno.* Paris: Institut d'Ethnologie.

Pomeroy, Cheryl
n.d.   "The Meaning of Salt for Andean Ecuadorian Cultures." Unpublished MS.
1986   "Environment, Economics, and Family Farm Systems: Farm Expansion and Adaptation on the West Andean Slopes of Ecuador." Ph.D. dissertation, University of Illinois at Urbana-Champaign.

Prieto, Mercedes
1980   "Haciendas estatales: Un Caso de ofensiva campesina 1926–1948." In *Ecuador: Cambios en el agro serrano,* pp. 101–132. Quito: FLACSO-CEPLAES.

Ramburger, O.
1979   "The Deep Grammar of Haute Cuisine." *Linguistics* 17:169–172.

Revel, Jean-François
1979   *Un Festin en paroles.* Paris: Société Nouvelle des Éditions Jean-Jacques Pauvert. *Culture and Cuisine: A Journey Through the History of Food.* Helen R. Lane, trans. Garden City, N.Y.: Doubleday, 1982.

Richards, Audrey I.
1964   "Food as a Symbol." In *Hunger and Work in a Savage Tribe: A Functional Study of Nutrition Among the Southern Bantu,* chapter 7. Cleveland: World Publishing Company.

Ricoeur, Paul
1977   "The Model of the Text: Meaningful Action Considered as a Text." In *Understanding and Social Inquiry,* Fred R. Dallmayr and Thomas A. McCarthy, eds., pp. 316–334. Notre Dame, Ind.: University of Notre Dame Press.

Rivadeneira A., Mauro
1980   *La Situación nutricional en el Ecuador.* Quito: Agency for International Development.

222

Robertson Smith, W.
1889   *Lectures on the Religion of the Semites.* New York: D. Appleton.
Robinson, Carol Ann
1968   "An Analysis of Contemporary Ecuadorian Highland Indian Dress."
M.A. thesis, Cornell University.
Root, Waverley and Richard de Rochemont
1976   *Eating in America: A History.* New York: Morrow.
Rowe, John Howland
1963   "Inca Culture at the Time of the Spanish Conquest." In *The Handbook
of South American Indians,* Julian Steward, ed., volume 2: *The Andean
Civilizations,* pp. 183–330. New York: Cooper Square Publications.
Rubinstein, Moshe F.
1975   *Patterns of Problem Solving.* Englewood Cliffs, N.J.: Prentice-Hall.
Sahlins, Marshall
1981   *Historical Metaphors and Mythical Realities.* Ann Arbor: University of
Michigan Press.
Salomon, Frank
1975   "Don Pedro de Zámbiza, un varayuj del siglo XVI." *Cuadernos de his-
toria y arqueología* 42:285–315.
1980   *Los Señores étnicos de Quito en la epoca de los Incas.* Colección Pen-
doneros 10A. Otavalo: Instituto Otavaleño de Antropologia.
1981   "Killing the Yumbo: a Ritual Drama of Northern Quito." In *Cultural
Transformations and Ethnicity in Modern Ecuador,* Norman E. Whitten Jr., ed., pp. 162–208. Urbana: University of Illinois Press.
1984   "El Quichua de los Andes ecuatoriales." *Revista andina* 1(2):393–406.
Sapir, J. David
1977   "The Anatomy of Metaphor." In *The Social Use of Metaphor,* David
J. Sapir and J. Christopher Crocker, eds., pp. 3–32. Philadelphia: Uni-
versity of Pennsylvania Press.
Saussure, Ferdinand de
1916   *Cours de linguistique générale.* Lausanne: Payot. Translated by Wade
Baskin as *Course in General Linguistics.* London: Peter Owen, 1959.
Schieffelin, Edward L.
1976   "I'm Sorry, Brother, I Don't Eat That." In *The Sorrow of the Lonely
and the Burning of the Dancers,* pp. 46–72. New York: St. Martin's
Press.
Scott, James C.
1985   Weapons of the Weak: Everyday Forms of Peasant Resistance. New
Haven: Yale University Press.
Sharon, Douglas
1978   *Wizard of the Four Winds: A Shaman's Story.* New York: Free Press.
Sherbondy, Jeanette Evelyn
1982   "The Canal Systems of Hanan Cuzco." Ph.D. dissertation, University
of Illinois.

Simons, Frederick J.
  1967   *Eat Not This Flesh: Food Avoidances in the Old World.* Madison: University of Wisconsin Press.
Sokolov, Raymond
  1984   "Oat Cuisine." *Natural History* 93(4):108–111.
Stavenhagen, Rodolfo
  1975   *Social Classes in Agrarian Societies.* Garden City, N.Y.: Doubleday Anchor Books.
Stewart, Susan
  1983   "Shouts on the Street: Bakhtin's Anti-Linguistics." *Critical Inquiry* 10(2):265–282.
Stone, L.
  1978   "Food Symbolism in Hindu Nepal." *Contributions to Nepalese Studies* 6(1):47–65.
Strathern, Andrew.
  1977   "Melpa Food-Names as an Expression of Ideas on Identity and Substance." *Journal of the Polynesian Society* 86:503–511.
Stutzman, Ronald
  1974   "Black Highlanders: Racism and Ethnic Stratification in the Ecuadorian Sierra." Ph.D. dissertation, Washington University, Saint Louis.
  1981   "*El Mestizaje:* An All-Inclusive Ideology." In *Cultural Transformations and Ethnicity in Modern Ecuador,* Norman E. Whitten Jr., ed., pp. 45–94. Urbana: University of Illinois Press.
Tannahill, Reay
  1973   *Food in History.* New York: Stein and Day.
Taussig, Michael T.
  1980   *The Devil and Commodity Fetishism in South America.* Chapel Hill: University of North Carolina Press.
  1984   "Culture of Terror-Space of Death: Roger Casement's Putumayo Report and the Explanation of Torture." *Comparative Studies in Society and History* 26:467–497.
Thomas, L. V.
  1960   "Essai d'analyse structurale appliquée à la cuisine diola." *Bulletin de l'Institut Française d'Afrique Noire* 22:328–45.
Thomas, R. Brooke
  1976   "Energy Flow at High Altitude." In *Man in the Andes: A Multidisciplinary Study of High Altitude Quechua,* Paul T. Baker and Michael A. Little, eds, pp. 379–404. Synthesis Series 1. Philadelphia: Hutchinson.
Thompson, E. P.
  1966   *The Making of the English Working Class.* New York: Vintage Books.
Towle, Margaret Ashley
  1961   *The Ethnobotany of Pre-Columbian Peru.* Chicago: Aldine Press.
Turner, B. S.
  1982   "The Discourse of Diet." *Theory, Culture, and Society* 1(1):23–32.

Bibliography

Turner, James
  1984 "'True Fruit' and First Fruits: Rituals of Increase in Fiji." *Ethnology* 23(2):133–142.
Turner, Victor
  1967 *The Forest of Symbols: Aspects of Ndembu Ritual.* Ithaca, N.Y.: Cornell University Press.
  1974 *Dramas, Fields, and Metaphors.* Ithaca, N.Y.: Cornell University Press.
Valcarcel, Luis
  1963 "The Andean Calendar." In *The Handbook of South American Indians,* Julian H. Steward, ed., volume 2: *The Andean Civilizations,* pp. 471–476. New York: Cooper Square.
Varea Teran, Marco and José Varea Teran, eds.
  1974 *Nutrición y desarollo en los Andes ecuatorianos.* Quito: Investigaciones Medico-Sociales del Ecuador.
Vesquez, Mario C.
  1956 "La Chicha en los países andinos." *America indígena* 27:265–282.
Villavicencio Rivadeneira, Gladys
  1973 *Relaciones Interétnicas en Otavalo, Ecuador.* Mexico City: Instituto Indigenista Interamericano.
Vogt, Evon Z.
  1976 *Tortillas for the Gods: A Symbolic Analysis of Zinacantecan Rituals.* Cambridge, Mass.: Harvard University Press.
Weismantel, Mary
  1983 "Everyday Life, Everyday Death: Cannibal Mouths and Bread Babies in the Ecuadorian Andes." Paper in lieu of M.A. thesis, Department of Anthropology, University of Illinois at Urbana-Champaign.
Whitten, Dorothea S. and Norman J. Whitten, Jr.
  1985 *Art, Knowledge and Health: Development and Assessment of a Collaborative Auto-Financed Organization in Eastern Ecuador.* Cambridge, Mass.: Cultural Survival, Inc. and Sacha Runa Foundation.
Whitten, Norman E., Jr.
  1965 *Class, Kinship, and Power in an Ecuadorian Town: The Negroes of San Lorenzo.* Stanford: Stanford University Press.
  1974 *Black Frontiersmen: A South American Case.* New York: Halsted.
  1976 (with the assistance of Marcelo F. Naranjo, Marcelo Santi Simbaña, and Dorothea S. Whitten) *Sacha Runa: Ethnicity and Adaptation of Ecuadorian Jungle Quichua.* Urbana: University of Illinois Press.
  1981 (with the assistance of Kathleen Fine) Introduction to *Cultural Transformations and Ethnicity in Modern Ecuador,* Norman E. Whitten, Jr., ed., pp. 1–41. Urbana: University of Illinois Press.
  1985 *Sicuanga Runa: The Other Side of Development in Amazonian Ecuador.* Urbana: University of Illinois Press.
Williams, Raymond
  1977 *Marxism and Literature.* Cambridge: Cambridge University Press.

Bibliography

Wolf, Teodoro
  1892 *Geografía y geología del Ecuador.* Leipzig: F. A. Brockhaus. Translated by James W. Flanagan as *Geography and Geology of Ecuador.* Toronto: Grand and Toy, 1933.
Yalman, Nur
  1969 "On the Meaning of Food Offerings in Ceylon." In *Forms of Symbolic Action,* Robert F. Spencer, ed., pp. 81–96. Seattle: University of Washington Press.
Young, M.
  1971 *Fighting with Food.* Cambridge: Cambridge University Press.
Zuidema, R. T.
  1980 "El Ushnu." *Revista de la Universidad Complutense* (Madrid) 28(117):317–362.

INDEX